Bergheim, West Germany

Ibadan, Nigeria

Bombay, India

Hartcliffe, Bristol, England

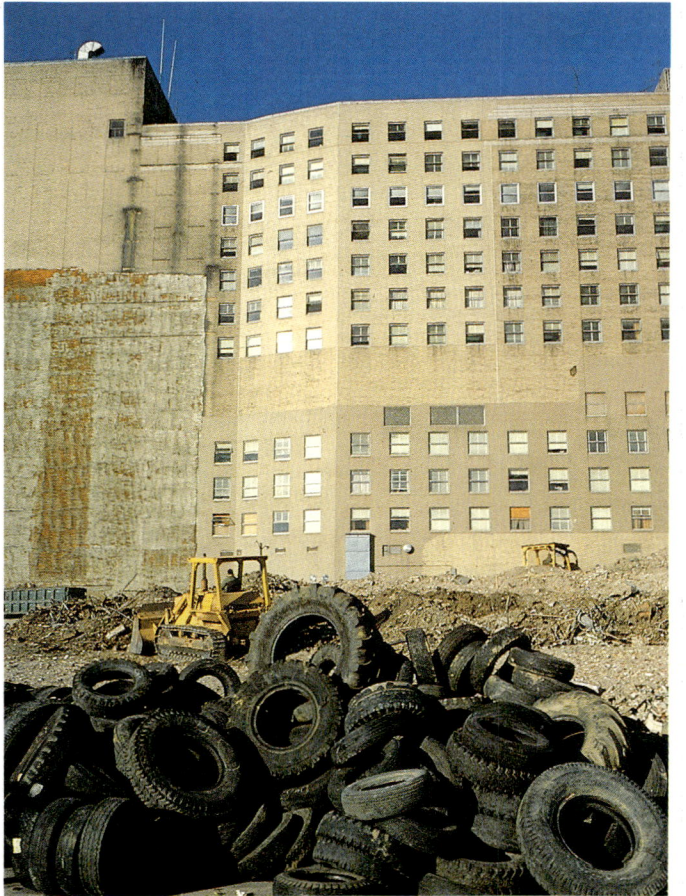

Washington DC, USA

5

2 IMAGES OF THE CITY

1 Think for a moment about Britain's six largest cities: London, Birmingham, Glasgow, Liverpool, Sheffield and Manchester.

a) Write down three things which come to mind when you think of each city.

b) Compare what you have written with what your neighbour has written. Are there many similarities?

c) Did you feel that you had more mental pictures for some of the cities than for others? Why?

These mental pictures or images of different places are built up from a variety of sources. We remember certain things about places we have visited. Our memories also take note of what other people say. Newspapers, radio and television provide many other images. The use of these mental images to recognize places and other things is known as perception.

Apart from building up images of different urban places, we also develop images of areas within towns and cities. The areas where we live, work and shop tend to be those areas that we know best. The most detailed images that we have are of these areas. Young children have more limited images than adults because they do not very often travel beyond their own neighbourhood. However, as the four sketch maps opposite show, we all have incomplete images of the urban environment. These *mental maps* only seem to emphasize those things which are important to us and leave out many features of our towns and cities.

Whatever images people have of towns and cities, they usually identify features which fall into one of five groups:

○ PATHS Channels along which people move, such as roads and footpaths.

○ EDGES Boundary lines which restrict movement, such as rivers and urban motorways.

○ DISTRICTS Sections of the city which are easily recognized because of the people who live there or the activities taking place there, such as central shopping areas and residential areas.

○ NODES Points which act as a focus for routes, such as major road junctions and squares.

○ LANDMARKS Distinctive buildings or features, such as churches and hospitals.

2 Write short definitions for the following terms:

a) perception and b) mental maps.

3 Study the maps shown opposite.

a) Describe the main features identified by each of the four mental maps.

b) How do the maps differ?

c) Which of the four maps most closely resembles the plan of central Durham? Give reasons for your answer.

d) In what ways is the plan of central Durham more useful than the mental maps?

4 a) Make a note of why the following features are important in people's mental maps of urban areas: paths edges districts nodes landmarks.

b) Which of these features stand out the most on the maps of Durham?

c) For your own town or city, list three examples of each feature.

5 Look at the survey results shown in Visual 1.

a) Describe how the inhabitants and outsiders perceived Hull. Suggest reasons for some of the differences.

b) Carry out a survey of people in your class to find out what are the most common images of your town or city.

c) Do you think that outsiders might have a different perception of where you live?

6 Look at Visual 2. If direction signs did not exist, how would we get from place to place? How would we know when we had arrived?

2 Our sense of place develops from the information that we gather from many sources

INHABITANTS % OF THOSE SURVEYED WHO MENTIONED:		OUTSIDERS % OF THOSE SURVEYED WHO MENTIONED:	
Good shopping centre	85	Docks	90
Working-class city	84	Working-class city	85
Docks	81	Ships	79
Large council estates	75	Fishy	75
Friendly	74	Heavy industry	67
Trees, parks	74	Slums	63
Ships	65	Large council estates	59
Low wages	61	Unemployment	57
Fishy	58	Cold	56
Congested traffic	57	Smoke	53
Tower block flats	56	Congested traffic	50
Redevelopment	55	Drabness	49

1 A recent survey carried out in the city of Hull revealed differences in perception for local and non-local people

PEOPLE IN THE

URBAN LANDSCAPE

STEVE CROSSLEY

Deputy Headteacher

Dene Magna School Mitcheldean

Formerly Head of Geography and Economics

Ryde High School

Consultant editors

Richard Kemp   County Adviser for Humanities Buckinghamshire

David Maclean   County Inspector for Geography Essex

Macdonald Educational

A MACDONALD BOOK

Text © Steve Crossley 1988

Design & artwork © Macdonald & Co (Publishers) Ltd 1988

First published in Great Britain in 1988 by
Macdonald & Co (Publishers) Ltd
London & Sydney
A member of Maxwell Pergamon Publishing Corporation plc

Typesetting by
Swanston Graphics Ltd
Derby

Printed in Great Britain by
Waterlow Ltd
Dunstable
A member of the BPCC Group

Macdonald & Co (Publishers) Ltd
Greater London House
Hampstead Road
London NW1 7QX

British Library Cataloguing in Publication Data

Crossley, Steve
     People in the urban landscape.—
     (Geography for GCSE)
     1. Cities and towns
     I. Title   II. Kemp, Richard   III. Maclean,
     David, *1948*—   IV. Series
     307.7′6   HT151

ISBN 0–356–11472–4

Series editor John Day
Editor Elizabeth Clarke
Design and art direction Liz Black
Picture research Kathy Lockley and Caroline Smith
Production David Meads

Cover illustration Brian Grimwood
Illustrators
Liz Black 11(BL), 21(T), 28, 52, 58, 71(B), 75
Matthew Doyle/David Lewis Management 11(T), 50
Jeremy Ford/David Lewis Management 42, 44, 92
Bob Harvey/David Lewis Management 46, 84
Fraser Shaw/David Lewis Management 45
Jerry Watkiss 10(R), 16(TR), 23(B), 78
Swanston Graphics Ltd all maps and other diagrams

Glossary

Terms which readers may be meeting for the first time or which
have a special meaning in the context of this book are listed in the
glossary on pages 94 and 95. The first time such a term appears it is
printed in *italic* type (except in the case of illustrations).

Acknowledgements
*The author and publisher thank the following for permission to reproduce
their photographs and other copyright materials. The numbers refer to
pages and L, R, T, B, C indicate left, right, top, bottom and centre.*

Photographs and prints
Aerofilms 24(TR), 40, 64(TR); A.D.E. Barker 20(TL); BBC Hulton Picture
Library 62(L); John Bethell 64(BL); Nick Birch 8(T), 9(T); Birmingham City
Council 48(TR); Birmingham City Council/Harrison Cowley Advertising
(Midlands) Ltd 27; John Day 46(B); Docklands Community Poster Project
61(B); Esso 31(T); Mary Evans Picture Library 32; Sally and Richard Greenhill
8(TL), 9(T), 12(TL); Handford Photography 61(T); Robert Harding Picture
Library 24(TL), 74(L, C); Hutchison Picture Library 5(TR), 12(TR), 66, 74(R),
79(R), 87; Impact 48(TR); Methuen/Norman Thelwell 13; Pilgrim Pres/New
Lanark Conservation 64(TL); Popperfoto 53, 58(T, B); Reflex/Piers Cavendish
80; Reflex/David Lurie 85(L); Rex Features 58(CR); Sealand Aerial
Photography 18, 20(TR), 34, 41(BL); Select/C. Grandjean 5(BR); Select/
Richard Olivier 57, 85(R); Select/Julian Simmonds 41(BR), 46(T); South
American Pictures/Tony Morrison 76, 78(L); Spectrum Colour Library 39,
83(C); Frank Spooner Pictures 78(R); Streetwork 52, 59; Universal Pictorial
Press 58(CL); ZEFA 5(TL, CL, BL), 6, 62(R), 64(BR), 83(T, B), 86, 88

Maps, diagrams and extracts
Birmingham City Council/Harrison Cowley Advertising (Midlands) Ltd 27;
Blackwell/T. Wilson 14; Brazilian Embassy, London 79(C); Cambridge
University Press/D.M. Smith 85(CR, B); Cergy-Pontoise Information Centre
67(B); Collins/Gareth Owen 50; Collins Educational/A. Kirby 89(T); Croom
Helm/D.M. Smith 45(T); C.A. Doxiadis 91(T); The Economist 40, 41, 57; The
Financial Times 63; Friends of the Earth 29; David Fulton Publishers/D.
Burtenshaw 67(T); Geographical Press/J. Eyles 51(B)/F.E. Hamilton 87(BR)/
S. Waterman and B. Kosmin 51(T, C); Mary Glasgow Publications 21(B), 31;
Guardian Newspapers 28(B), 59(T); Halifax Building Society 41(T); Hamlyn
Publishing Group: Lionheart Books 38(T); Harper and Row/S.D. Brunn and
J.F. Williams 72(TR), 75(C), 91, 93(B); Information and Documentation
Centre for the Geography of the Netherlands 70, 71; Jan Kaplicky and David
Nixon/Future Systems 92(T); London Docklands Development Corporation
60(T); Macmillan/D. Pocock and R. Hudson 7 (insets); Edward B. Marks
Music Corporation/Lois Lenski 28; Michigan State University 93(B); National
Housing and Town Planning Council 42; Nelson/D. Waugh 8, 18; New
Internationalist 77; News Group Newspapers/British Library Newspaper
Library 55; Newspaper Publishing plc 47; The Observer Newspaper/British
Library Newspaper Library 54; Ordnance Survey 13, 43; Ordnance Survey/
Land Use Survey 17; Oxford University Press/M. Simons 79(B); Penguin
Books/N. Fairbrother 44; Pergamon Press/UN Department of Economic and
Social Affairs 75(C); Eleanor and John Rawling, Geography 16-19 Project/
School Curriculum Development Committee 22, 23; M. Renwick 26(C);
Scientific American/L. Long and D. DeAre 89(C); Times Newspapers 30, 39,
93(TR); US News and World Inc. 72(TL); Unwin Hyman/P. Gould and R.
White 19(T); Weatherall Green & Smith 25(B); Yale University Press/M.
Girouard 33(B).

*The author and publisher are also much indebted to the following whose
cited publications were consulted during the preparation of this book.*

J. Bale, *The Location of Manufacturing Industry*, Oliver and Boyd; G.
Barraclough, *The Times Atlas of World History*, Times Books; Brazilian
Embassy, London *Brazil: São Paulo*; S.D. Brunn and J.F. Williams, *Cities of the
World*, Harper and Row; D. Burtenshaw, *The City in West Europe*, David
Fulton Publishers; A. Church and J. Hall, 'Discovery of Docklands',
Geographical Magazine, 1986, p.633; Consortium Developments, *Tillingham
Hall: Outline Plan*; P. Daniel and M. Hopkinson, *The Geography of Settlement*,
Oliver and Boyd; J. Eyles, 'Black and British', *Geographical Magazine*, 1982,
p.277; S. Fothergill and J. Vincent, *The State of the Nation*, Pan; M. Girouard,
Cities and People, Yale University Press; Mary Glasgow Publications, *Geofile*
(2) 1982, (25) 1984, (46) 1985, (7) 1986; P. Gould and R. White, *Mental Maps*,
Unwin Hyman, p.29; P. Hall, 'Urban Growth in Britain 1809-1939', in *The
City Experience*, Ward Lock; F.E. Hamilton, 'The East European and Soviet
City', *Geographical Magazine*, May 1978, p.515; M. Kidron and R. Segal, *The
State of the World Atlas*, Pan; A. Kirby, 'The American City Today', in *People
and Environments*, Collins Educational, p.68; L. Long and D. DeAre, 'The
Slowing Down of Urbanisation in the US', *Scientific American*, July 1983; H.
Meijer, *Randstad Holland*, Information and Documentation Centre for the
Geography of the Netherlands; *New Internationalist*, June 1978, p.8 and June
1980, p.23; National Housing and Town Planning Council, 'New
Settlements', *Housing and Planning Review*, Vol.39, No.5, 1984; Office of
Population Censuses and Surveys, *OPCS Monitor: 1981 Census*; Ordnance
Survey, *National Atlas of Great Britain*, Hamlyn Publishing Group,/Lionheart
Books, p.61; J. Paxton, *The Statesman's Yearbook 1982-83*, Macmillan; D.
Pocock and R. Hudson, *Images of the Urban Environment*, Macmillan; M.
Simons, *Poverty and Wealth in Cities and Villages*, Oxford University Press; F.
Slater (ed.), *People and Environments*, Collins Educational; D.M. Smith,
Apartheid in South Africa, Cambridge University Press and *Where the Grass is
Greener*, Croom Helm; M. Storm, *Urban Growth in Britian*, Oxford University
Press; S. Waterman and B. Kosmin, 'The Jews of London', *Geographical
Magazine*, 1986, p.21; D. Waugh, *The British Isles*, Nelson, p.69, 108; D.
Wilcox, *London – The Heartless City*, Thames TV; T. Wilson, *Settlement –
Location and Links*, Blackwell; World Bank, *World Development Report 1982*,
Oxford University Press, p.148.

CONTENTS

Towns and cities seem to be a success story. But are they?

Most people in Britain live in towns and cities and an increasing number of people throughout the world are living in urban areas. By the year 2000, the majority of people in the world will live in towns and cities. As the pictures on these pages show, urban landscapes can vary a great deal. The world's towns and cities offer both some of the best and some of the worst conditions for people to live in.

1 Write short definitions for the terms 'urban' and 'rural'.

2 Looking at the table which classifies settlements:

a) What is the population of the settlement where you live? According to the table, in which type of settlement do you live?

b) For each of the urban settlements, find an example near to where you live. Make a list of these settlements and find out their population size.

3 Look at all the pictures.

a) Write down the location for each picture. Now write a few words to describe your first reaction to each urban scene.

b) Compare your notes with those of your neighbour. Did you have similar or different feelings about the pictures?

c) How much would you like to live in each of the urban areas pictured here? List them in your choice order. Explain the reasons in choosing the way you did.

d) These pictures show only a few aspects of a small number of urban settlements. Form a group of four people and discuss what other pictures could be included to build up a detailed visual record of urban life.

WHAT IS URBAN?

Dictionaries usually define *urban* as 'of a city or town' and *rural* as 'of the country'.

Although this seems straightforward many countries use different population sizes to define their urban areas. Here are some European examples.

DENMARK	200	FRANCE	2000
SWEDEN	200	BELGIUM	5000
ALBANIA	400	GREECE	10 000
IRELAND	1500	SPAIN	10 000
EAST GERMANY	2000	NETHERLANDS	20 000

Clearly, there is little agreement about how large a settlement needs to be before it can be called urban.

The table on the right shows one way of classifying settlements according to population size.

RURAL SETTLEMENTS	POPULATION
Isolated farm or house	1 – 10
Hamlet	11 – 100
Small village	101 – 500
Large Village	501 – 2000

URBAN SETTLEMENTS	POPULATION
Small town	2001 – 10 000
Large town	10 001 – 100 000
City	100 001 – 1 000 000
Millionaire city	1 000 001 – 5 000 000
Supercity	5 000 001 and more

Young Child

castle
river
country side
my house
river bank
school
leading to newcastle
v cottage
motorway where cars going
Dell
Wood
Railway Station
park
police station

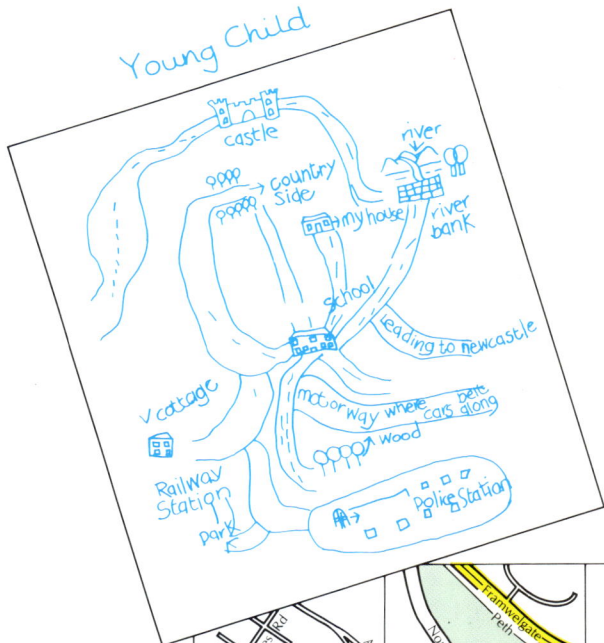

University Student

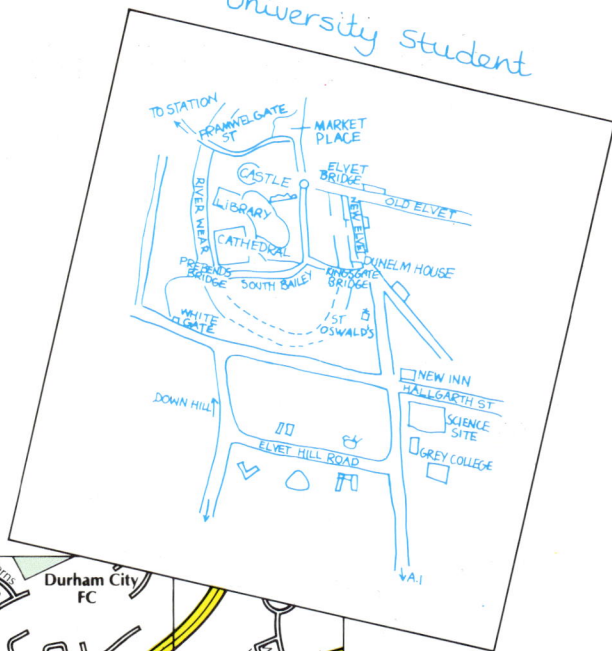

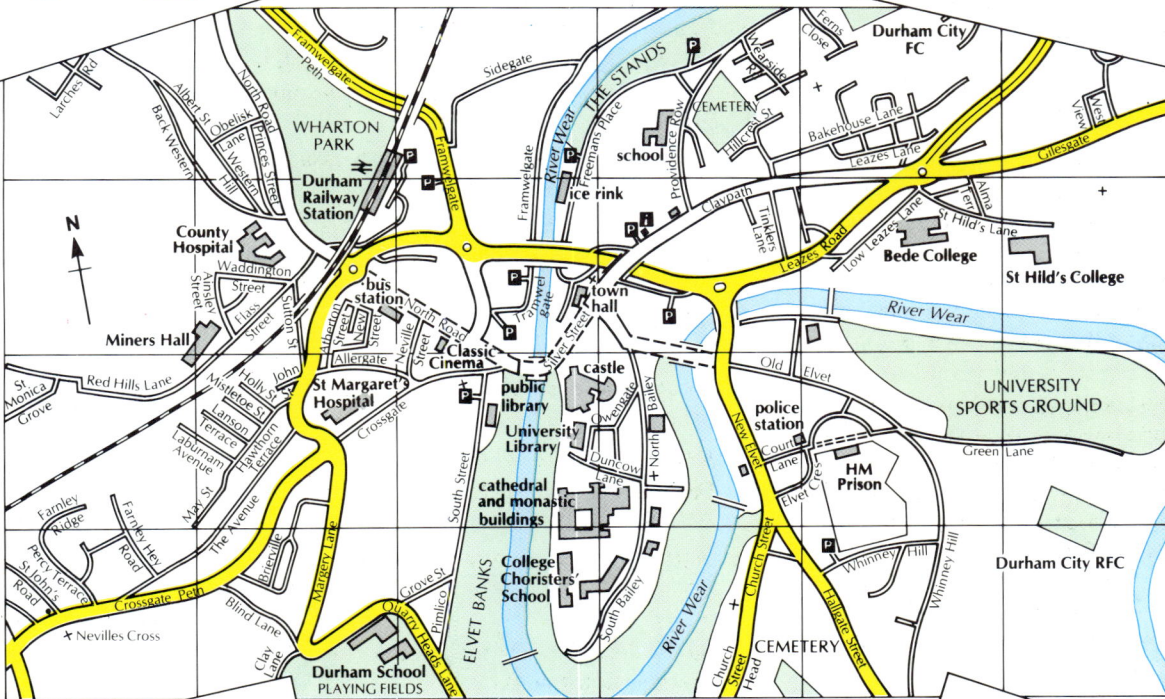

TO STATION
FRAMWELGATE ST
MARKET PLACE
CASTLE
ELVET BRIDGE
LIBRARY
OLD ELVET
CATHEDRAL
RIVER WEAR
DUNELM HOUSE
PREBENDS BRIDGE
SOUTH BAILEY
KINGSGATE BRIDGE
WHITE GATE
ST OSWALD'S
NEW INN
HALLGARTH ST
DOWN HILL
SCIENCE SITE
ELVET HILL ROAD
GREY COLLEGE
TO A.1

Adult Resident

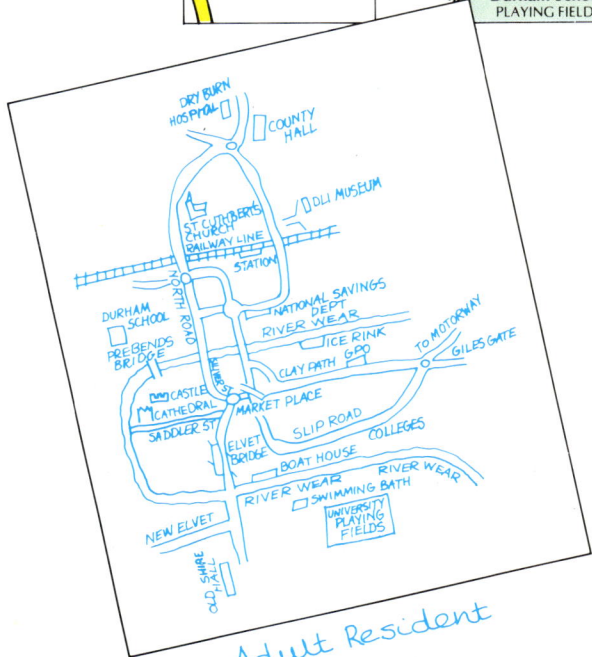

DRY BURN HOSPITAL
COUNTY HALL
ST CUTHBERTS CHURCH
DLI MUSEUM
RAILWAY LINE
STATION
NATIONAL SAVINGS DEPT
RIVER WEAR
DURHAM SCHOOL
NORTH ROAD
ICE RINK
TO MOTORWAY
PREBENDS BRIDGE
CLAY PATH
GPO
GILES GATE
CASTLE
CATHEDRAL
MARKET PLACE
SADDLER ST
SLIP ROAD
COLLEGES
ELVET BRIDGE
BOAT HOUSE
RIVER WEAR
RIVER WEAR
NEW ELVET
SWIMMING BATH
UNIVERSITY PLAYING FIELDS
OLD SHIRE HALL

Tourist

REDEVELOPMENT AREA
MARKET AREA
SUNDERLAND
RIVERSIDE RESTAURANT
SHOPS
SHOPS
POLICE BOX
DARLINGTON
DOUGLAS
BRIDGE
STONE
Castle
SHOPS
SHOPS
TO CASTLE
KEEP
Green
Cathedral
RIVER

(central 'proper' map of Durham)

Framwelgate Peth
Sidegate
THE STANDS
River Wear
Freemans Place
CEMETERY
Hillcrest
Close
Ferns
Durham City FC
Riverside
West View
Larches Rd
Albert St
Obelisk
North Road
Princes Street
Western Hill
Back Western
Framwelgate
school
Providence Row
Bakehouse Lane
Leazes Lane
Leazes Lane
Gilesgate
WHARTON PARK
Durham Railway Station
ice rink
Claypath
Tinklers Lane
Low Leazes Lane
Alma Place
St Hild's Lane
County Hospital
Waddington Street
Ainsley Street
Sutton St
Flass Street
bus station
North Road
Neville Street
North Road
town hall
Leazes Road
Bede College
St Hild's College
Miners Hall
Red Hills Lane
Holly St
John Street
Allergate
Classic Cinema
Framwelgate
Silver Street
castle
Old Elvet
River Wear
St Monica Grove
Mistletoe St
Crossgate
public library
University Library
Oswald
North Bailey
Duncow Lane
police station
Court Lane
HM Prison
New Elvet
Green Lane
UNIVERSITY SPORTS GROUND
St Margaret's Hospital
Laburnum Avenue
Lanson Terrace
Hawthorn Terrace
May St
cathedral and monastic buildings
South Street
Elvet Cres
Elvet Street
Farnley Ridge
Farnley Hey Road
The Avenue
Briarville
Grove St
Pimlico
ELVET BANKS
College Choristers School
South Bailey
River Wear
Church Street
Whinney Hill
Church Street
Halgate Street
Durham City RFC
Percy Terrace
St John's Road
Crossgate Peth
Blind Lane
Clay Lane
Margery Lane
Quarry Heads Lane
CEMETERY
Church Head
Nevilles Cross
Durham School PLAYING FIELDS
N

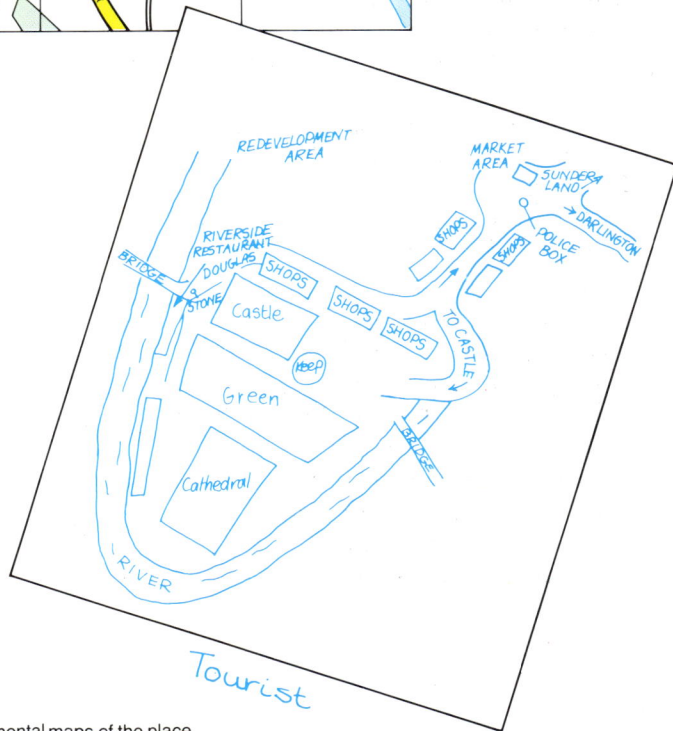

3 A 'proper' map of the centre of Durham and people's mental maps of the place

A SENSE OF BELONGING

Is there a neighbourhood feeling in the area in which you live? Do you live in an area which people feel they belong to? Is there a sense of community?

People living in a village would probably answer 'Yes' to all of these questions. Small settlements usually produce strong community feelings. In larger urban settlements, fewer people experience this feeling of belonging. Big towns and cities are somehow less personal and getting to know people is more difficult. However, *neighbourhood* or *community areas* do exist within many towns and cities. These 'urban villages' are settlements within settlements.

It is possible to distinguish between different types of neighbourhood:

° Physical neighbourhoods have houses of the same age and style. Or they may be clearly defined by boundaries such as main roads or railway lines.

° Social neighbourhoods contain residents from a similar social and economic class or from an ethnic minority group.

° Functional neighbourhoods revolve around shops, schools, churches and recreational facilities. These act as a focus for the area.

° Community neighbourhoods result from people developing a 'sense of togetherness' because movement into and out of such an area is limited.

Planners have tried to develop a sense of community in many of the new towns that have been built in Britain. This has been done by grouping housing and other amenities together into a *neighbourhood unit* (Visual 1). By having its own shops, community centres and open space, the neighbourhood unit reduces the need to travel elsewhere in the town and this helps to develop a local community spirit.

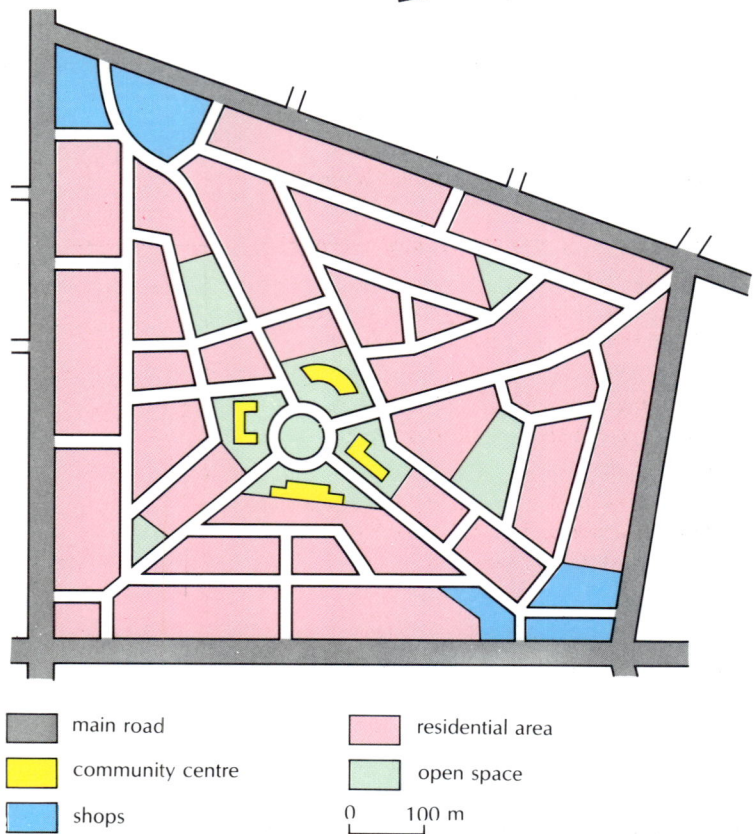

▨ main road	▨ residential area
▨ community centre	▨ open space
▨ shops	0 100 m

1 A neighbourhood unit in a new town. Many units like this one would be found in a new town

1 Look at the plan of the neighbourhood unit in Visual 1.

a) Make your own copy of the plan.

b) Add brief notes underneath your plan to explain how the neighbourhood unit:
   i) Reduces the need for transport.
   ii) Reduces the time and cost involved in shopping and using community and recreation facilities.
   iii) Reduces traffic congestion in the area.
   iv) Provides a safer environment for the young and elderly.

2 The three photographs above show facilities for shopping, education and recreation.

a) Write a paragraph to explain why these facilities are important in encouraging a neighbourhood or community feeling.

b) Make a list of other neighbourhood facilities which you think might also be important in encouraging a sense of community.

c) Think about the area where you live. Does it have any of the facilities you have listed? Do they help to make it more of a neighbourhood or community area?

3 Working in pairs:

a) Carry out a survey in your town or city to find out whether urban social areas exist. Use copies of the survey sheet shown in Visual 2 to collect the information.

b) As a class, discuss ways in which the information collected could be presented and analysed.

c) What conclusions can you draw about social areas in your town or city?

4 Elderly people often have a good memory for how neighbourhoods and communities have grown up and changed. You may have elderly relatives or neighbours who could provide you with some interesting information.

a) Try to arrange some interviews and record them on tape.

b) If you have access to a video camera, you might wish to do the interview on video tape.

c) Play back some of the interviews to the whole class and discuss some of the issues raised.

2 An example of a survey sheet for an investigation of urban social areas

URBAN SOCIAL AREAS SURVEY

1. IS THERE AN AREA AROUND HERE, IN WHICH YOU LIVE, THAT YOU CAN CALL A NEIGHBOURHOOD OR COMMUNITY AREA?   YES_____   NO_____

2. WHAT IS THE NAME OF THIS AREA?

_____

3. WHAT IS IT ABOUT THIS AREA THAT MAKES YOU FEEL IT IS A NEIGHBOURHOOD OR COMMUNITY?

_____

4. IF YOU HAD TO MOVE AWAY FROM THIS AREA WHAT DO YOU THINK YOU WOULD MISS THE MOST?

_____

THANK YOU FOR YOUR HELP WITH THIS SURVEY.

ASSIGNMENT ONE
A Good Place to Live?

There are many aspects of our urban surroundings that can be studied through first-hand investigations. This assignment is concerned with fieldwork exercises which can be carried out in urban areas. Throughout this book you will study many topics which offer possibilities for urban fieldwork. Besides working through this assignment, you may wish to design your own fieldwork investigations.

Your Assignment
○ Carry out your own urban fieldwork.
○ Consider the differences in environmental quality among selected neighbourhoods within your town or city.

Resources
1 The information on pages 8 and 9 on urban social areas.
2 Copies of the Environmental Quality Assessment Sheet shown here.
3 Visuals 1 and 2.
4 Clipboard and pencil.
5 Local street maps.
6 Camera.

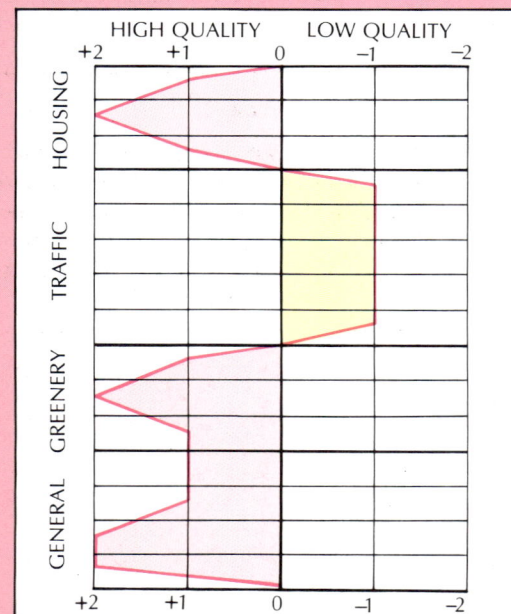

1 Assessing environmental quality. This imaginary neighbourhood is generally of high quality, although it seems to have traffic problems

ENVIRONMENTAL QUALITY ASSESSMENT SHEET

Name of streetworker _____   Group _____
Name of neighbourhood_____   Date/time
Weather conditions _____   _____

	HIGH QUALITY	+2	+1	0	−1	−2	LOW QUALITY
H O U S I N G	Well designed						Badly designed
	Good external condition						Poor external condition
	Expensive						Cheap
T R A F F I C	Uncongested streets						Congested streets
	Easy to park						Difficult to park
	Quiet						Noisy
	Safe for people						Dangerous for people
	Little pollution						Heavy pollution
G R E E N E R Y	Large gardens						Small gardens
	Plenty of trees and shrubs						Few trees and shrubs
	Plenty of public parks and gardens						Few public parks and gardens
G E N E R A L	Attractive						Ugly
	Little vandalism						Much vandalism
	Tidy						Untidy
	Good reputation						Poor reputation

TOTAL SCORE = [ ]

NOTE: to calculate the total score, add up all the + scores, next add up all the − scores, then find the difference between the two numbers. Remember to include a + or − sign in the total score.
Maximum possible score = +30
Minimum possible score = −30

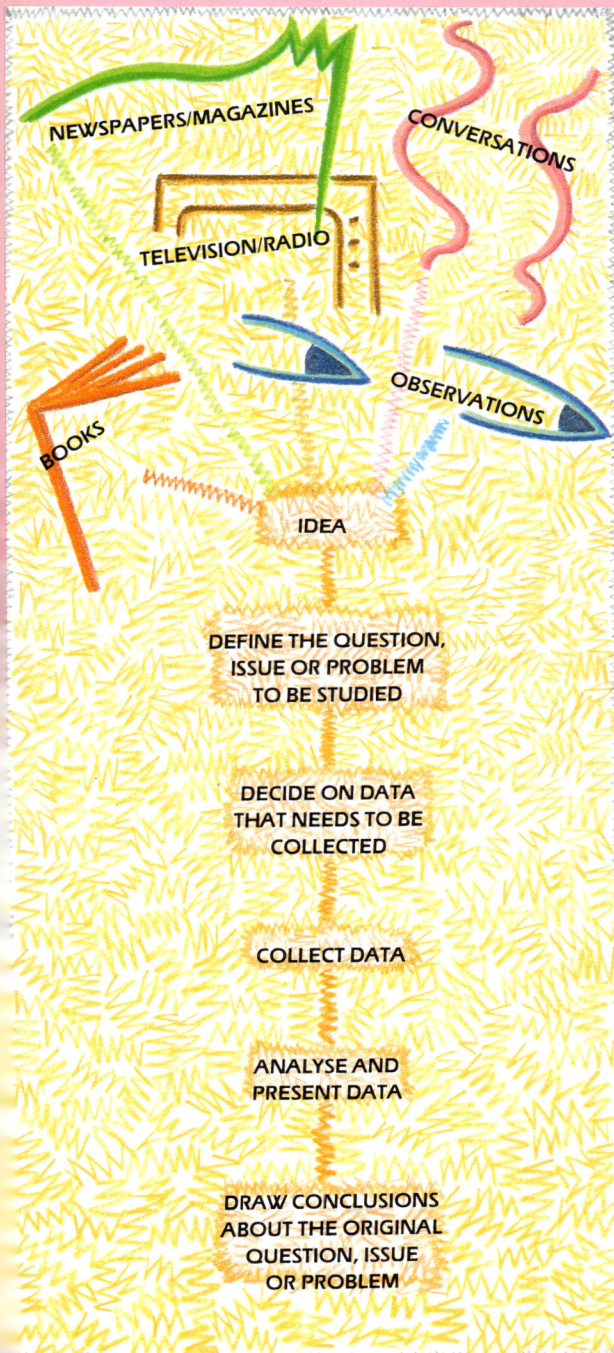

2 The main stages involved in a fieldwork investigation

NEWSPAPERS/MAGAZINES

CONVERSATIONS

TELEVISION/RADIO

OBSERVATIONS

BOOKS

IDEA

DEFINE THE QUESTION, ISSUE OR PROBLEM TO BE STUDIED

DECIDE ON DATA THAT NEEDS TO BE COLLECTED

COLLECT DATA

ANALYSE AND PRESENT DATA

DRAW CONCLUSIONS ABOUT THE ORIGINAL QUESTION, ISSUE OR PROBLEM

Work Programme A

1 a) Look back through the information on urban social areas on pages 8 and 9. Discuss the types of neighbourhood which exist in your local area. Are there many differences among neighbourhoods?

b) Choose four local neighbourhoods in which to collect data for your fieldwork investigation. Try to include:

- A council housing estate.
- An area of older terraced housing.
- A modern private estate.
- Another distinctive neighbourhood.

2 Working in groups of four, visit each of the neighbourhoods in turn.

a) First, take a good walk round each area to build up a general impression.

b) Complete your Environmental Quality Assessment Sheet. For each pair of words or statements, tick the box that best describes the neighbourhood. For example, if the area has very well designed housing, you might give it a score of $+2$. An area of very badly designed housing might get a score of only -2.

c) Calculate the total score for each neighbourhood.

3 Now you need to present and analyse the fieldwork data.

a) Draw bar charts to show the total scores for the four neighbourhoods.

b) For each neighbourhood, construct a diagram like the one shown in Visual 1.

c) Discuss what the bar charts and diagrams show about the neighbourhoods which you have surveyed. What conclusions can you draw?

Work Programme B

Work in groups of four.

1 Choose two of your neighbourhoods for further investigation. Try to select two contrasting neighbourhoods: for example, a council estate and a private estate, or an area of older housing and an area of newer housing.

2 Using a street map of each area, make a road-by-road survey to locate all the local facilities. Include such things as schools, shops, doctors, etc. Take photographs of the facilities in each area so you can build up a visual record.

3 Design a short questionnaire to find out whether people are happy with the facilities in their neighbourhood. Interview 20 people in each area.

4 Prepare a short report in which you display and write about your findings.

Work Programme C

Working in groups of four, look through some of the other chapters in this book to find ideas that could be developed into fieldwork investigations. Visual 2 shows the stages you should follow. Now carry out your own urban fieldwork.

4 ZONES OF LAND USE

1 Look at Visual 1, which shows two ways in which land is used in towns and cities.

a) You are going to make a list of different types of urban land use. Write down 'residential' and 'recreational' as the first two items on your list.

b) Now think of other ways in which land is used in urban areas. Add these to your list.

c) Compare your list with your neighbour's list. Can you get any further ideas from each other?

Within towns and cities different zones exist where the land has a particular kind of use. Town and city centres are full of shops, offices, hotels and public buildings. Most of the land within urban areas is taken up by housing. Space is also needed for industry and recreational facilities.

Land use zones are particularly well developed in older and larger towns and cities. In London or Birmingham, for example, the following main zones are formed by different land uses:

○ The central business district is at the heart of the city and easily recognized by its tall buildings. This is the shopping and business centre of the city.

○ Industrial areas are near the main road and rail routes. Older industries are usually found nearer the city centre, newer industries on the outskirts.

○ Old housing areas are near the city centre and are made up of terraced houses built around a grid pattern of narrow streets. In some places, the houses have been replaced by blocks of flats.

○ New housing areas are on the outskirts of the city. They are made up of detached and semi-detached houses built around a less regular pattern of streets. The houses tend to be larger than the old terraced houses.

○ Recreational areas are scattered throughout the city. They include public parks and gardens, sports facilities and open spaces.

The land use zones develop for logical reasons. Land is scarce near the city centre, for example, and this makes the cost of land high. Shops and businesses take over this central area because they do well from all the people (potential customers) passing through the centre. A shop or business can make big profits from a small amount of space. By contrast, there is no room for spacious new houses in city centres and newer housing areas are located on the outskirts of the city. Here there is room to build at lower densities. Many people prefer to live in these areas because they are closer to the countryside.

Visual 3 shows how different urban land uses do not always fit together easily. The first cartoon shows how today's road users need fast, modern roads which sometimes need to cross older housing areas to get to the city centre. In this case, there is a conflict between the housing need and road transport need. Examples of these conflicts of land use can be found in all towns and cities.

2 Visual 2 lists six major urban land uses and some specific examples of each.

a) Draw up a table with six columns and put a different major urban land use at the top of each column.

b) Now put each of the specific land use examples in the correct column.

3 Look at Visual 3. Working in a small group:

a) Discuss the message behind each of the cartoons.

b) Think of some other examples of conflicts of land use in towns and cities. You may be able to think of some good examples from your local area.

c) Design a cartoon to illustrate a conflict of urban land use.

4 Study the 1:50 000 Ordnance Survey map extract of Luton shown in Visual 4. Look carefully at the five marked grid squares.

a) What are the main land uses shown in each of the five marked grid squares?

b) Why are the land uses found at these particular locations in Luton?

c) Using evidence from the map, explain the land use pattern in Luton.

1 Residential and recreational land uses like these are important in all towns and cities

TYPES OF LAND USE

Residential
Industrial
Transport
Recreation and open space
Shops and offices
Public buildings and services

LAND USE EXAMPLES

House
Primary school
Newsagent
Park
Bank
Supermarket
Hospital
Factory
Railway station
College
Flats
Butcher
Travel agent
Bus station
Golf course

2 The main types of urban land use and some specific examples

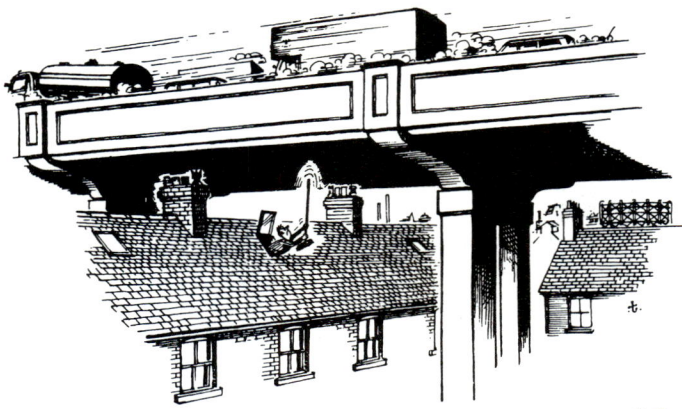

3 Some urban land uses are in conflict with others, as these cartoons show

"They'll have to do something soon. It's affecting the polar bears in the Arctic."

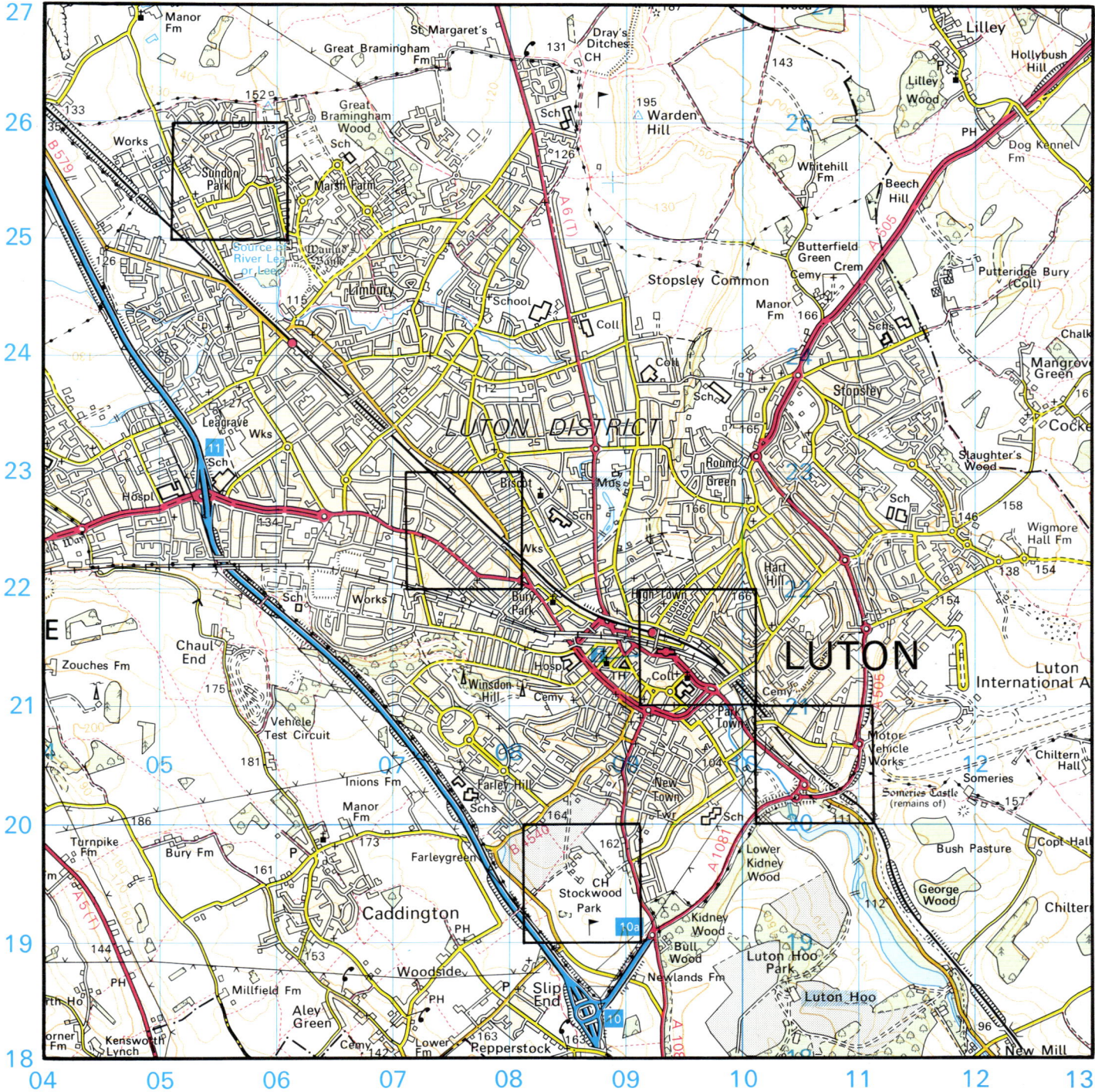

© Crown copyright 1987

4 Luton, Bedfordshire, is a city with 164 000 inhabitants. Luton shows a pattern of land use typical of many large urban areas

MODELS OF URBAN LAND USE

All towns and cities are different. Each has its own special features and landmarks. However, there are certain patterns which are common to all cities. In 1844, a German called Friedrich Engels visited the growing industrial city of Manchester. He was studying the conditions in which working people lived, and wrote about what he found. Although he did not realize it, Engels was setting down some of the first ideas about general land use in all cities.

Engels noticed that Manchester's business district was at the centre of the city and extended for almost 800 m in all directions. The housing areas were located according to social class. The houses of the working people were mixed in with factories and extended for 2.4 km around the central business district (CBD). Beyond this zone, were the homes of the wealthier middle classes. On the very edge of the city were the houses of the upper classes. Engels thought that this general pattern was typical of all cities.

Since then, many others have suggested theories to describe and explain the patterns of land use found within cities. Visual 1 shows the three main theories which have been developed. The ideas behind the theories are best shown in the form of diagrams which are called *models* because they are simplified and scaled-down versions of reality. These *urban land use models* have been used to explain the patterns found mainly in the cities of North America and Western Europe.

The first model suggests that cities grow outwards from the CBD in a series of circular zones. As the CBD grows, it invades the next zone and people have to move out. In this way, the circular zones expand and grow outwards. This was the sort of pattern that Engels described for Manchester and it was typical of the compact industrial cities of the 1800s. Later on, with the arrival of modern transport, people saw the advantage of locating industry along major roads and railways. Sectors of industry grew outwards along these transport routes, giving some cities a sector pattern of land use. Finally, there is the multi-centred model. In large cities which have grown up more recently, development has taken place around several centres. These cities have a much more mixed pattern of commercial, industrial and residential land use.

Circular pattern of land use zones

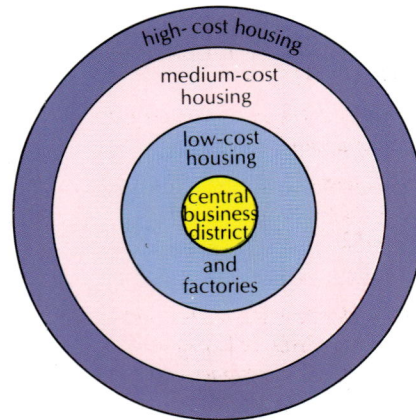

high-cost housing
medium-cost housing
low-cost housing
central business district
and factories

Sector pattern of land use zones

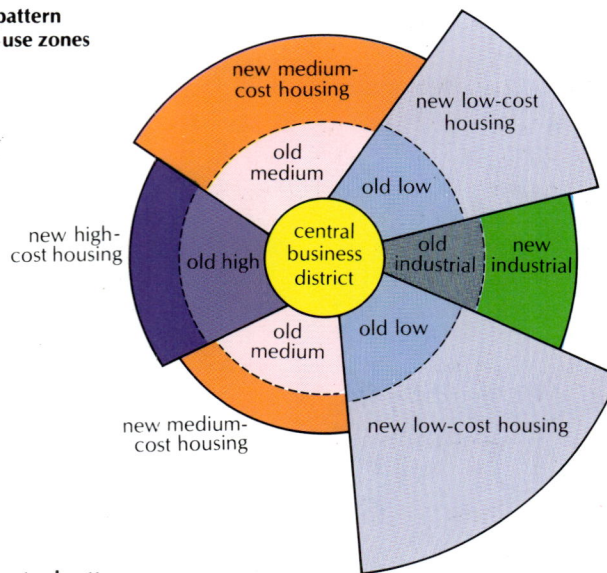

new medium-cost housing
new low-cost housing
old medium
old low
new high-cost housing
old high
central business district
old industrial
new industrial
old medium
old low
new medium-cost housing
new low-cost housing

Multi-centred pattern of land use zones

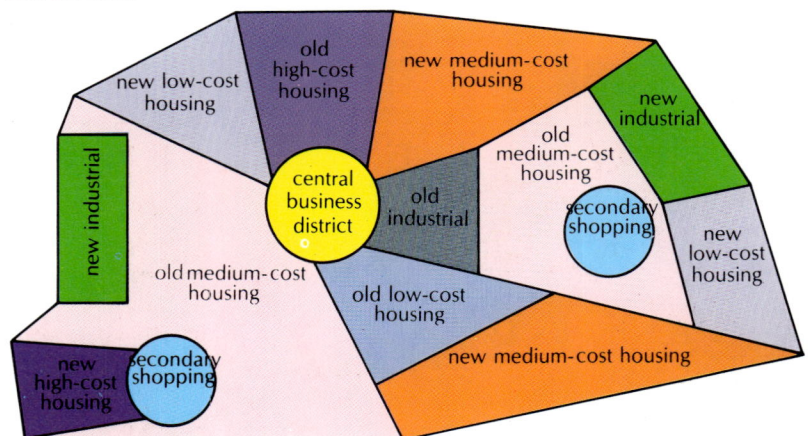

new low-cost housing
old high-cost housing
new medium-cost housing
new industrial
new industrial
central business district
old industrial
old medium-cost housing
secondary shopping
new low-cost housing
old medium-cost housing
old low-cost housing
new medium-cost housing
new high-cost housing
secondary shopping

1 These three models of urban land use have been used to describe and explain the growth and structure of cities

1 Look back at the information in the first two paragraphs.

  a) Describe the pattern of urban land use that Friedrich Engels found in Manchester in 1844.

  b) Why were his findings important?

2 Study the models in Visual 1 and read again the paragraph which explains them.

  a) Using the titles from Visual 1 as subheadings, list the main features of each of the three urban land use models.

  b) Think of your nearest town or city. Which model best describes the pattern of land use there?

  c) How have changes in society in the last 200 years led to changes in the pattern of urban land use?

3 Sometimes the growth and layout of a city are influenced by its location or some other special features. Some examples are shown in Visual 2.

  a) Make a copy of the four sketch maps.

  b) Think how each city might develop. Remember that cities grow outwards from the CBD, industry is attracted to transport routes, and the higher-cost housing gets the better land away from the CBD and industrial areas.

  c) Complete your sketch maps by drawing in a likely pattern of land use.

4 Look at Visual 3, which shows an urban land use model for cities in South America.

  a) Describe the pattern of land use.

  b) Suggest reasons for the location of the high-cost housing area and the zone of squatter settlements.

  c) Most models of urban land use have been developed in North America and Western Europe. Suggest some reasons why they may not be very useful in explaining the pattern of land use in cities in the countries of the South.

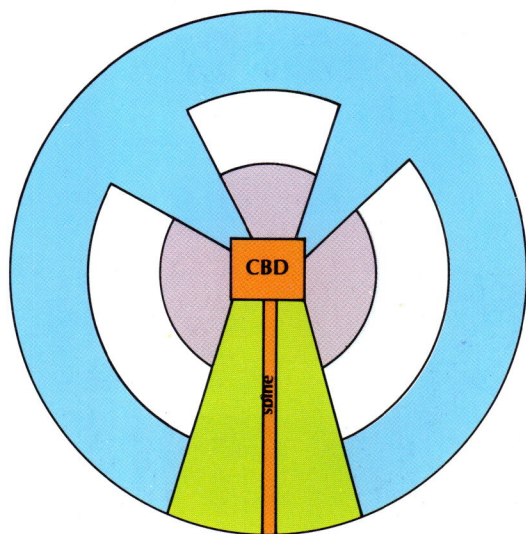

- commercial/ industrial
- high-class housing
- middle-class housing
- working-class housing
- squatter settlements

3 The pattern of urban land use is often very different in cities of the South, as this model shows

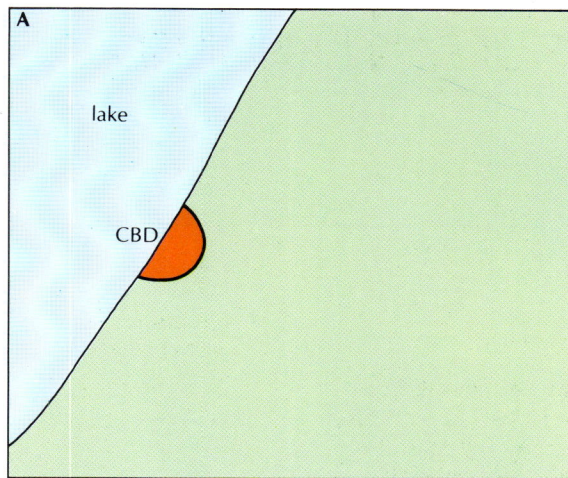

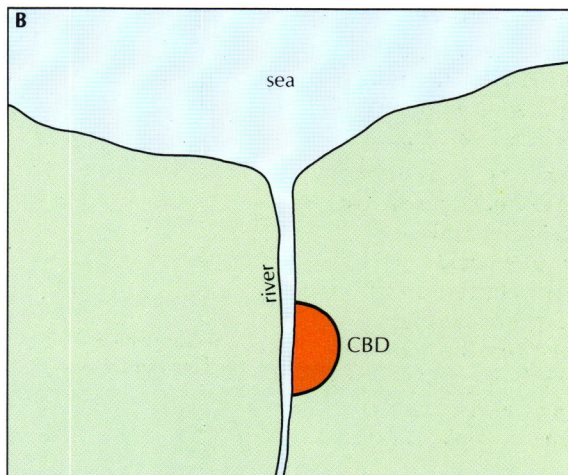

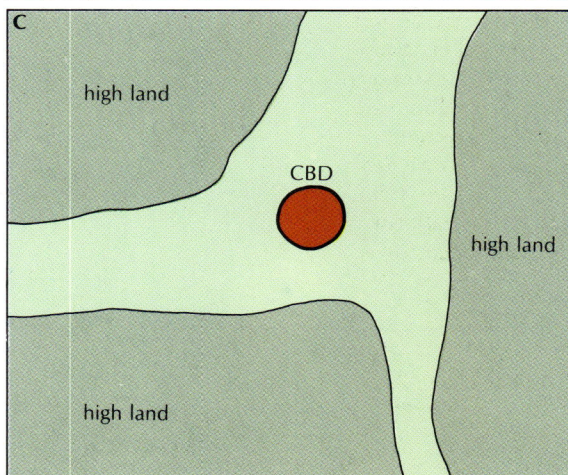

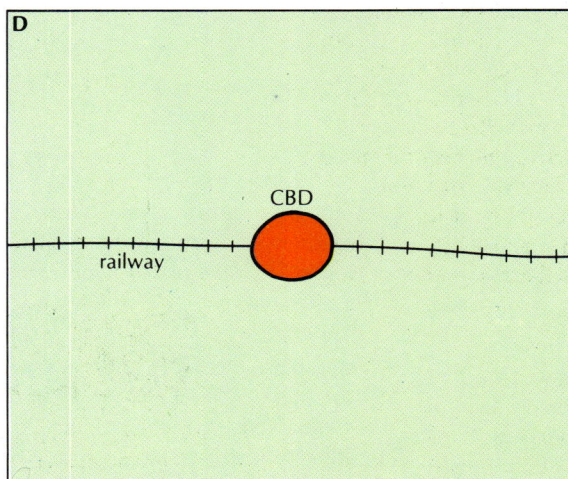

2 The pattern of urban land use in these four cities will be affected by
A the lake
B the river
C the high land
D the railway

ASSIGNMENT TWO
Land Use Survey

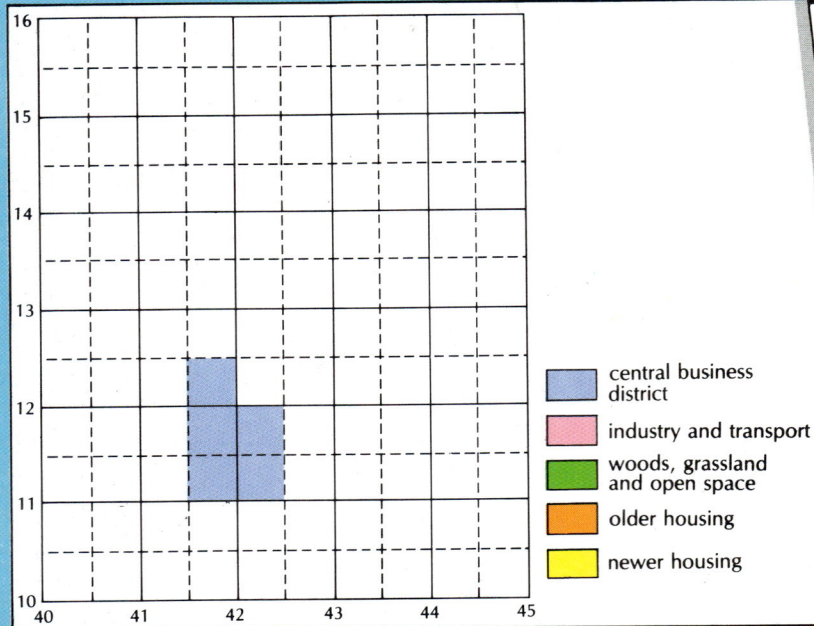

1 Your grid and colour code for plotting the general pattern of land use in Southampton

Legend:
- central business district
- industry and transport
- woods, grassland and open space
- older housing
- newer housing

Your Assignment

You work in a small team of three people in the Technical Support Unit at the Ordnance Survey Headquarters in Southampton. You have been asked by the head of your unit to produce some of the exhibition material requested by the head of Information and Public Relations Department.

Resources

1 The memo from the head of the Information and Public Relations Department.
2 Visuals 1 and 2.
3 The information on pages 14 and 15 on urban land use patterns.
4 The map of southern England in your atlas.

Work Programme

1 a) Read the memo.
   b) Discuss the type of material that would be best for an exhibition open to the general public.

2 Prepare the following visual material which could be photographically enlarged for display in the exhibition:

   a) A labelled sketch map of southern England to show the location and regional setting of Southampton.

   b) A copy of the urban land use models shown on page 14. Make sure that they have titles and are fully labelled.

   c) A map to show the general pattern of land use in Southampton. A copy of Visual 1 can be used for this map. Look at each quarter grid square in

   Visual 2 and decide which is the dominant land use. Using the key in Visual 1, fill in your map.

   d) Detailed sketch maps to show the distribution of two of the following:
   - Public open space.
   - Transport facilities.
   - Industry.
   - Old housing.

3 Use the information given here, together with your maps and diagrams, to prepare a list of key ideas related to urban land use in Southampton. For example:
   - Southampton's CBD is not centrally located.
   - Older housing is mainly located near the city centre.

Legend (map key):
- Housing, Shops and Offices
- Manufacturing Industry
- Public Utilities
- Tips
- Derelict Land
- Docks and Transport
- Major Roads
- Minor Roads
- Open Space
- Woodland
- Grassland
- Rough Land
- Allotments
- Nurseries
- Water

2 Extract from 1965 land use map of the Southampton area. (Based on Ordnance Survey 1:25 000 map with permission of the Controller of Her Majesty's Stationery Office. Crown Copyright reserved)

6 THE CITY CENTRE

1 The city centre of Birmingham

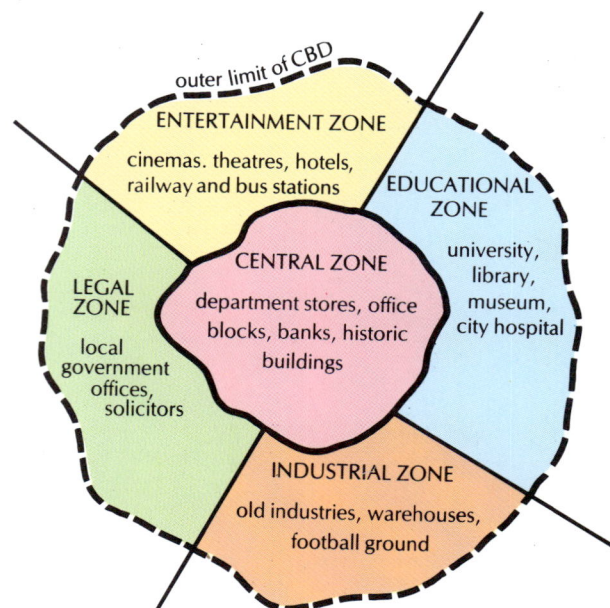

2 A model to show functional zones in central business districts

Diagram labels:

outer limit of CBD

ENTERTAINMENT ZONE
cinemas. theatres, hotels, railway and bus stations

EDUCATIONAL ZONE
university, library, museum, city hospital

CENTRAL ZONE
department stores, office blocks, banks, historic buildings

LEGAL ZONE
local government offices, solicitors

INDUSTRIAL ZONE
old industries, warehouses, football ground

Central business districts or CBDs grow up in the centre of towns and cities where major road and rail routes converge. These transport routes make the city centre easy to get to (accessible) from the suburbs and the region around the city. Space is in short supply in the city centre and competition for space pushes up the value of the land. Only shops, banks and other commercial enterprises can afford the high land values, so these dominate the CBD. Shops, banks and other services group together within the CBD because more customers can be attracted to a limited area. Some of the main features of the CBD are shown at the top of page 19.

Birmingham, the second largest city in Britain, has a city centre that has undergone massive changes during the last 40 years. The slums and the old Victorian heart of the city have been cleared to make way for new roads, office blocks and shopping centres. Visual 1 shows what Birmingham city centre looks like today.

Birmingham's CBD is the core of a city of one million people and much of the redevelopment has been designed to reduce traffic congestion. New multi-storey and roof-top car parks have eased parking problems and an inner ring road has improved traffic flow. The Bull Ring and New Street Station shopping centres opened in the 1960s. These areas have shops, offices, open air markets and gardens and provide covered shopping halls on seven floors. The nearby mainline railway station and bus station make these areas accessible to the entire West Midlands region.

Not everyone is happy with the changes in the centre of Birmingham. Some local people say that the city centre has lost its individuality and now looks like many other city centres. There are other pressures on the CBD as well. Since the 1960s, many people and jobs have moved out of central Birmingham into the suburbs and surrounding region. Shopping centres and hypermarkets have been built on the edge of the city. The competition from these could force the CBD to change again in the future.

MAIN FEATURES OF CENTRAL BUSINESS DISTRICTS

Concentration of Shops

Large department stores, such as Marks and Spencer, C&A and British Home Stores, are found at the heart of the CBD. They attract large numbers of people from a wide area. Other specialist shops, such as book shops and jewellers, are also concentrated in the CBD

Concentration of Offices

Regional and head offices of large companies concentrate in the CBD. They are attracted by the accessibility of the city centre. Well-known companies like a well-known location for their head offices.

Little Manufacturing Industry

The CBD is not a suitable location for most manufacturing industries. However, a few specialized industries, such as newspaper and magazine publishers, do locate in the CBD. They need to be near to other CBD services and to have access to road and rail transport for distribution.

Growth of Functional Zones

Similar activities tend to concentrate in certain parts of the CBD. It is usually possible to find areas given over almost entirely to entertainment, banks and financial services, educational facilities and shops.

Multi-storey Development

The CBD has to grow upwards as well as outwards because of high land values. The most expensive sites have the tallest buildings. In a multi-storey block different activities may often occupy different floors.

Low Residential Population

There is little housing in the CBD because of the high land values. However, a few people live in luxury flats and apartments.

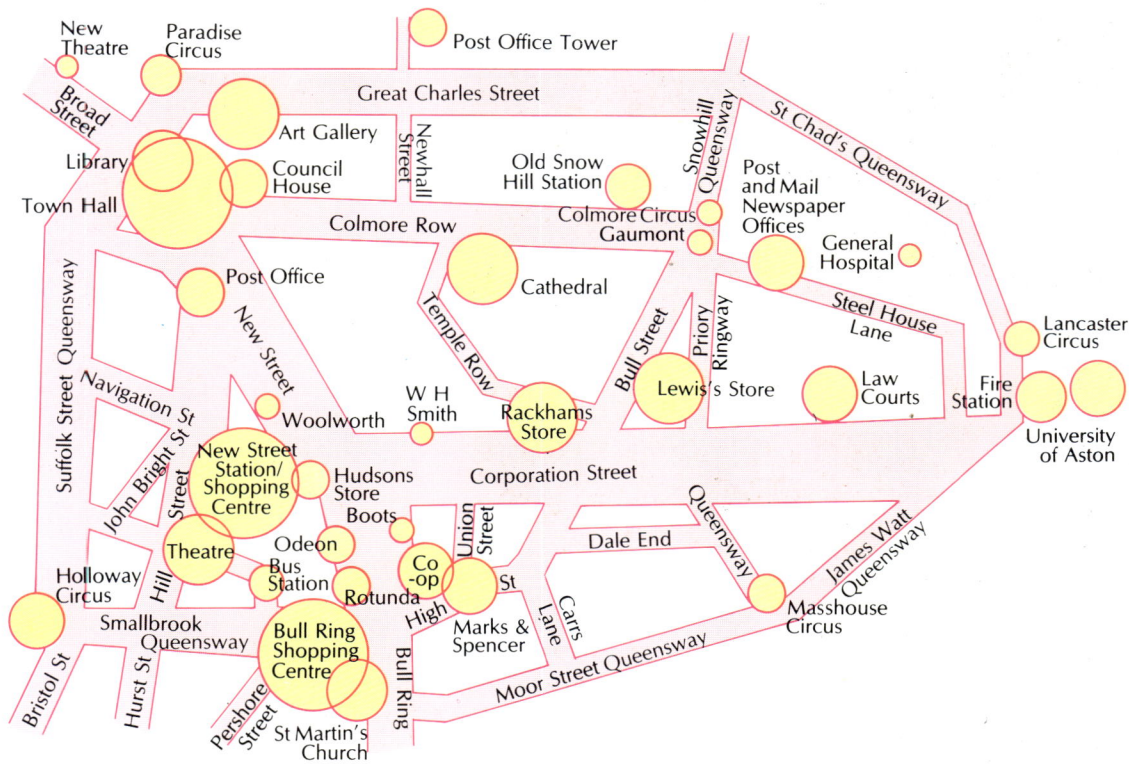

1 a) Write a short definition for the term 'central business district'.

   b) In your own words, describe the main features of CBDs.

2 Study the CBD of Birmingham shown in Visual 1. Make a sketch of the area shown and add labels for the following: inner ring road, Rotunda Tower, office blocks, car parks, shops. Give your finished sketch a suitable title.

3 Visual 2 shows how functional zones develop in central business districts.

   a) Copy Visual 2.

   b) Now think about the centre of a town or city near you. Do some land uses form groups along certain roads or in certain areas?

   c) Draw a simple sketch map of your nearest town or city to show any functional zones that exist.

4 Look at Visual 3, which shows a map of how Birmingham people see their own city centre.

   a) Which buildings and streets are the most important to Birmingham people?

   b) Why do you think that some buildings and streets are more important than others?

   c) Is there any evidence of functional zones in Birmingham's CBD?

   d) Why might a map, like the one in Visual 3, be useful to city planners?

5 Write a short essay with the title 'The CBD of the Future'. Describe how you see city centres developing over the next 50 years. Suggest reasons for any changes you describe.

3 This map of central Birmingham is based on the results of a survey of city residents. The size of the circles and the width of the streets in this map show the importance they attached to certain streets and buildings

1

2

In the days before motor transport, most people's shopping needs were satisfied by small *corner shops*. Each corner shop served a small area and people went there regularly for foodstuffs and other necessities. Most things, such as tea, coffee and butter, were not sold in packets. They had to be weighed out and then wrapped up for the customer. The first self-service grocery shops, called 'Humpty Dumpty' stores, were opened in the United States in 1912. The first grocery store with a check-out at the exit was the 'Piggly Wiggly', opened in Memphis in 1916. These early *supermarkets* were a huge success and within seven years there were 2800 'Piggly Wigglys' in the States. In 1948 the Coop opened their first British supermarket at Manor Park in London.

During the last 20 years, other far-reaching changes have taken place in the location and type of retail activity in Britain. The major urban redevelopment which affected the centres of many British cities during the 1960s and 1970s has now died down. Today, there is an increased demand for out-of-town shopping centres. People now spend a smaller proportion of their income on shopping than they did 20 years ago. The attitudes of shoppers are changing as well. A recent survey found that supermarket shoppers rate convenience of store location as more important than price in deciding where to shop.

These social changes are leading to different types of retail complex being built.

City centre shopping areas are centrally located and purpose-built and covered to provide protection from the weather all year round. Access to them is good and they have multi-storey car parks. Large department stores, such as Boots and Debenhams, act as 'anchor shops', attracting customers for the smaller retailers. The Queensgate Shopping Centre in Peterborough and the Arndale Centre in Manchester are examples of these.

Out-of-town shopping centres have been the trend in recent years. Sometimes these feature a large *superstore* or *hypermarket*, such as Asda or Tesco, which offers a wide range of food and non-food products in a single-level, self-service store (Visual 2). Free car parks are provided and other facilities, such as petrol stations, are common.

Discount warehouses sometimes occupy out-of-town sites. Here, two or more stores selling bulky, household goods operate from a single site with a shared car park. B&Q and MFI are examples of superstore groups that operate from discount warehouses. Out-of-town shopping centres are located on important roads, often near major intersections so that people can get to them easily.

Speciality shopping centres are small developments, containing shops that sell specialized goods, such as clothes and jewellery. This type of centre has its own individuality, so it needs no large stores to act as 'anchors'. There are often many catering outlets. London's Covent Garden is perhaps the best-known speciality shopping centre in Britain. Others can be found in, for example, Edinburgh, Liverpool and Leicester.

Multi-purpose centres are the latest idea in retailing. Here, shopping is linked with other activities such as leisure or education. The Metrocentre in Gateshead, near Newcastle upon Tyne, is a good example. It includes a Marks and Spencer store, a Carrefour hypermarket, 130 smaller shops in a glass-covered mall, an undercover funfair, a ten-screen cinema and an antiques market. A nearby hotel, office and business park complex will complete the Metrocentre. We will probably see much more of this type of mixed development over the next few years.

1 High streets are looking more and more alike because each chain store or group, such as McDonald, uses the same kind of frontage and logo everywhere

2 Tesco started as a market stall. Then it became a chain of high street supermarkets. Today Tesco is tending to occupy out-of-town sites. The addition of non-food products and more floor space is turning Tesco into a group of superstores

3 Some well-known superstores, department stores and discount warehouses

1 Write short definitions for the following terms:
corner shop   supermarket   superstore
department store   hypermarket   discount warehouse.

2 Look at Visual 1. Working in pairs, make a list of chain stores which you would easily recognize in any town because of their distinctive shop fronts and logos.

3 Look at Visual 3. Working with your neighbour:

a) Draw up a table like the one below and sort the store names into the correct column.

SUPERMARKET/ SUPERSTORE	DEPARTMENT STORE	DISCOUNT WAREHOUSE
Tesco	Debenhams	B & Q

b) Which ones were difficult to place? Why was this?

4 Visual 4 shows the layout of a new city centre shopping complex in South London.

a) What is the purpose of the anchor stores?

b) What do you notice about their location?

c) What types of shop are likely to occupy the smaller retail units?

d) What other facilities would you like to see in a shopping centre such as this?

5 Write a short report in which you summarize the main developments in retailing during the last 20 years.

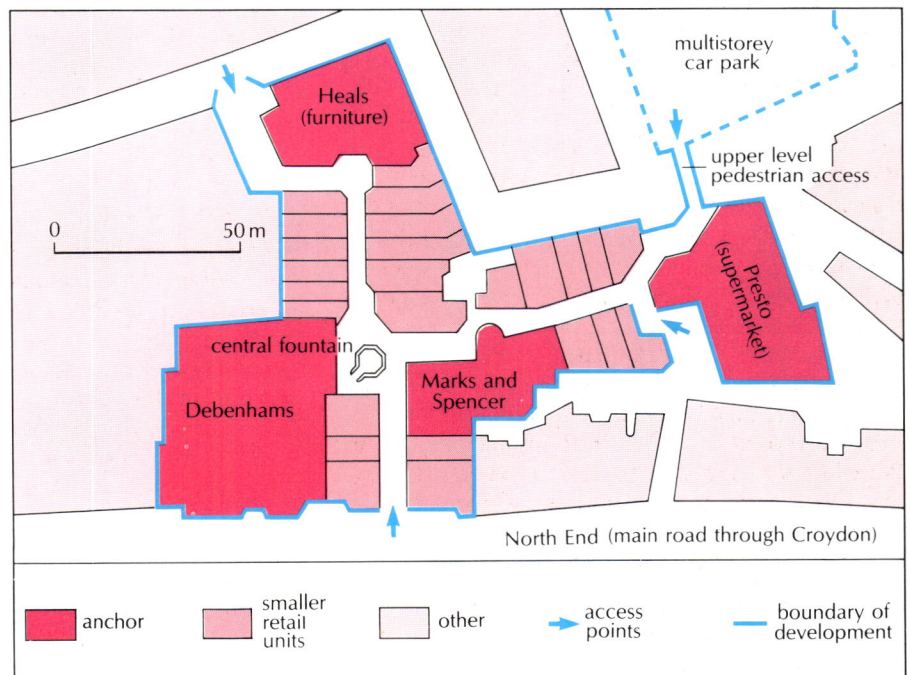

4 The Drummond Place Shopping Centre in Croydon

21

Locating a Superstore

Abingdon is a thriving market town in Oxfordshire. In recent years its population growth has been rapid, both in the town and in the surrounding area. There is now an urgent need for further shopping development in the town to meet increasing demand.

A further 8000 square metres of shop floor-space is needed if Abingdon is to continue its present role as a shopping centre. Only three sites in the town are capable of accommodating this scale of development. Several leading foodstore groups are interested in establishing new premises in Abingdon. The minimum floor-space requirement would be 4000 square metres, although the premises could be larger.

Any development of this kind is bound to have a considerable economic, social and environmental impact on the town. Opposition is likely to come from small shopkeepers, conservationists and other interested groups of people. However, any foodstore group that can successfully establish premises in Abingdon is likely to earn large profits in the coming years.

Your Assignment

You work for the Crossmac Foodstore Group. Your job is to find profitable new sites for supermarkets, superstores and hypermarkets throughout Britain. At the moment, you are looking at the possibility of establishing new premises in Abingdon. You have just received some background information on Abingdon from Parker and Unwin Property Surveys plc.

The competition from other foodstore groups is fierce. They probably have their sights set on Abingdon as well. You need to weigh up the possibilities quickly and report to your managing director as soon as possible.

Resources

1 Abingdon Shopping Survey – summary of findings.

2 Map showing location of possible sites.

3 Extracts from letters to the local newspaper.

Parker & Unwin Property Surveys PLC

EXISTING SHOPPING FACILITIES

1 Quantity

The present shopping catchment area (ie the town and immediate surrounding villages) includes a population of about 45 000 and is served by 174 establishments with 18 580 m^2 of shop floor space. Some shopping is also done by Abingdon people in the regional centre of Oxford. Average spending per person in Abingdon shops is £1500 per year.

2 Location

The heart of the shopping area is in the town centre. Much of this is pedestrianised and forms a compact area. Shops give way to other commercial premises along Ock Street, and towards the River Thames tourist facilities dominate. Because the town centre is so compact, shops on the fringe of the town centre are not as successful commercially. Removal of a great deal of the town centre traffic by the A34(T) bypass has improved the attractiveness of the town as a shopping area.

At the moment there are no large district shopping centres in Abingdon, though there are local shopping facilities in most of the residential areas. There are four neighbourhood centres providing everyday needs. The new residential areas growing up to the north and east of Abingdon are, at present, not served by shopping facilities.

3 Quality

Abingdon is overshadowed by Oxford, which is an important regional shopping centre. Its range of goods and facilities are therefore limited. Convenience goods (eg food, newspapers) are poorly represented for a town of its size. The range of comparison goods (eg carpets, furniture) is also limited.

FUTURE REQUIREMENTS AND POSSIBILITIES

1 Quantity

By 1991 the shopping catchment area will include a population of about 55 000. If it is assumed that, in line with national trends, spending will increase to about £1750 per year, then an additional 8 000 m^2 of shop floor space will be needed by 1991 in order for Abingdon to continue its present role.

2 Location

On the basis of a technical study carried out, it appears that three sites in Abingdon are suitable for further shopping development on this scale. These sites (A, B and C) are shown on the enclosed map. The main features of the sites are given in the table below.

SITE	DESCRIPTION	MAXIMUM CAPACITY
A	Edge of town. Junction of A415 and new A34(T) north/south route. A major development site with room for expansion.	12 000 m^2
B	Town centre. Traditional route centre and main shopping area. Would involve demolition of cattle market and some housing.	8 000 m^2
C	Neighbourhood. Within new residential development on north-eastern edge of town.	4 000 m^2

3 Quality

Possible shopping developments fall into three main groups:

(a) District supermarket: size about 4 000 m^2 to serve a population of about 7 000.

(b) Town superstore: size about 8 000 m^2 to serve a population of about 25 000.

(c) Regional hypermarket: size about 12 000 m^2 to serve a population of about 55 000.

Parker & Unwin Property Surveys PLC

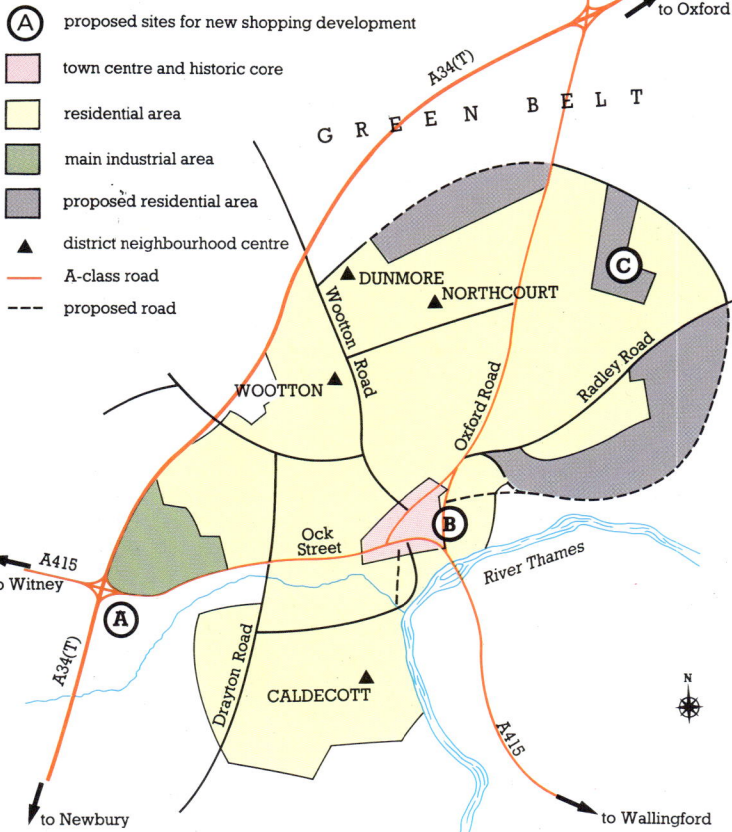

Map Legend

- Ⓐ proposed sites for new shopping development
- town centre and historic core
- residential area
- main industrial area
- proposed residential area
- ▲ district neighbourhood centre
- A-class road
- proposed road

to Oxford

A34(T)

GREEN BELT

▲ DUNMORE

▲ NORTHCOURT

Ⓒ

Wootton Road

WOOTTON

Oxford Road

Radley Road

Ock Street

Ⓑ

River Thames

A415 to Witney

A34(T)

Drayton Road

Ⓐ

CALDECOTT

▲

A415

N

to Newbury

to Wallingford

Parker & Unwin Property Surveys PLC

ABINGDON FACTSHEET

- Historic market town lying in the Thames Valley, some six miles to the south of Oxford.
- Acts as a shopping, administrative, recreation, education and employment centre for its inhabitants and the surrounding rural area.
- Recent growth: the population has risen from 14,287 in 1961 to 18,610 in 1971 and 22,686 in 1981, accommodated mainly in new residential developments on the southern and eastern fringes of the town.
- Further population growth is envisaged to 31,500 in 1991. Much of this growth is planned for the northern and eastern edges of Abingdon.
- Fine historic buildings and cobbled market place in the town centre, much of which is protected by Conservation Area status.
- Growing traffic congestion in the town centre has been relieved by the completion of an inner relief road and the A34(T) by-pass.
- Attractive riverside location adds to Abingdon's role as a tourist centre.

Friends of Abingdon

Honorary Secretary: Mrs C. Pendleford-Jones
48 East Saint Helen Street
Abingdon on Thames
Oxfordshire

12 September 1987

Dear Sir

I am deeply concerned about the rumours concerning a proposed shopping development for Abingdon's historic town centre. As you will be aware, the 'Friends of Abingdon' have been working tirelessly to protect Abingdon's ... town centre ...

WESSEX HOMES (Ltd)

24 Dorset Terrace, Salisbury, Wiltshire

15 September 1987

Dear Sir,

You will be aware that Wessex Homes have played a leading role in promoting attractive homes at reasonable prices for the growing number of people who wish to live in this area. He... there is an urgent need for new shopping developments for... new housing areas we are developing ... north-east Abingdon...

HUTCHINSONS of ABINGDON
specialist grocers of distinction
founded 1854

8 September 1987

Dear Sir

The attractive atmosphere and compact nature of the Abingdon town centre shopping area is something that must be preserved at all costs. The building of a new supermarket or superstore on the outskirts of Abingdon would greatly harm town centre trade ...

John Day
48 Drayton Road
Caldecot
South Abingdon
Oxon

21st September 1987

Dear Sir,

I have been following stories in your newspaper about future shopping development in the town with great interest. I live on the south-west side of the town where shopping facilities are very poor and have thought about this p...

Work Programme

Your job is to prepare a report for Crossmac's managing director on whether to establish premises in Abingdon. Draw upon information from any of the resources and illustrate your report where possible. Use the following sections in your report:

1. **The Abingdon Scene.** Describe Abingdon, its existing shopping facilities and future shopping needs.

2. **The Abingdon Alternatives.** Outline the sites available for development and what types of development are possible.

3. **Crossmac in Abingdon.** Consider the different types of development that Crossmac could offer at each site. What impact would this company have on Abingdon? Which ones are best for Crossmac?

4. **The Crossmac Decision.** State what types of shopping development should take place and at which site. Give full reasons for your decision.

INDUSTRY IN BRITAIN'S CITIES

1 Office block development in London is booming. In recent years, office-based service industries have grown more quickly than factory-based manufacturing industries

2 Manufacturing industry is attracted by urban locations where labour supply, good transport links and a market are all available. This photograph, taken in 1937, shows factories and housing along the Great West Road, about 20 km west from the centre of London. The photograph was taken looking west

Urban areas are natural sites for many industries. Industry needs a labour supply and a market for its products. Towns and cities provide both of these in one concentrated area. Industry also needs good communications for moving raw materials and finished products. Again, towns and cities are ideal because they often grow up where major road and rail routes meet.

Industry in urban areas is constantly changing. Until the 1700s, the main industries in British towns and cities were retailing (usually small, individually-owned shops) and craft industries (producing clothes, metalwares and household items on a small scale). During the Industrial Revolution, large-scale manufacturing industries developed rapidly in the cities of the Midlands, the North, South Wales and Scotland. These industries included iron and steel making, textiles and engineering. All this activity led to a need for more services in banking, insurance and commerce.

London is the place where many of these service industries concentrate and most of the head offices of major companies are based there. Today, service industries are becoming increasingly important in all of Britain's cities, while manufacturing industries are in decline. This is a national trend.

Industry has made its mark on cities, and certain industrial patterns can be picked out in most large urban areas. Visual 3 shows, in simplified form, the general pattern of industrial location in Britain's urban areas. Some industries need to be sited in and around the central business district. Most city centre employment is in offices (Visual 1). Financial services (banking, shipping and insurance), government departments, law firms and specialist technical and scientific services take up most of the office space. Specialist manufacturing industries also have central locations. Examples include printing and publishing, jewellery-making and the clothing trade. Industries that use the whole of the city as a market place, such as bakeries and breweries, also occupy central sites.

From 1918 to 1939, people and jobs started to move outwards from city centres towards the suburbs. Many newer industries grew up along major roads. This type of industrial *ribbon development* was common in North and West London (Visual 2). Food processing and light manufacturing industries grew along the Edgware Road, Western Avenue, Great West Road and North Circular Road. Some manufacturing industries needing plenty of space, such as metals and chemicals, have grown up in suburban locations as well.

Waterfront locations are important for industry where an urban area has a major river or a stretch of coastline. Shipbuilding and ship-repairing obviously need to be on waterfronts. Other industries that prefer a waterfront location include those that handle bulky raw materials. Examples are oil refining, flour milling, sugar refining, timber mills and chemical works.

CITY EDGE DEVELOPMENT: *industrial estates beyond the city boundary at the intersection of major arterial roads and new motorways.*

NEW TOWNS: *purpose-built industrial areas beyond the city boundary on 'greenfield' sites in satellite towns.*

ENTERPRISE ZONES: *older run-down areas near the city centre which are undergoing redevelopment.*

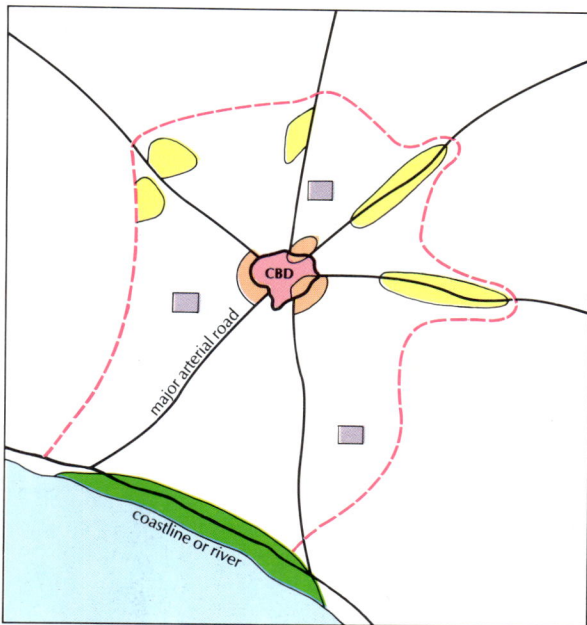

- centrally located industries
- suburban industries
- waterfront industries
- randomly located industries
- – – – limit of urban area

3 A model of industrial location in a typical British city

1 Study the business and industrial environments shown in Visuals 1 and 2. Working in pairs:

 a) Discuss the advantages and disadvantages of working in each area.

 b) Which area would you prefer to work in? Why?

2 Look back through the information in this chapter and answer the following:

 a) Why are urban areas a natural location for many industries?

 b) What types of industry were found in urban areas before the Industrial Revolution?

 c) What types of industry developed in urban areas during the Industrial Revolution?

 d) Why are service industries more important in urban areas nowadays than manufacturing industries?

 e) What does a national trend mean?

3 a) Make your own copy of the diagram shown in Visual 3. Remember to give your diagram a title and full key.

 b) Why might some industries be located randomly?

 c) Add two examples to your key of industries found in each location.

4 Locations which have become important for industry in recent years are shown in the table on the left.

 a) Using the appropriate symbols and labels, mark these developments and locations on your diagram.

 b) Write a paragraph to summarize the main features of your diagram.

5 Look at the information in the advertisement (Visual 4).

 a) Write a short paragraph to describe the location of the industrial estate.

 b) What types of industry have moved into the estate? Do they fit into certain industrial groups?

 c) Make a list of the main advantages which this location has for industry.

 d) What evidence is there in the advertisement that the developers are trying to provide an attractive environment for industry and its workers?

At the heart of the Midlands and minutes from the M1...

Already the Braunstone Industrial Estate numbers among its tenants some of the biggest names in British Industry.

Braunstone is sited on the edge of a large residential estate, is well served by public transport, and only 2½ miles from the centre of Leicester with its 285,000 inhabitants.

Mackenzie Hill have industrial units from 20,000 sq. ft. to let.

Mackenzie Hill
International property developers

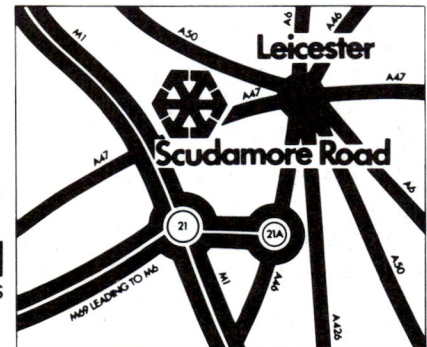

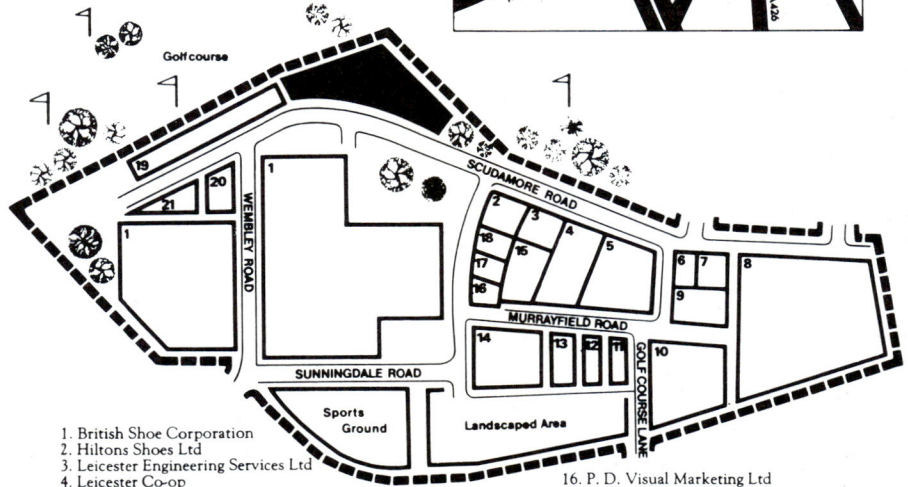

1. British Shoe Corporation
2. Hiltons Shoes Ltd
3. Leicester Engineering Services Ltd
4. Leicester Co-op
5. Decca Radio & Television Ltd
6. Cadbury-Schweppes
7. English Glass Co
8. GEC-Elliot Process Automation Ltd
9. Marwin Hardmetals Ltd
10. Stibbes Ltd
11. Sylvan Fabrics Ltd
12. Milk Marketing Board
13. Olivers Shoes Ltd
14. Rowntree-Mackintosh Ltd
15. Budgen Cash & Carry
16. P. D. Visual Marketing Ltd
17. Crompton Parkinson Ltd
18. Eden Vale Dairy Food (Ski Yoghurt)
19. Nursery Units, mainly occupied by private companies
20. United Carriers Ltd
21. R.S.P.C.A.

4 A purpose-built industrial estate with a city edge location

Is there much to do where you live? What do you, your friends and family do in your spare time? Some areas seem to have better facilities than others for sport, entertainment and leisure. If you live in a large town or city, the chances are that you will have a wide range of leisure activities and facilities to choose from. Exactly where you live has an impact on what you do for leisure.

Like many countries in the North, Britain has to meet an increasing demand for leisure and recreational facilities. This is due to several important changes that have occurred in society over the past 30 years:

° The population has increased.

° Annual holidays are now longer and working hours shorter.

° Incomes have risen.

° Car ownership has increased.

° Educational opportunities exist for more people.

So we now live in a country where many people have more free time and money for leisure and recreation. People are generally better informed about what leisure activities and facilities are available and many have their own means of transport.

The distribution of these facilities is often uneven throughout a city. For example, cinemas and theatres are usually found near the centre. Museums and art galleries are also found here. Parks and other public open spaces are often scattered throughout a city. Larger areas of open space are often on the edge where the land is cheaper because of less competition from other land uses. Recreation grounds and small play spaces are found throughout urban areas.

Until recently, planners concentrated on providing recreation and leisure facilities for city dwellers in areas outside cities. However, the growing number of visitors to parts of our coastline and countryside has led to their becoming over-used. Pressure from people is also causing problems in Green Belt areas around large cities and conurbations. Today, recreation planners are trying to provide extra facilities either within urban areas or in nearby country parks. Leisure facilities and combined shopping leisure complexes are just some of the ways in which leisure is being promoted nowadays in towns and cities.

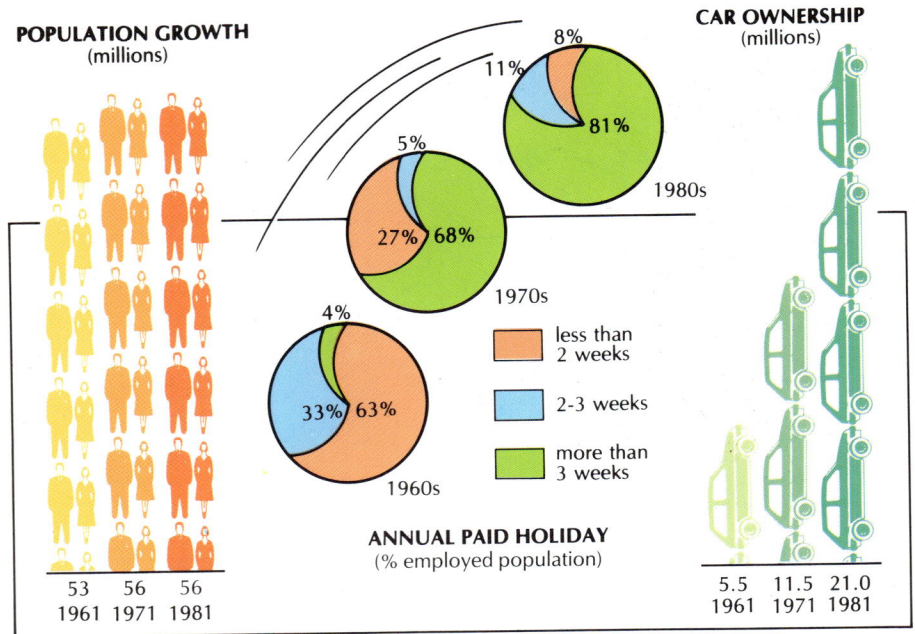

POPULATION GROWTH (millions)

53 / 1961   56 / 1971   56 / 1981

CAR OWNERSHIP (millions)

5.5 / 1961   11.5 / 1971   21.0 / 1981

ANNUAL PAID HOLIDAY (% employed population)

1980s: 81%, 11%, 8%
1970s: 68%, 27%, 5%
1960s: 63%, 33%, 4%

less than 2 weeks
2-3 weeks
more than 3 weeks

1 Changes in British society have changed the demand for leisure and recreation

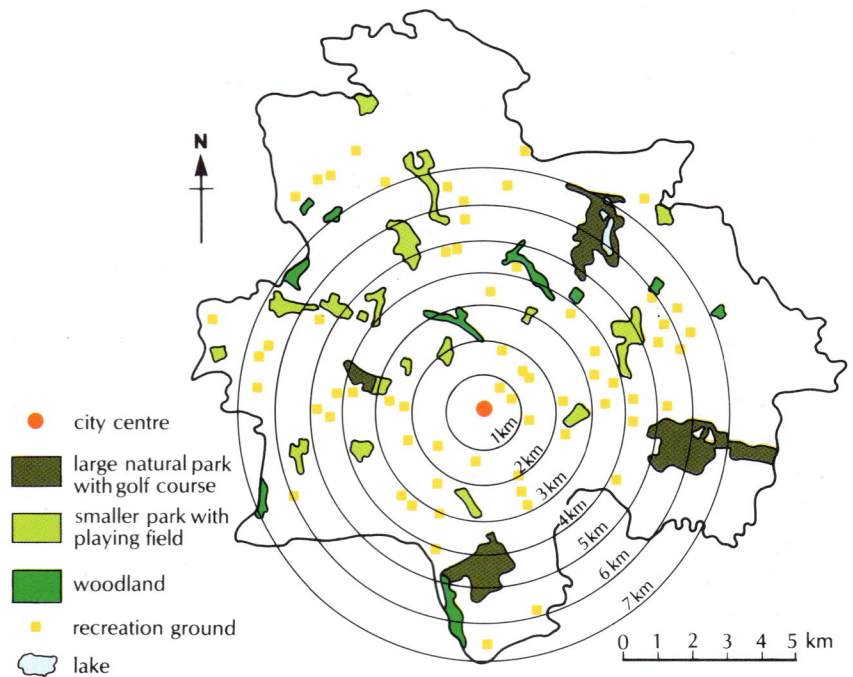

city centre
large natural park with golf course
smaller park with playing field
woodland
recreation ground
lake

0 1 2 3 4 5 km

2 The distribution of public open space in the city of Leeds

	LEISURE CENTRES/ SPORTS STADIA	GOLF COURSES	SWIMMING POOLS	NETBALL COURTS	HOCKEY PITCHES	RUGBY PITCHES	FOOTBALL PITCHES	CRICKET PITCHES	CRICKET NETS	BOWLING GREENS	FISHING AREAS	BOATING AREAS	
City of Birmingham	6	8	21	21	6	15	181	49	14	43	18	5	Birmingham is Britain's second largest city. It first developed during the Industrial Revolution and has grown steadily ever since. Its population in 1981 was 920 389.
Milton Keynes Development Corporation	4	4	13	36	13	13	98	24	20	9	12	4	Milton Keynes is one of Britain's most successful new towns. It has grown up rapidly since it was first designated in 1967. Its population in 1981 was 106 974.

3 The provision of selected sporting facilities in Birmingham and Milton Keynes

Imagine New York without Central Park. Or Paris without the Bois de Boulogne.

All great cities of the world have their open spaces. And Birmingham is no exception.

Not content with one of Britain's largest natural parklands, totalling some 2,500 acres, Birmingham boasts almost another 4,000 acres of England's green and pleasant land.

Every single acre is within minutes of the city's bustling centre.

Kept with the meticulous care that has won gold medals year after year at the internationally-renowned Chelsea Flower Show.

Much as the wildlife of Birmingham might revel in this splendid habitat, so its more cultured inhabitants can take even greater advantage of these wide-open spaces.

Edgbaston Reservoir, for instance, is the focal point for anglers, sailors and skiers.

Land-based sportsmen have their pick of 183 soccer pitches, 214 tennis courts and just about every other game in town.

In 1985, the world's best golfers went to town in competition for the Ryder Cup at the Belfry, home of the Professional Golf Association.

To all those who have so often heard Birmingham described as the cradle of modern industrial society, this information must surely come as a breath of fresh air.

City of Birmingham, Council House, Victoria Square, Birmingham. 021-235 2903.

BIRMINGHAM ONE OF THE WORLD'S GREAT CITIES

The Big Heart of England

1 Using Visual 1:

a) Make a note of the figures for population growth, car ownership and annual paid holiday for the dates shown.

b) In what ways, shown by Visual 1, has society changed since the early 1960s?

c) Suggest some reasons why these changes have affected the demand for leisure and recreation.

d) What other changes in society may have affected the demand for leisure and recreation?

2 Working in small groups of three or four:

a) List as many different leisure and recreation activities as you can.

b) Sort out your list by classifying each item under one of the following headings:
   i)   Indoor sport
   ii) Outdoor sport
   iii) Entertainment
   iv) Parks/open spaces
   v)   Miscellaneous.

c) How many of the activities on your list are important in towns and cities? Are some more important in urban areas than in rural areas?

3 Look at Visual 2.

a) List the four main types of open space found in Leeds.

Write next to each one how it might be used for leisure and recreation.

b) What types of open space are found at 1 km intervals from the city centre? Record your results in a table or on a graph.

c) As far as public open space is concerned, where is the best place to live in Leeds?

4 Birmingham and Milton Keynes both pride themselves on good facilities for leisure and recreation. Some of these are shown in Visual 3.

a) Compare the two sets of figures.

b) What is the total number of facilities for each city?

c) Why are these total figures surprising when you take into account the size of the cities?

d) Suggest reasons why a new town might find it easier to provide better leisure and recreation facilities than an older town or city.

5 Look at Visual 4.

a) What is the main message behind the advert?

b) What things are there in the photograph which help to give you a good impression of the city?

c) What other information about leisure and recreation is given in the advert which helps Birmingham to claim that it is one of the world's great cities?

4 An advertisement like this was published in various magazines as part of a campaign to promote Britain's second largest city

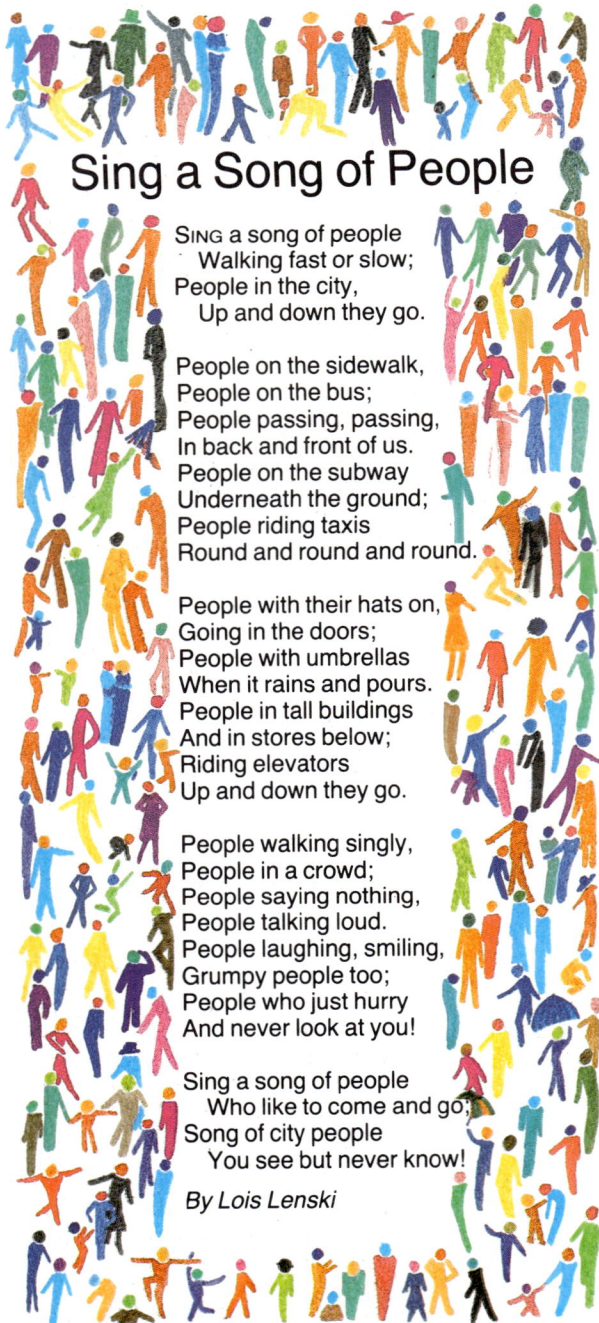

Sing a Song of People

SING a song of people
   Walking fast or slow;
People in the city,
   Up and down they go.

People on the sidewalk,
People on the bus;
People passing, passing,
In back and front of us.
People on the subway
Underneath the ground;
People riding taxis
Round and round and round.

People with their hats on,
Going in the doors;
People with umbrellas
When it rains and pours.
People in tall buildings
And in stores below;
Riding elevators
Up and down they go.

People walking singly,
People in a crowd;
People saying nothing,
People talking loud.
People laughing, smiling,
Grumpy people too;
People who just hurry
And never look at you!

Sing a song of people
   Who like to come and go;
Song of city people
   You see but never know!

By Lois Lenski

As towns and cities have grown larger, so has the amount of traffic. People have to move around in order to get to work, to shop and to satisfy their need for leisure and recreation. This increased mobility, and the volume of traffic it creates, are causing serious transport problems in many urban areas.

Until quite recently, most people got from one place to another by walking, cycling or using public transport. In 1971, 51% of people travelling to work went by bus, train or on foot. Only 35% travelled by car. By 1981, the situation had almost reversed with 50% of all workers travelling by car and only 38% travelling by bus, train or on foot.

Traffic problems call for public funds

By John Ardill, Environment Correspondent

Densely populated areas of Inner London need investment in roads and public transport to make life more tolerable and prosperous, the British Road Federation says in a report published yesterday.

The four areas surveyed, Harlesden, Leytonstone, Stratford and Wandsworth, all have above-average population densities, and disappearing industry and rising unemployment are common problems.

An extract from *The Guardian* for 11 November 1986

About 100 residents of each area from streets near shopping centres and industrial estates were interviewed last summer. A separate survey was made of shoppers on the streets, local firms and their employees. A BRF spokesman said: "These places are already at crisis point as far as traffic is concerned, and any development has got to take account of a desire for better mobility."

The report, which focuses on traffic congestion, says that 71 per cent of the Harlesden residents questioned considered traffic conditions a nuisance. The other areas were Wandsworth 61 per cent, Stratford 58 per cent, and Leytonstone 42 per cent.

Although Stratford has a new, pedestrianised shopping area, the other three have congested shopping streets and about half the residents were dissatisfied with arrangements for shoppers.

The use of cars for shopping varied little between the four areas even though Stratford and Wandsworth have multi-storey car parks beside their shopping centres and the other two have acute parking problems.

Households with cars range from 50 per cent in Harlesden to 78 per cent in Wandsworth and the proportion of people driving to work ranged from 33 per cent in Harlesden and Wandsworth to 70 per cent in Leytonstone.

"In all four study areas many people who own a car are nevertheless conscious of traffic nuisance. They would welcome measures to reduce the environmental impact of traffic, but not by being deprived of the ownership and use of their own cars."

Residents considered that many bus services were unreliable, particularly in Wandsworth and local firms found congestion a problem.

In Britain, the greatest use of public transport is in the larger urban areas and in the built-up regions around towns and cities. This situation is, however, changing as car ownership increases. Cities have spread outwards with the growth of suburbs and this has led to an increase in the number of people *commuting* to work. Many commuters prefer to travel by car, adding greatly to the volume of traffic on the roads – especially during peak hours.

The growth of urban population, the trend away from public transport towards private transport, and the increase in the level of commuting are all helping to put more traffic on our roads. The environmental impact of this traffic – congestion, accidents, pollution – is there for all to see.

1 Read the poem 'Sing a Song of People'.

   a) *What types of transport are mentioned in the poem?*

   b) *What other ways of moving around can you think of?*

   c) *What are the poet's conclusions about city people?*

2 Look at the newspaper item on the right.

   a) *Make a list of the traffic problems mentioned.*

   b) *What are the main causes of these traffic problems?*

   c) *What is suggested to help solve these urban transport problems?*

3 Some environmental pressure groups are trying to draw attention to urban transport problems. Study the information from Friends of the Earth on page 29 and then, working in small groups:

   a) *Discuss how the illustrator has used the idea of 'Cities for Cars or Cities for People'?*

   b) *Imagine that your group works in the publicity department at Friends of the Earth head office. You have been given a two-minute slot on local radio for your 'Cities for People' campaign. Decide on the key points you wish to get across and then write the script. Each group should then choose someone to 'broadcast' their group's version to the class.*

CITIES FOR CARS, OR...

...CITIES FOR PEOPLE?

CONGESTION
The theory is that we need new roads to relieve traffic congestion. In fact, new roads often encourage more traffic, which means **more** congestion! Even widening existing roads can draw large amounts of additional traffic into city centres, many of which are ill-equipped to deal with the problem. And it's often the car commuters that cause so much of the problem. One person's car can easily become another person's traffic jam!

ACCIDENTS
More than 5,000 people are killed every year on Britain's roads, at a cost to the country of £2.9 billion, according to Department of Transport figures. In London alone, 566 people were killed and 50,000 injured during 1984.

DISRUPTION
New road schemes, or even the threat of them, can cast a terrible planning blight over large parts of local communities. Whole areas can rapidly become very tatty, property values fall, businesses move out and the vandals move in. When the roads do come, as happened with the Westway, they can literally rip the com-munity apart, slicing through residential areas, cutting off homes from shops, schools, hospitals and places where peo-ple work. As always, it tends to be the old, the disabled, the young, and women who suffer the most.

EMISSIONS
Car exhaust fumes are unpleasant, dirty and dangerous. They are a threat to human health, even involving certain cancer forming agents, and a threat to the environment through the acid rain they help to cause. And **lead** still won't be taken out of petrol until the EEC directive is complied with in 1989.

EMPLOYMENT
As far as the local community is con-cerned, new roads usually destroy more jobs than they create. Houses and factor-ies may be knocked down, never to be rebuilt; firms can locate outside the area and drive their products into the city from there. As if the lorries weren't already enough of a problem, as they thunder through our cities, polluting the atmos-phere, deafening us, and causing untold damage to our homes and roads.

PUBLIC TRANSPORT
A proper balance between cars and cities **is** possible. This applies just as much to local residents with cars and to drivers of essential vehicles, as to those who do **not** drive. With the right kind of planning and investment, public transport **works**. Train, bus, tube, metro, tram – these are the most reliable ways of moving large numbers of people efficiently. Local au-thorities such as Sheffield, Newcastle and (when they were allowed to!) the GLC, have shown just what can be done to provide clean, fast and frequent public services.

LORRIES
Many countries now ban most lorries in their towns at weekends and on public holidays. Our local authorities have the power to ban heavy lorries too, and the GLC has just introduced a night-time and weekend lorry ban. And much more of our freight could be moved by rail.

ROAD SAFETY
Road safety and better streets go hand in hand. Local authorities can create 'play streets' or 'environmental areas' where through-traffic is kept out with road closures and one-way systems, without seriously inconveniencing local traffic. Both cycling and walking are healthy, cheap and much better for the environ-ment than over-dependence on the motor car. But they need to be positively encouraged, as they are in Europe.

JOBS
Many authorities are now putting more emphasis on setting up local environment initiatives, but we could still be doing far more in terms of repairing and renovating our housing, tidying up derelict land, planting more trees, or providing more allotments for people to grow food. 'Greening the city' means we should **all** benefit!

COMMUNITIES
Communities are held together by invisi-ble threads, by neighbours helping each other out, by being able to recognise people in the street rather than everyone being strangers, with kids being able to walk to school and people using the shop on the corner rather than driving miles to the nearest hypermarket. That's what many people believe **quality of life** is really about.

IT'S **YOUR** CHOICE!

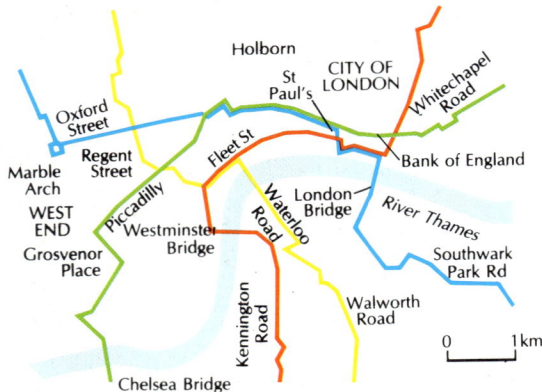

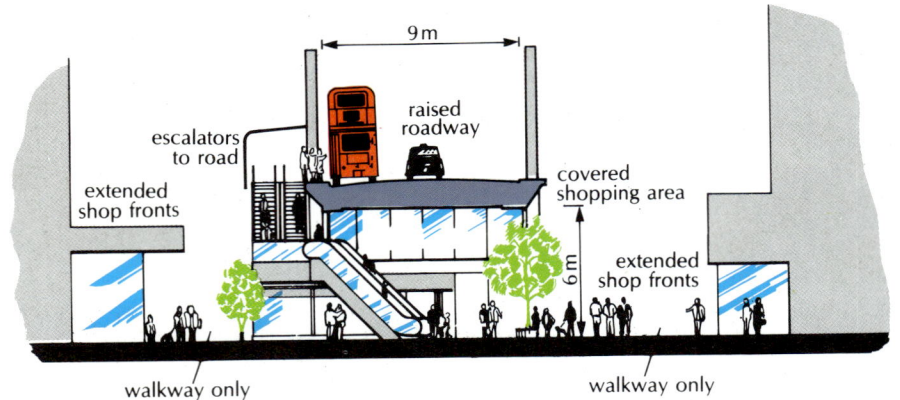

1 Two possible solutions to Central London's chronic traffic problems: a minibus network (left) and a raised vehicle-way in Oxford Street (right)

Transport planners and traffic engineers have the difficult job of trying to solve some of our urban transport problems. Solutions that have been tried so far include:

- Reduce congestion and improve traffic flow.
- Improve road safety for both drivers and pedestrians.
- Improve the quality of the environment.

Traffic problems in a large city such as London are many and complex. The worst problems are found in the central part of the city, which is the focus for the capital's shops, offices and places of entertainment. Every day, millions of people clog up the mainline railway stations, the underground and the roads. Traffic moves at an average speed of 12 miles per hour throughout the day – the same speed as in 1908!

For many years, planners and traffic engineers concentrated on trying to reduce congestion by improving traffic flow. One-way streets, bus lanes and linked sets of traffic lights all help to keep traffic moving. However, these solutions have neither reduced the amount of traffic nor created more routes. Some recent proposals are more adventurous.

One suggestion is that some of London's under-used railway lines could be converted into new roads. This might ease congestion on many existing roads. Raised roadways have been suggested for some of London's busier streets (Visual 1). Improvements to the capital's public transport system might also reduce the number of cars on the roads. The difficulty with this idea is that people enjoy using their cars and would not want to pay higher taxes for better public transport that they would rarely use.

Not everyone wants to get to the heart of the capital. Some traffic wants to get from one side of London to another without being caught in the congestion of the central area. The idea of a ring road around London was first suggested in the 1960s. Work on the first section of the M25 was finished in 1975 and the motorway was finally completed in 1987 (Visuals 2 and 3). The M25 represents *transport planning* on a grand scale and few capital cities have such a giant ring road.

London's orbital motorway seems to have solved some problems but created others. The M25 has provided a new route – but new journeys are filling it to bursting point. The traffic (mainly lorries) that has been taken out of central London has been rapidly replaced by cars driven by people who would have used public transport beforehand. Finally, the M25 is turning out to be a ring road paved with gold for property developers. People are clamouring for nearby land for housing and industry.

1 *Think about traffic problems in your town or in any other urban areas that you know well.*

a) *Draw up a table like the one below. Add a few more examples to each column to show how planners are trying to find solutions to these problems.*

TRAFFIC FLOW IMPROVEMENTS	ROAD SAFETY IMPROVEMENTS	ENVIRONMENTAL IMPROVEMENTS
One-way streets Bus lanes	Cycle paths Pelican crossings	Lorry bans Pedestrianized shopping precincts

b) *Could some solutions fit into more than one column?*

c) *What types of urban transport problem cause concern for the following groups of people? What solutions would be helpful to them? Write a short paragraph for each group.*
   i) *Parents with young children*
   ii) *Lorry drivers*
   iii) *Disabled people*
   iv) *Commuters using cars*
   v) *Pensioners*
   vi) *People on low incomes.*

2 *Look at Visual 1.*

a) *What advantages would minibuses have compared with other types of road transport?*

b) *Which groups of people might use the minibuses most?*

c) *Who might object to the introduction of a minibus scheme? Why might they object?*

2 A section of the M25, at Junction 2, looking north towards the River Thames and the Dartford Tunnel

M25 – London's Ring Road

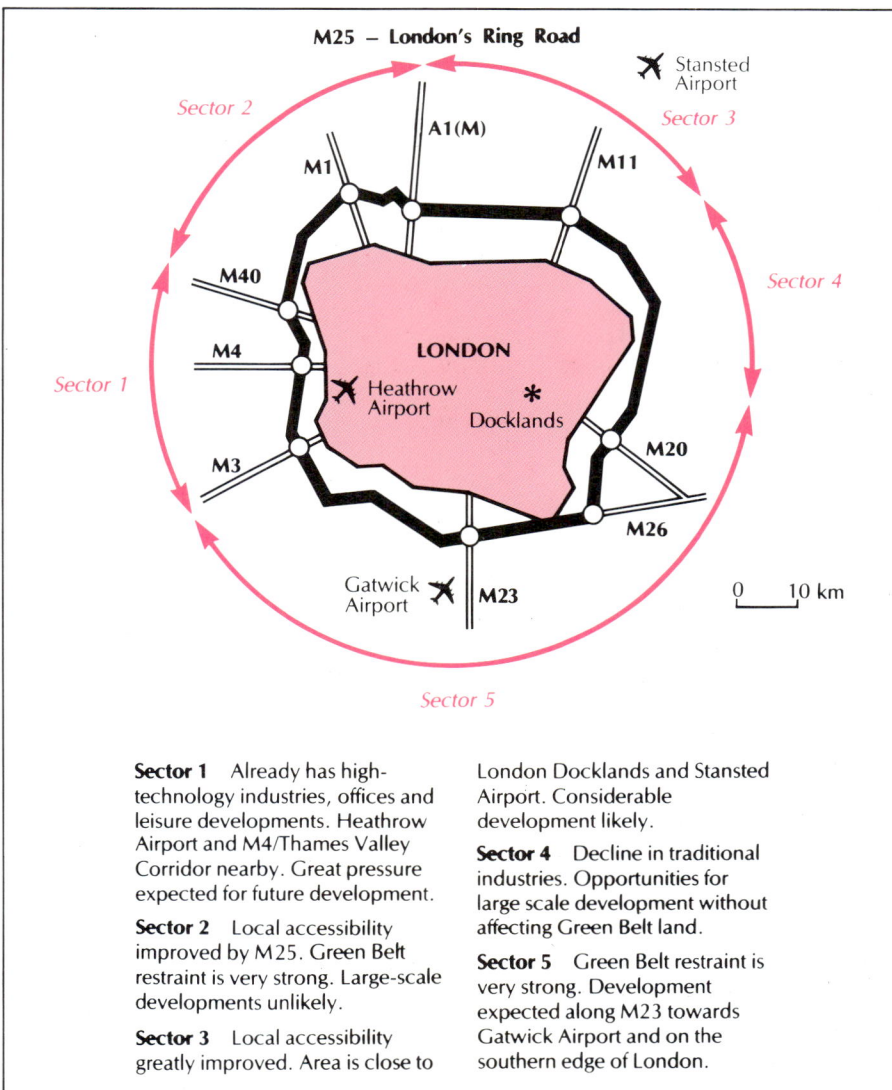

Sector 1 Already has high-technology industries, offices and leisure developments. Heathrow Airport and M4/Thames Valley Corridor nearby. Great pressure expected for future development.

Sector 2 Local accessibility improved by M25. Green Belt restraint is very strong. Large-scale developments unlikely.

Sector 3 Local accessibility greatly improved. Area is close to London Docklands and Stansted Airport. Considerable development likely.

Sector 4 Decline in traditional industries. Opportunities for large scale development without affecting Green Belt land.

Sector 5 Green Belt restraint is very strong. Development expected along M23 towards Gatwick Airport and on the southern edge of London.

d) *What are the advantages of separating traffic and shoppers in Oxford Street?*

e) *Can you think of any disadvantages for this proposal?*

3 *Study the information shown in Visual 3.*

a) *Make your own copy of the map to show London's ring road.*

b) *Use your atlas to find out where the other motorways lead. Mark this information on your map.*

c) *Add labels to explain how areas around London could be affected by the M25 in the future.*

4 *Look at Visual 2.*

a) *Make a simplified, labelled sketch of the area shown. Draw a frame for your sketch and add each of the following:*
   i)   *M25 motorway*
   ii) *M25/A2 intersection*
   iii) *A225 road*
   iv) *Built-up areas*
   v)   *Non-productive land on each side of the M25*
   vi) *Housing most affected by the building of the motorway*
   vii) *Possible sites for future industrial development.*

b) *Think about how the triangle of land between the M25, A2 and the A225 might be developed in the future. Make a list of the main arguments for developing the site as a:*
   i)   *High-technology industrial estate*
   ii) *Superstore complex*
   iii) *Leisure park*
   vi) *Conservation area.*

3 The last section of London's orbital M25 motorway was opened in 1987. The M25 is already having a major impact on the London region

1 Manchester in the 1800s: already an industrial city

1801 was a special year for Britain. In that year, the first official population census was carried out. Information was collected on the number of people living in Britain and on where they lived. A census has been carried out every ten years since then. The last one was in 1981. These population censuses give a detailed picture of the growth and movement of population over a period of nearly 200 years.

Britain was a very different country in the early 1800s from the country we know today. In 1801 the total population of England and Wales was only nine million. The majority of people (83%) lived in the countryside, in small villages, where they made a living by farming. The largest city was London with a population of just over one million. Most other cities and towns were very small and acted as market centres for the agricultural areas around them.

During the 1800s great changes occurred in British industry. The so-called Industrial Revolution was going full steam ahead. At the same time, an 'explosion' took place in population growth. Water, which had previously provided the power for industry, gave way to steam power using coal as a fuel. Factories sprang up on coal-field areas and Britain became the first industrialized nation producing textiles, iron and steel, machinery and other finished goods. Farm workers, attracted by the higher wages, flooded into the industrial towns to find work in the factories. As local craft industries

declined, even more workers left the countryside for the towns. The result was a period of incredible urban growth, when places such as Liverpool, Manchester and Birmingham changed from small towns to major industrial cities. This rapid growth brought with it terrible housing and living conditions, as cities tried to cope with the flood of migrants and the rapid population increase.

The 1800s also saw a big change in the percentage of urban and rural populations. By 1851, 50% of the population of England and Wales were living in towns and cities. By 1901, 77% of the population were living in urban areas. In less than 100 years, Britain had changed from a country with a rural population, based on agriculture, to a country with an urban population based on industry.

The population of Britain continued to grow during the 1900s. By 1951, the population of England and Wales had grown to five times the 1801 level and 81% of the population lived in urban areas. The peak year of growth for London and other major cities was 1951. Since then Britain's large cities have declined in population, as people gradually moved to rural areas surrounding the large cities. The drift of population from rural to urban areas, known as urbanization, now seems to have slowed down in most places and in some has stopped altogether. Increasingly, British people want to live in rural areas and smaller towns.

1 The terms 'urban growth' and 'urbanization' mean different things. Re-read this chapter to find out exactly what they mean. In your own words, write a definition for each term.

2 Look at Visual 2.

a) Copy the bar chart.

b) Use the figures above the bars to subdivide each bar into an urban and rural section. Colour the urban sections red and the rural sections green.

c) Write a paragraph to describe what your finished graph shows. Mention both the overall change in population and the changing percentage of urban rural populations.

3 The figures in the table below show the population of three of England's industrial cities for selected census years:

YEAR	LIVERPOOL	MANCHESTER	BIRMINGHAM
1801	82 000	75 000	71 000
1851	376 000	303 000	233 000
1951	789 000	703 000	1 100 000
1981	510 000	449 000	1 007 000

a) Draw a line graph to show the growth and decline of populations in the three cities. Use a different coloured line for each city.

b) Write a paragraph to explain why the city populations grew so rapidly in the 1800s but have fallen in the late 1900s.

4 Read through the extracts in Visual 3 and look at Visual 1.

a) Make a list of the problems found in Manchester in the 1800s.

b) Imagine that you live in the early 1800s. You have just moved to Manchester, from a village in the nearby countryside, in search of work. Write a letter to relatives at home describing the working and living conditions in the city.

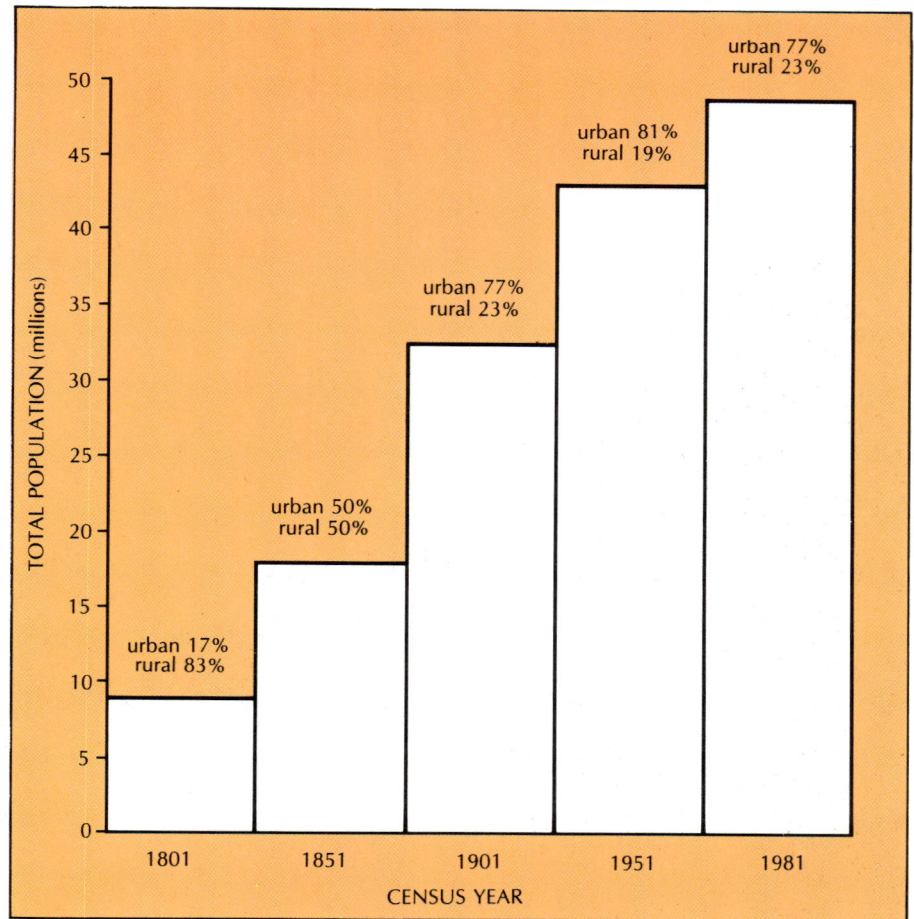

2 The changing share of the urban and rural populations in England and Wales

Earth and air seem impregnated with fog and soot. The factories extend their flanks of fouler brick one after another, bare, with shutterless windows, like colossal prisons ... and inside, lit by gas-jets and deafened by the uproar of their own labour, toil thousands of workmen, penned in, regimented, hands active, feet motionless, all day and every day, mechanically serving their machines... What dreary streets! Through half-open windows we could see wretched rooms at ground level, or often below the damp earth's surface. Masses of wild children, dirty and flabby of flesh, crowd each threshold and breathe the vile air of the street ... Even to walk in the rich quarter of the town is depressing ...

People were fascinated, amazed and appalled by it. For a newcomer the first distant view of Manchester and its smoking chimneys must have been as extraordinary as a first view of Constantinople in the tenth century, or of New York in the early twentieth century ... In Manchester factory chimneys far outnumbered church towers, eight-storey mills towered over squalid little houses, opulent warehouses, some of them as large as the mills, were grander and bigger than the town hall. From 1830, when the first passenger railway line in the world joined Manchester to Liverpool, viaducts carried steaming and smoking trains above the roofs of the smaller houses and added another large, bizarre and unfamiliar element to the townscape ...

3 Manchester in the 1800s has been described as the 'shock city of its age'. The extract above was written by a visitor to Manchester in 1859. The extract on the left is by a recent writer

1 The centre of Nottingham

Wherever you live in Britain, you will not be far away from a town or city. Only the upland parts of Scotland, England and Wales lack any large settlements. Most of the rest of Britain is densely populated and most people are 'townies'. Seventy-seven per cent of the population of England and Wales is urban in the 1980s. In fact, Britain is one of the most urbanized countries in the world.

The last population census in 1981 showed that over 56 million people lived in Britain. Of these, 19.5 million (or 35% of the total population) lived in the conurbations of Greater London, the West Midlands, South Yorkshire, West Yorkshire, Greater Manchester, Merseyside, Tyneside and Central Clydeside (Visual 2). A conurbation is a very large urban area, formed when a number of nearby cities or towns merge together. For example, in the West Midlands conurbation the city of Birmingham has spread outwards and merged with the nearby towns of Wolverhampton, Walsall, West Bromwich, Dudley and Solihull to form one giant urban area.

Many people in Britain live outside the conurbations in medium-sized urban areas. The cities, with a population of more than 100 000, are spread throughout Britain, although most are found in England (Visual 2). Together they contain about 6.5 million people or 12% of the total population. Finally, about 15.6 million people (28% of the total population) live in the smallest urban areas, which are called towns. Towns usually have more than 10 000 people.

Britain's population, therefore, is highly concentrated, with most people living in one of the three types of urban area. Britain has the second highest *population density* in Europe after the Netherlands. The highest population densities are found in urban areas. In Greater London there are more than 4000 people per square kilometre (more than 10 000 per square mile). It is no wonder that people occasionally feel the need to get away from the crowded towns and cities.

1 Look at Visual 2.

a) Make a note of your nearest city and nearest conurbation.

b) Choose two of the conurbations shown. Using your atlas, make a list of the main cities and towns which are to be found in each conurbation.

c) On a blank outline map of Britain mark the conurbations and cities. Use your atlas to find the names of the cities whose initial letters are shown in Visual 2. Add these names to your map.

2 Look at the table.

	CONURBATIONS	CITIES	TOWNS	RURAL AREAS
NUMBER		36	375	not applicable
TOTAL POPULATION (MILLIONS)	19.5		15.6	
% OF BRITAIN'S POPULATION				33.0

a) Make a copy of the table.

b) Using information from these pages, complete the table.

c) Say briefly what the table tells you about where people live in Britain.

3 The table below shows the population of each urban area in Nottinghamshire, which had more than 10 000 people at the 1981 census.

URBAN AREA	POPULATION
Arnold	37 242
Beeston and Stapleford	64 599
Carlton	46 456
East Retford	19 348
Eastwood	11 700
Hucknall	28 142
Kirkby in Ashfield	24 467
Mansfield	58 949
Mansfield Woodhouse	26 725
Newark	24 091
Nottingham	271 080
Sutton in Ashfield	41 270
Warsop	13 675
West Bridgford	28 073
Worksop	36 893
NOTTINGHAMSHIRE	982 631

a) Work out the percentage of urban population in Nottinghamshire. How does this compare with the country as a whole?

b) What percentage of Nottinghamshire's population lives in the largest urban area?

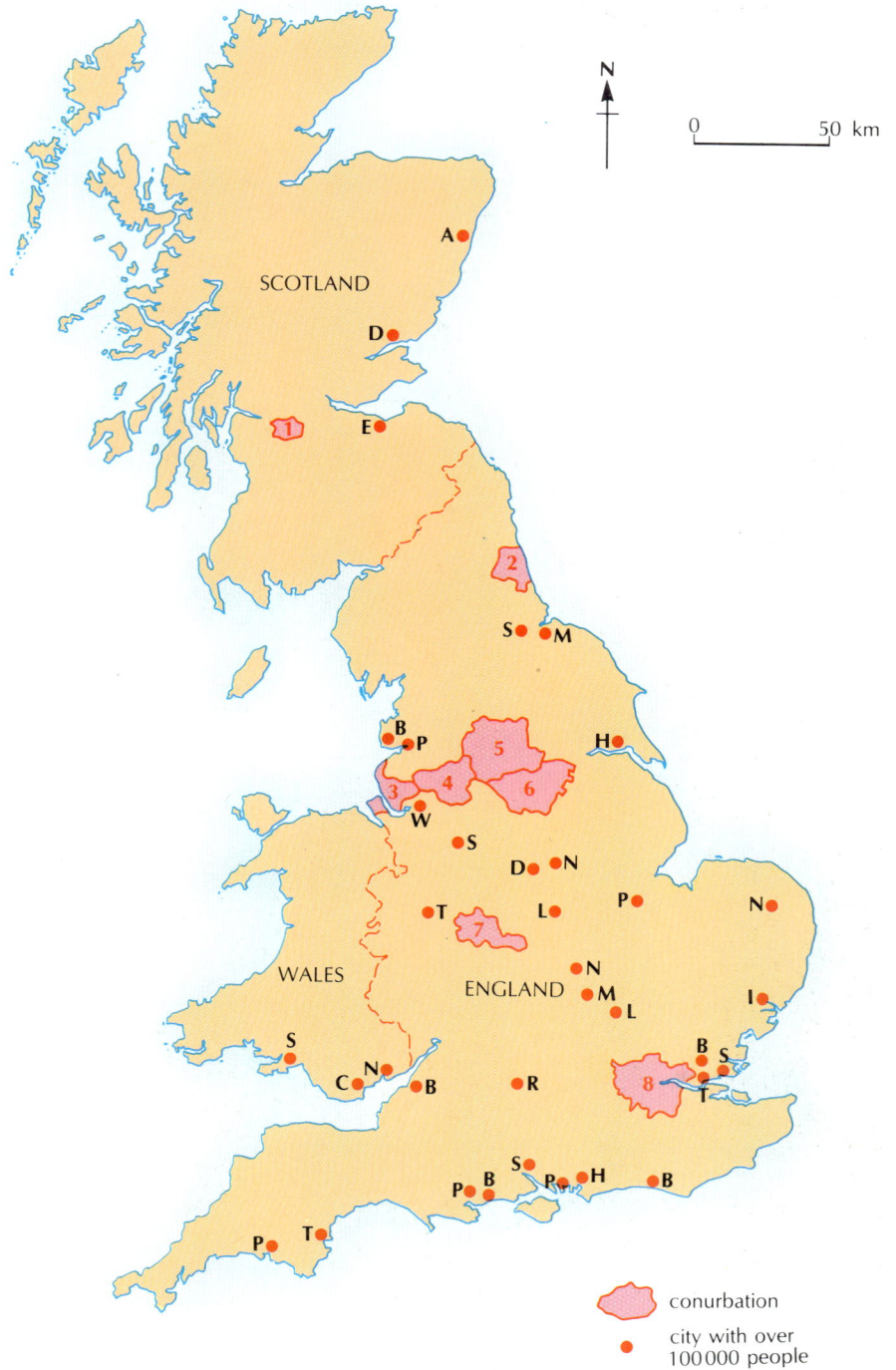

c) Using census information for you own county:
   i) What percentage of the population lives in urban areas?
   ii) How does your county compare with the country as a whole?
   iii) What percentage of the population of your county lives in the largest town or city?

4 Working in small groups:

a) Produce a large map which can be used for display purposes, showing the distribution of towns and cities in your county. Use proportional symbols so that the size of each symbol relates to the population size of the urban area it represents. Give the finished map a title and a full key.

b) Use photographs from local newspapers and magazines, postcards and other resources to build up a wallchart display showing urban environments in your county. Try to include material about small and large urban areas.

conurbation

● city with over 100 000 people

Conurbations
1 Clydeside
2 Tyneside
3 Merseyside
4 Greater Manchester
5 West Yorkshire
6 South Yorkshire
7 West Midlands
8 Greater London

2 The location of Britain's major urban areas. Notice how most of Britain's cities are concentrated in England. There are eight major conurbations (not shown to scale)

LONDON BOROUGH	POPULATION (THOUSANDS)		% CHANGE
	1951	1981	1951-1981
Barking	189	150	−21
Barnet	320	293	− 8
Bexley	205	215	+ 5
Brent	311	253	−19
Bromley	268	297	+11
Camden	258	172	−33
Croydon	310	318	+ 3
Ealing	311	280	−10
Enfield	288	259	−10
Greenwich	236	212	−10
Hackney	265	180	−32
Hammersmith	241	148	−39
Haringey	277	204	−26
Harrow	219	197	−10
Havering	192	241	+26
Hillingdon	210	230	+10
Hounslow	211	201	− 5
Islington	271	161	−41
Kensington & Chelsea	219	139	−37
Kingston upon Thames	147	133	−10
Lambeth	347	246	−29
Lewisham	303	231	−24
Merton	200	166	−17
Newham	294	209	−29
Redbridge	257	226	−12
Richmond upon Thames	188	160	−15
Southwark	338	212	−37
Sutton	176	169	− 4
Tower Hamlets	231	143	−38
Waltham Forest	275	216	−21
Wandsworth	331	255	−23
Westminster	300	191	−36
GREATER LONDON	8 197	6 713	−18
Rest of England & Wales	35 561	42 315	+19

1 Population changes in the London boroughs, 1951–1981. London reached its peak population in 1951 and since then has lost people every year

inner London boroughs

outer London boroughs

2 London's inner boroughs were built largely in the 1800s and early 1900s. The outer boroughs were built mainly between the two World Wars

0   10 km

1 Look at Visual 1.

   a) What happened to the population of England and Wales between 1951 and 1981?

   b) What happened to the population of Greater London between 1951 and 1981?

   c) How many of the 32 London boroughs lost people between 1951 and 1981?

The events occurring in Greater London over the past 30 years are not unique to London. They have been mirrored in virtually every other conurbation and major city in the country. Instead of growing, our major urban areas are now losing people at a rapid rate. This movement away from our major cities is known as urban depopulation.

As early as the 1600s, people began to notice that London was spreading outwards. As buildings sprang up on the edge of London, richer people left the more central areas to live in the newer suburbs. In the 1800s London spread outwards even further. The development of the railways enabled many to work in central London but live in Victorian suburbs, such as Haringey and Hammersmith. Between the First World War and the Second World War, the population of inner London began to decline seriously. A great house-building boom was taking place and those who could afford it moved to the new sprawling suburbs, such as Enfield, Barnet and Harrow. The population of outer London doubled from two to four million and London's built up area nearly tripled through this process of suburbanization. After the Second World War, the ring of population growth moved out beyond London itself. Motorways and faster, more modern railways enabled commuters to live as far away as Bedford to the north, Newbury to the west, and Brighton to the south. Between 1971 and 1981 all of the London boroughs (inner and outer) lost people, while new towns and market towns around London grew rapidly.

Urban depopulation is causing many problems for both the urban areas involved and the surrounding regions. As the population of London falls, so does the number of jobs. Industries are moving to cheaper locations outside the capital where there is room for expansion. Decisions now have to be taken about when and where to close schools, hospitals and other services. These are the problems of urban decline. Meanwhile, the areas surrounding London need extra services to cope with the increasing population. Another problem is that the 'flight from the cities' is not evenly spread among different sorts of people (social groups). Those who move out of London tend to be younger, richer and in work. As a result, London is left with an increasingly large share of the poor and disadvantaged.

2 Using information from Visuals 1 and 2:

a) On your own outline map of the London boroughs, mark the boundary between the inner and outer boroughs.

b) Using the key below and four colours, shade your map to show the population changes in each borough. Add the key to your map.

very high rate of population decrease	over −20%
high rate of population decrease	−19% to −10%
low rate of population decrease	−9% to 0%
population growth	0% to +26%

c) Write a few sentences to describe the pattern shown by your map. Try to explain this pattern.

3 Look at Visual 3.

a) Which type of area shown in Visual 3 do you live in?

b) Working with a neighbour, discuss the population changes shown in the different urban and rural areas.

c) Draw up a table like the one below and note the percentage population changes for the areas shown.

AREA	POPULATION	% POPULATION CHANGE (1971–81)	COMMENT
Greater London	6.7m	−9.9%	Most decline in the inner city

4 Visual 4 shows how population has changed between the last two censuses.

a) What does this map tell you about recent population trends in the conurbations?

b) Using your atlas, write a paragraph to describe recent population changes in England and Wales.

c) What is happening to the population of your county?

5 Write a short report on population changes in London, using the information provided here.

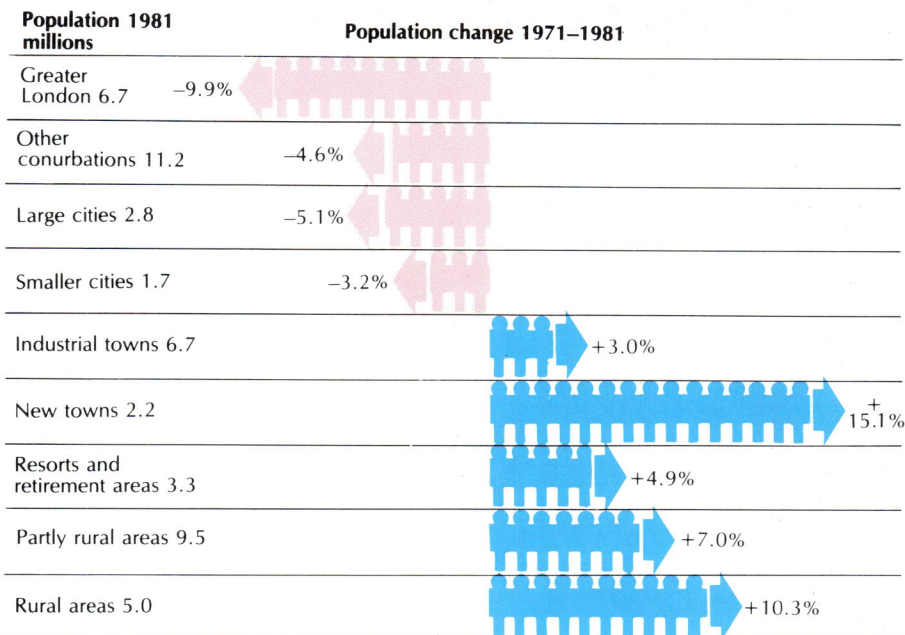

4 Population change by county in England and Wales, 1971–1981. The extremes were Buckinghamshire (+18.8%) and Greater London (−10.1%)

Population 1981 millions	Population change 1971–1981	
Greater London 6.7	−9.9%	
Other conurbations 11.2	−4.6%	
Large cities 2.8	−5.1%	
Smaller cities 1.7	−3.2%	
Industrial towns 6.7	+3.0%	
New towns 2.2	+15.1%	
Resorts and retirement areas 3.3	+4.9%	
Partly rural areas 9.5	+7.0%	
Rural areas 5.0	+10.3%	

3 Population change in England and Wales over a decade. Recent population changes are unlike those of earlier times. Today's conurbations and cities are losing people, while small towns and rural areas are gaining them

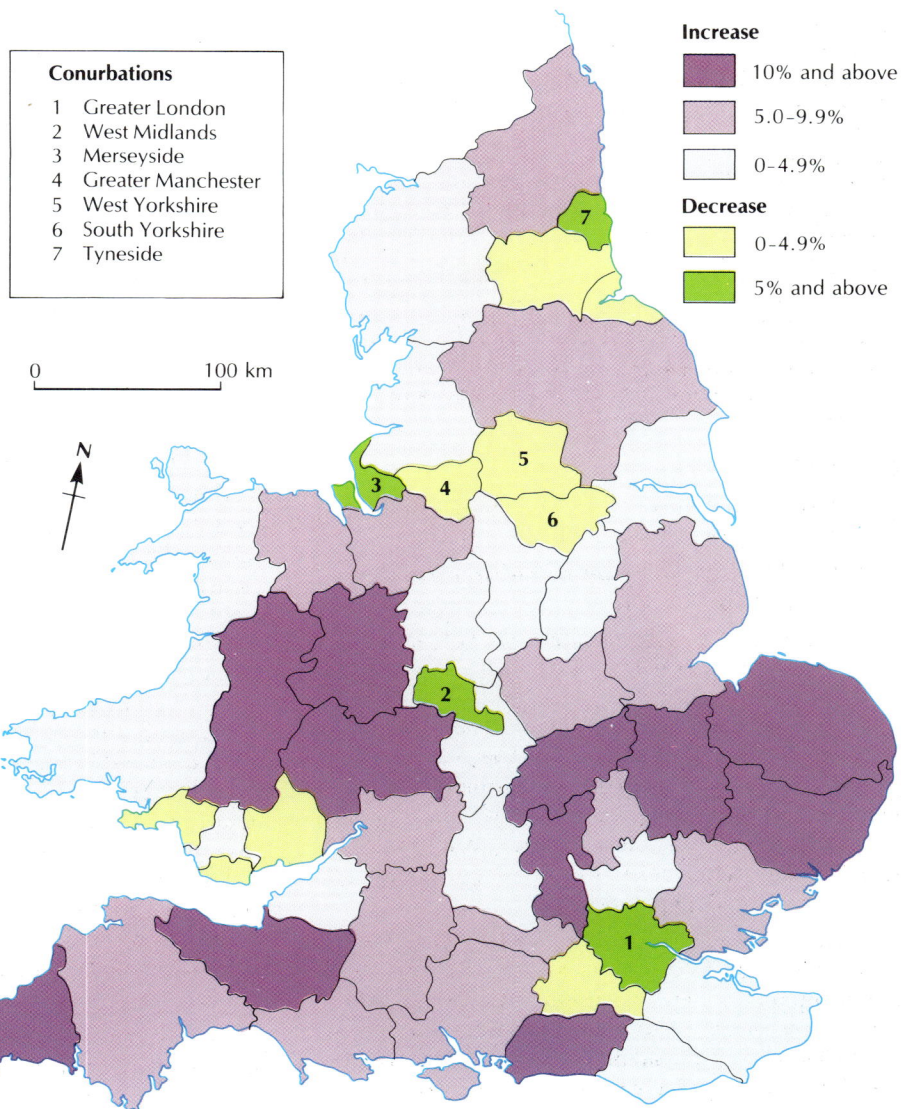

Conurbations
1 Greater London
2 West Midlands
3 Merseyside
4 Greater Manchester
5 West Yorkshire
6 South Yorkshire
7 Tyneside

Increase
10% and above
5.0–9.9%
0–4.9%

Decrease
0–4.9%
5% and above

0   100 km

N

37

1800s

1900s

1 In the 1800s, when cities were growing, population movements tended to form a cone-shape – the density of population increased towards the centre of a city. Today, these cities resemble an expanding ring, as population moves from the inner city to the suburbs and beyond

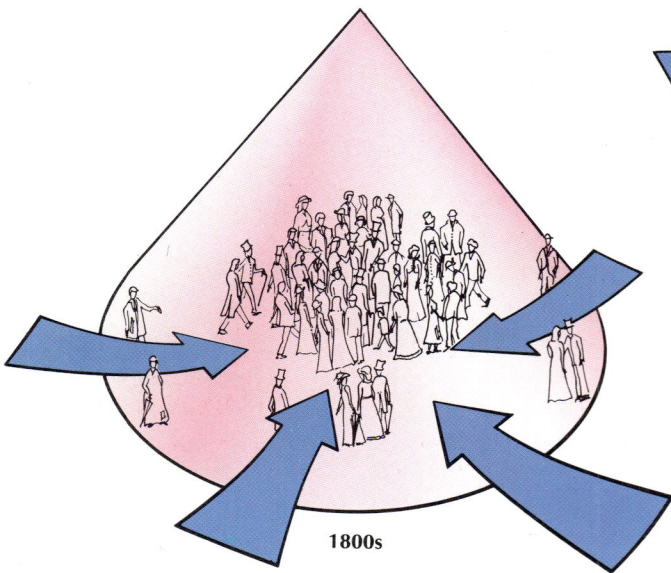

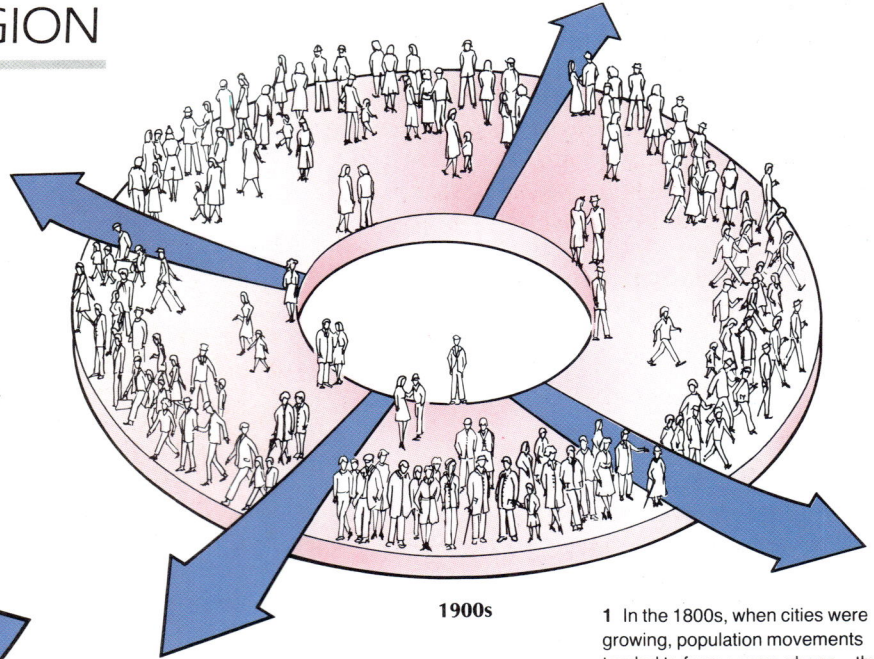

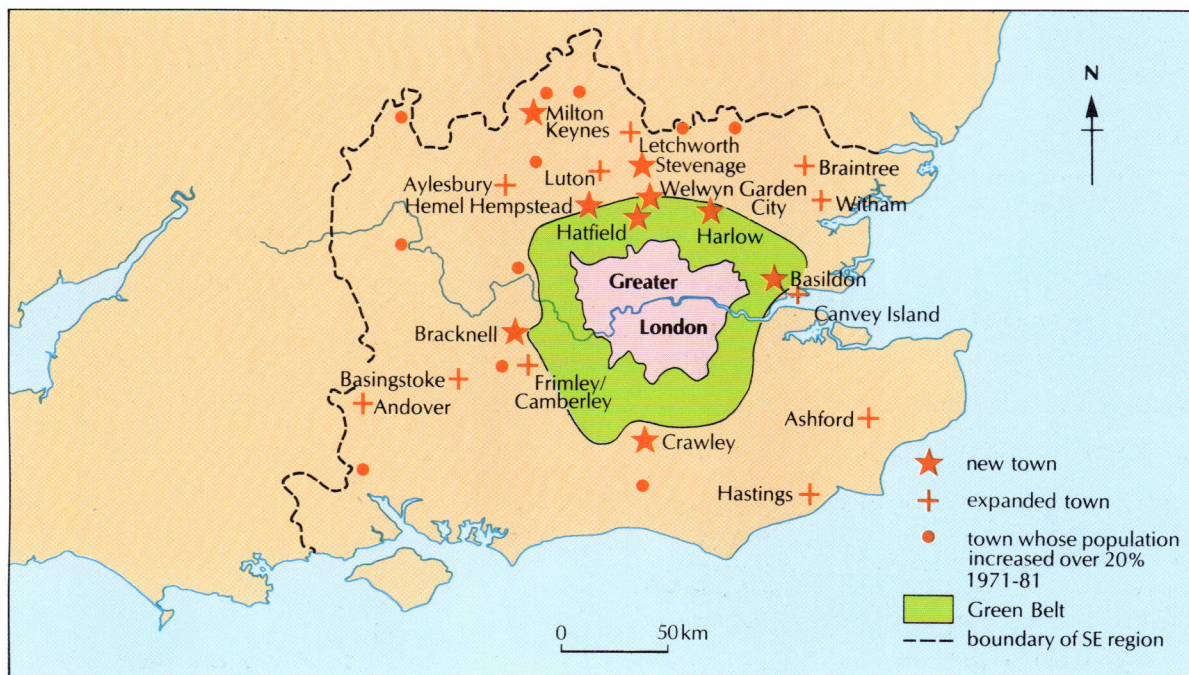

Towns and cities are constantly changing. While some urban areas grow, others decline. Towns and cities in the 1800s were quite compact because most people got about by walking. Today, towns and cities are spreading outwards, largely due to fast roads and railways. Until the 1950s people in Britain were still moving into large cities; since then they have been moving away. The diagrams in Visual 1 summarize these changes.

The trend over the centuries has been for towns and cities to increase in size. London, for example, had a population in the 1981 census six times larger than its 1801 population. The size of the built-up area had increased by over 30 times in the same period. As people move out of London into surrounding small towns and rural areas, the city is declining – but the London region is growing. Many of those who have

moved may still commute to work in London and use the city for shopping and entertainment.

Visual 2 shows the location of major urban developments in the London region during the past 40 years. The outward spread of London has been halted by the creation of a zone of land which is used only for farming, recreation or open space. This is called the Green Belt. But people leaving London have gone beyond the Green Belt. Nine new towns have been built in the London region. These have been major centres of population growth since the 1950s. Also, a number of existing towns have expanded by building new housing areas for people moving out of London. Eleven towns in the London region have recorded an increase in population of more than 20% between 1971 and 1981. A large part of this increase has come from ex-Londoners.

2 Urban developments in the London region. The towns shown on the map have received much of the outward population movement from London

The expansion of London is now causing many problems for those areas on the edge of the city, known as the urban fringe, and for those areas beyond the Green Belt. The main problems are:

° An increase in population which produces a need for more houses, jobs and services.
° A rapid growth of built-up areas along the edge of the Green Belt and along major transport routes away from London.
° The loss of land to motorways and linked developments, such as service areas and industrial sites.

1 Write short definitions for the following:

a) A city region

b) The Green Belt

c) The urban fringe.

2 a) On your own copy of Visual 2, place an overlay of tracing paper. Using your atlas, or an AA Handbook, mark on the following motorways and trunk roads:

M25 M1 A1(M) M11 A12 A127 M20/A20 M23/A23 M3 M4 M40.

b) What do you notice about the location of most towns?

c) In which direction does London seem to be expanding most? Can you think of any reasons for this directional expansion?

d) What would be the effect of each of the following on urban growth in the south-east region:

i) The Channel Tunnel?
ii) London's third airport at Stansted?
iii) The abolition of the Green Belt?

Give reasons for your answers.

3 a) On an outline map of Britain, mark on the 21 new towns, using Visual 5 and your atlas.

b) Mark the position of the major conurbations (Visual 2, page 35).

c) Do you notice anything about the location of most of the new towns?

d) Add arrows to your map linking conurbations with nearby new towns to suggest the direction in which people are moving. Can this be done for all new towns?

4 Look at Visual 4 and discuss with a neighbour:

a) The problems which have created conflict in Yateley.

b) The objections to building new homes on under-used school fields.

c) How the school playing fields might be better used.

d) Why this type of problem is likely to exist throughout the London region.

3 Without laws to protect it, land like this in London's Green Belt might be developed for housing, roads and industry

Fighting on the playing fields

by Norman Harris

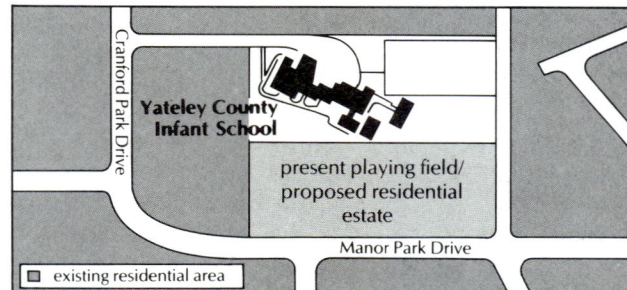

RESIDENTS of Yateley, a Hampshire 'growth' town close to the Surrey border, are fighting hard to prevent the sale of the playing field at a local infants' school. United under one banner are the local Conservative and Liberal groups, a parents' body, a preservation society and a residents' association. Even the board of governors at the school, Yateley County Infants, is up in arms.

"Yateley is growing at such a rate," says Colin Murton, chairman of the governors. "Green space is disappearing rapidly from Yateley and land lost is lost for ever."

Hampshire Education Authority is proposing to build 19 houses on the land. In Yateley it jogged memories of a similar plan to build 1,000 houses at nearby Frogmore Comprehensive – the local community only learnt of that when the builder asked for planning permission.

In the end, the Frogmore plan was refused. Yateley's, which hangs on a decision by the county education building sub-committee, still has a long way to go. But similar arguments over playing fields are happening in many other places up and down the country – and some have already been lost.

4 This type of local conflict is created by the outward spread of population from London

SCOTLAND	NORTH-EAST	NORTH-WEST	MIDLANDS	WALES
Glenrothes	Washington	Central Lancashire (Leyland-Chorley)	Telford	Cwmbran
Cumbernauld	Peterlee	Skelmersdale	Corby	Newtown
Livingston	Aycliffe	Runcorn	Redditch	
East Kilbride	Cramlington	Warrington	Northampton	
Irvine	Killingworth		Peterborough	

5 Britain's new towns outside the London region

ASSIGNMENT FOUR

Invading the Green Belt: Tillingham Hall

1 Tillingham Hall

In recent years, certain groups of people have tried to persuade the government to let them build on areas set aside as Green Belt. Shortage of space in cities has forced people to look towards the countryside for sites for housing. In south-east England, the problem has been getting worse. The shortage of building land is helping to push house prices higher and higher. Some people argue that one way of helping to provide more space for housing would be to scrap some parts of the Green Belts which surround many British towns and cities.

Your Assignment

○ Examine some of the arguments made by people and organizations for and against building in the Green Belt.
○ Design a small new town to be built in the Green Belt at Tillingham Hall in south Essex. Argue the case for this development.

Resources

The visuals and extracts on this two-page spread and the next one.

Work Programme A

Developing the Green Belt

You work for a development company, Pointing Enterprises plc, which is made up from a group of leading housebuilders. You want to build a small new town in the Green Belt at Tillingham Hall. Using the information on this two-page spread, together with your own knowledge and ideas, prepare a report in which you first outline the reasons why a new town should be built in the Green Belt.

Work Programme B

The case for Tillingham Hall

In the second part of you report, you will need to argue a case for the new town you propose to build at Tillingham Hall. To help you, look at the information on pages 42 and 43.

Scotland Edinburgh, Glasgow, Grangemouth, Prestwick

North Newcastle upon Tyne

North Leeds, Sheffield, Liverpool, Manchester

Midlands Birmingham, Stoke-on-Trent, Nottingham

South Cambridge, London, Oxford

South-West Bournemouth, Bristol

2 Where the Green Belts are located

Successive governments have repeated the semi-sacred utterance that development in the Green Belt cannot be allowed. Today there are 4.5 million acres of Green Belt in England within easy reach of city dwellers and over 0.25 million acres in Scotland.

4 An extract from 'Green Belt Battles', *Sunday Times*, 5 January 1986

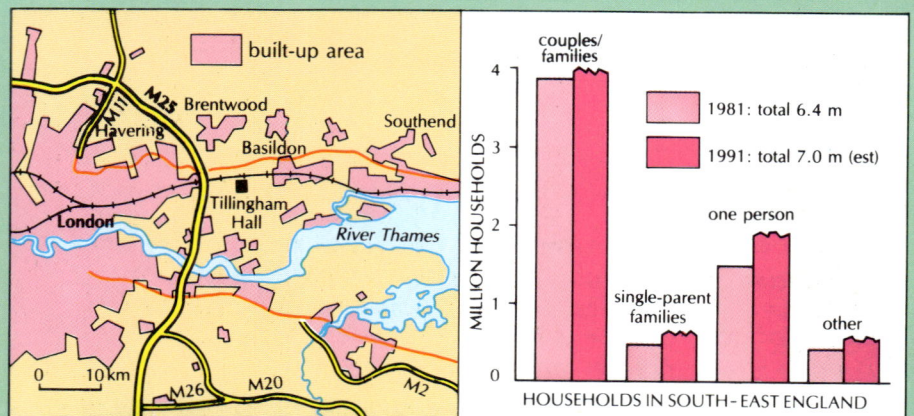

3 The crowded South-East: should building be allowed here and if it is, for whom?

built-up area

1981: total 6.4 m
1991: total 7.0 m (est)

couples/families
one person
single-parent families
other

MILLION HOUSEHOLDS

HOUSEHOLDS IN SOUTH-EAST ENGLAND

REGIONAL PRICES

The North-South gap has continued to widen. In the last quarter, house prices in Greater London increased by nearly three times the national average whereas in all the northern and midland regions they rose by less than the national average figure of 1.5%. In fact, house prices in Scotland and Wales actually fell during the same period.

THE NORTH-SOUTH DIVIDE – AN IRREVERSIBLE TREND?

In our last regional bulletin we discussed some of the reasons and consequences of an ever-widening house price gap between the north and the south. The high demand for houses has pushed up prices in London by almost 20% over the last year. The average price for a detached house in London is now over £115,000.

Relatively buoyant economic growth in the South East, lower unemployment, faster growth in personal incomes (in particular the recent explosion in City salaries) and a relative deficiency of available building land in the south are all reasons behind the North-South divide. The future projects to build a Channel Tunnel and expand Stansted Airport will tend to exacerbate further this problem.

CAN WE AFFORD THE GREEN BELT?

The determining factor of house prices is the availability of houses compared to demand, hence it is only by reducing the relative shortage of houses in the south that the house price gap can be narrowed. A major problem is the lack of building land. The loss of some of the Green Belt around London is perhaps the only short-term solution to the problem of first-time buyer access to reasonable homes and to the reduction of the house price gap between the north and the south.

TYPE OF HOUSE	Terraced	Semi-detached	Detached
GREATER LONDON	£65 000	£77 000	£130 000
SOUTH EAST	£45 000	£55 000	£92 000
WEST MIDLANDS	£21 000	£28 000	£51 000
NORTH WEST	£20 000	£29 000	£53 000
SCOTLAND	£31 000	£34 000	£48 000

5 Extracts from the 1986 *House Price Index* of the Halifax Building Society

(i) There is and will be a large, potentially unsatisfied demand for new housing in south-east England.
(ii) Housing must go where people want to live, not where planners think they ought to; and that means more round London than in it.
(iii) Anyway, land is not available at affordable prices in London, while surrounding counties refuse to release enough.
(iv) So additional land must be found.

6 From 'Green grows the South-East', *Economist*, 18 May 1985

7 An estate in Woodham Ferrers, Essex

9 Brentwood's urban sprawl

New towns may not (or not yet) be needed. Yet they might be better than suburban sprawl. They would probably be better planned; they would not swamp existing town centres and facilities; they would certainly attract new jobs. And just because it is green belt, a smart developer can buy the land (relatively) cheap – and offer correspondingly more in the way of public quality and infrastructure to the local authority and potential housebuyers.

8 From 'Green grows the South-East', *Economist*, 18 May 1985

Work Programme C

Designing a new town: what people think

To be successful, the new town you propose will have to appeal to a variety of people. Carry out a survey to help you to find out what people think a new town should be like. What questions would you want to ask? Draw up a questionnaire. You could survey a sample of people at home and/or at school. Among other things, you will need to find out about people's feelings towards housing, work and leisure.

41

Some ideas about New Towns in the 80s and 90s

THE NEW SETTLEMENTS

Each new settlement would ideally include sufficient land for between 5 000 and 7 000 homes. Depending on the mix of different house types and future changes in household size, the average population of such a settlement would be 13 000–18 000 people.

This definition of the size of the 'ideal' new settlement emerged after consideration of various factors including primary school catchment areas, health care facility catchments and neighbourhood planning principles. Most housing markets could not absorb a larger scheme and smaller schemes would not offer a sufficient range of choice.

A new settlement would **not** resemble the new towns built by Development Corporations under the New Towns Act with large target populations of between 88 000 and 200 000 people mainly in public sector housing for rent. The scale of a new settlement is similar to some of the town expansion schemes under the Town Development Act 1952. Yet a new settlement would differ considerably from a town expansion scheme which built primarily local authority rented housing for London overspill during their early years.

The new settlement will be privately developed mainly with housing for sale. No public sector subsidy will be required other than that arising from a local authority decision to develop a limited number of houses for rent or for shared ownership. Most housing in the new settlement would be developed by private housebuilders.

The quality of landscaping, estate layout and finishes which can be created in a new settlement, will prove to be superior to that which results from the development of small and medium sized sites.

The developer of a new settlement can make provision for the additional landscaping, public open spaces and children's play facilities in the original financial plan for the new settlement.

Housebuyers would like the quality of environment. Many regard owner occupation as an investment and the high quality environment will be reflected in future growth of the value of their home.

Housebuyers would also welcome the additional choice which a new settlement offers. As a result of the reductions in the supply of housing land in many communities in the South East, it is likely that the choice of new dwellings available in an area will dramatically increase the range of dwellings on offer to prospective purchasers.

In areas where new settlements are developed, land prices should stabilise. Land is one of the basic raw materials. When land costs are less, more resources are available for investment in the actual construction of the new settlement.

10 An extract from 'New Settlements', Housing and Planning Review, 1984

Work Programme D

Designing a new town: your proposals

1 On a copy of the map on page 43, draw up a plan to show the layout of your proposed new town at Tillingham Hall. When designing your new town, you will need to take into account:

  ◦ The results of your survey.
  ◦ The information on this page.

2 Say why you have planned your new town in this way. Give reasons for your suggested layout. Talk about the type of environment you will create. Sketches like those in the box on the right could be included to help illustrate some of your ideas.

Work Programme E

Conflicts of interest

Choose one of the following people:

◦ A local resident from the nearby village of West Horndon.
◦ Someone living in a run-down inner-city area in London.

Write a letter to the local newspaper saying why you support or oppose the proposed new town at Tillingham Hall. In preparing your letter, you will need to examine carefully the evidence provided in this assignment.

TILLINGHAM HALL SITE – 304 HECTARES

HOUSING APPROXIMATELY 160 HECTARES
5000 NEW HOMES, AT LOW, MEDIUM AND HIGH PRICE, TAKING 60–65% TOTAL AREA PROJECTED POPULATION OF 15 000

COMMERCIAL SHOPS, PUBS, GARAGES
5 HECTARES

COMMUNITY A RANGE OF SERVICES
2.4 HECTARES

EMPLOYMENT 2000 JOBS IN A VARIETY OF INDUSTRIES AND SERVICES – 14 HECTARES

EDUCATION 3 PRIMARY SCHOOLS (1.6 HECTARES)
1 SECONDARY SCHOOL (8 HECTARES)

OPEN SPACE TO PROVIDE FOR LEISURE NEEDS INCLUDING PLAYING FIELDS, WATER FEATURES 60 HECTARES

OTHER ROADS

THINGS TO CONSIDER EXISTING LAND USES (eg ROADS, FOOTPATHS)
THE QUALITY OF THE ENVIRONMENT
THE NATURE AND TYPES OF INDUSTRY/SERVICES
THE LOCATION OF EACH TYPE OF LAND USE

11 Detail of Tillingham Hall site (Based on Ordnance Survey
1:10 000 map with permission of the Controller of Her
Majesty's Stationery Office Crown. Copyright reserved)

WEST HORNDON

Engineering
Works

Sports
Ground

Post
Office

Station

Bulphan Bypass

Blue House
Farm

Little Tillingham
Hall (listed building)

Field House
(listed building)

Middleton
Hall

Brentwood Road

Moat (archaeological
find site)

Tillingham
Hall

Dunnings Lane

China Lane

Slough
House

BULPHAN

School

Bulphan
Hall

	0				500 m

N

- ▪▪▪▪ gas pipeline
- •••• oil pipeline
- ——— railway
- - - - footpath
- ═══ road
- —•—•— 132 kV overhead power line
- ▬▬▬ site boundary
- ♧ woodland

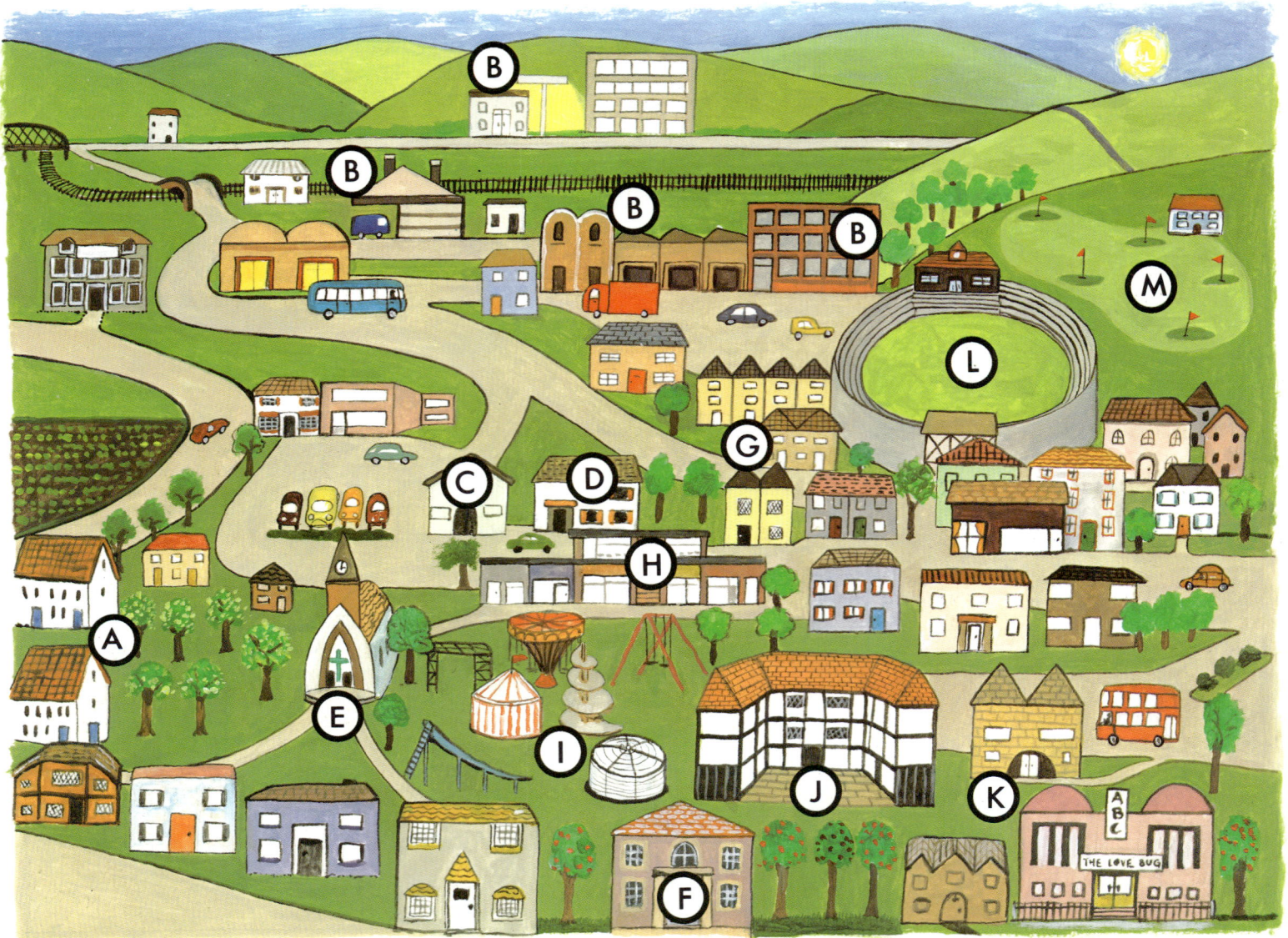

What attracts people to cities? What keeps them there? What do people want from an urban environment?

When Britain's towns and cities were growing rapidly in the 1800s, the main attraction for newcomers was the prospect of finding work. The same is true today for most countries of the *South*. The chance of finding a job, or a better job, is drawing people into urban areas in large numbers. People in these countries are also attracted by the better health care, schools, shops and services which towns and cities can offer.

Britain's major cities, however, no longer satisfy everyone. More than half the people living in London would like to move out because they do not like their neighbourhood. A recent national survey showed that 52% of Londoners wanted to move. Only 28% of those questioned elsewhere in the country wanted to move from where they lived. Thirty-three per cent of Londoners wanted to live in a town not too far away from the capital. Next came the outer London suburbs (30%) and then the countryside (16%). Only 5% said that they would like to live in central London. People in London do not simply think about moving – many actually do move out. The population of Greater London fell from 7 452 346 in 1971 to 6 713 165 in 1981.

What is the quality of life? It is hard to define and may differ from person to person. Different people seek different things from urban areas. Some people are just concerned about getting a job, a house with basic amenities and the cost of urban services such as public transport. Others may be concerned about the wider issues of their urban environment, such as pollution.

1 This town was planned by a group of junior school children

A senior citizens' flats
B work place
C police station
D public house
E church
F town hall
G council houses
H shopping centre
I recreation area
J school
K youth club
L sports ground
M golf course

1 a) By how much did London's population fall between 1971 and 1981? What do you think happened to most of these people?

   b) Draw a bar chart to show where dissatisfied Londoners would like to live if they were given the choice. Label each bar of your chart.

2 Look at Visual 2.

   a) Write a paragraph to describe the variations in quality of life in different parts of London.

   b) Do you think that the map confirms the findings of the national survey?

3 No house, neighbourhood or city is likely to have everything we want.

   a) Make a list of those things which you would like each of the above to have.

   b) Compare your list with your neighbour's list. Are they very different?

   c) How much agreement is there in the class as a whole? Draw up a table which shows the top six things which the class would like in a house, neighbourhood or city.

4 Visual 1 shows an ideal town and its facilities, as seen through the eyes of some young people.

   a) How do you think that some of the facilities shown would improve the quality of life for residents of this town?

   b) What else would you add if you were designing this town?

5 Look at these pictures of disadvantaged people. Working in small groups:

   a) Discuss what problems city life presents for people in each category.

   b) How could the quality of life be improved for each group of people?

   c) Summarize your ideas under two headings:

      i)   People – problems of city life.
      ii) People – improving the quality of life.

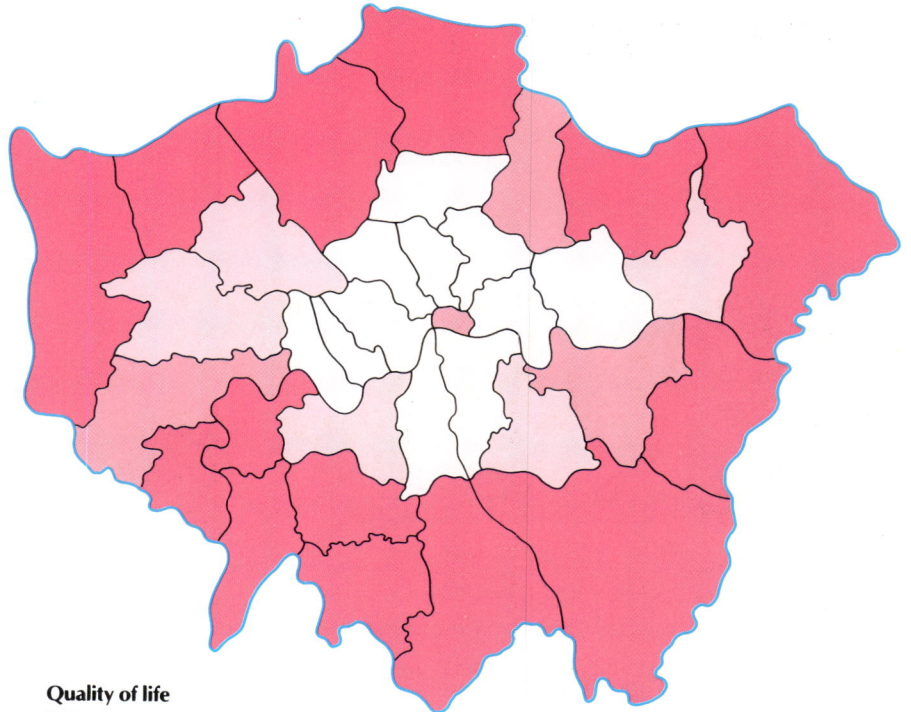

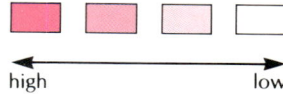

Quality of life

high ←——————→ low

0 _____ 5 km

2 The quality of life throughout the London boroughs is very uneven. This map is based on such factors as housing conditions, amount of unemployment and other social issues. For the key to London boroughs see page 36.

Mentally handicapped

Low paid

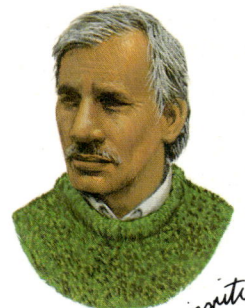

Ethnic minority

Lonely and depressed

Poorly housed

One parent family

Disabled

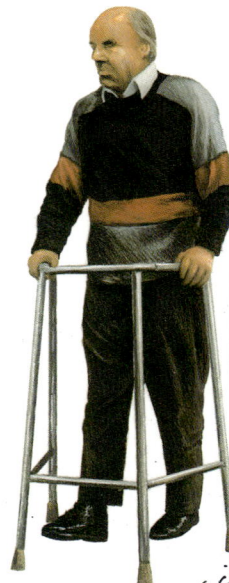

Senior citizen

Jobless

> Since moving to Britain from Jamaica 20 years ago I have lived in the Notting Hill area of London. Notting Hill has many problems, such as high unemployment and poor housing. But there is also a strong community feeling which makes it a good place to live.
> **EDDIE DOUGLAS HOSPITAL PORTER**

> I live in a large detached house in Northwood, London. This area has everything I need. It is near the countryside and has an excellent golf club. I commute to work in Central London, sometimes by train and sometimes by car.
> **ROGER BROWN COMPANY DIRECTOR**

> I live in a bedsitter in Clapham in South London. I share a kitchen and a bathroom with four other people who have bedsitters in the same house. I could do with more space but I can only afford a small bedsitter with my grant.
> **JULIA KING MUSIC STUDENT**

> When I was promoted to a top job at the banks head-quarters in the city, I moved into a new flat in Bromley in London. This means I need to commute to and from work every day, but I don't mind because at the weekends I am near the countryside.
> **SARAH WRIGHT BANK EMPLOYEE**

Rich and poor areas can be found in every town and city. The quality of life that people experience varies according to the sort of neighbourhood that they live in. In British cities there are many differences between the housing areas found near the city centre (inner city areas) and those found near the edge of the city (the suburbs). The inner city areas contain, in general, poorer people who usually have a lower quality of life than the wealthier people in the suburbs.

Housing in inner city areas developed mainly in the 1800s and was packed tightly around the city centre. Some of these buildings are now decaying and many have become slums as they lack modern facilities. Many of the larger houses have been made into flats and bedsitters. Traffic congestion is a problem because the tightly packed streets were not built to cope with today's level of traffic.

Nearly four million people live in inner city areas in Britain and the problems that they face include: poor housing, declining industries, poor services, poverty, a high concentration of young and old people, high unemployment, much vandalism and crime, and a poor physical environment. The population is usually not very stable and changes frequently, many people moving to other areas as soon as they can afford to do so.

Housing in suburban areas developed mainly in the 1920s and 1930s. More modern suburbs have also developed since the 1950s. Housing densities are lower than in the inner city areas and the houses have modern facilities and space for cars. There are open spaces and recreational areas. The millions of people who live in Britain's suburbs enjoy a higher standard of living and suffer few of the problems found in inner city areas. Many people living in suburbs own their houses, thus the population is generally more stable than in an area where most people rent their homes.

1 Two contrasting examples of housing in London

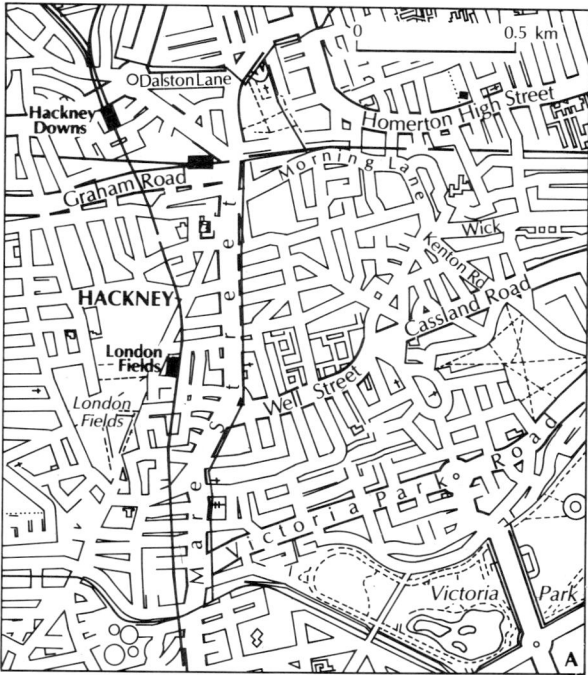

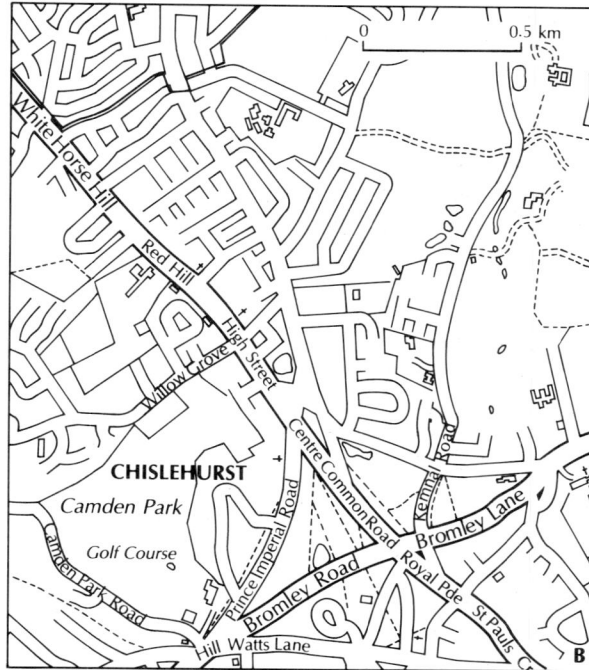

2 Map extracts of the two areas in which the housing shown in Visual 1 is located

1 Looking back through the information on these pages:

   a) Write a short definition of 'inner city area' and 'suburb'.

   b) Draw up a table listing some of the main differences between inner city areas and suburbs.

2 Look at the quotes at the top of page 46.

   a) In which part of a city would each of the people live – inner city or suburb?

   b) Can you locate Clapham, Northwood, Bromley and Notting Hill on a map of London?

   c) Can you suggest some reasons for your answers to part a) of this question?

   d) Write character sketches, like those at the top of page 46, for the following city dwellers:

      i)   Someone living rough
      ii) A 'jet set' millionaire
      iii) An old person living on a small pension.

3 Visual 2 shows the street pattern in an inner city and a suburban part of London.

   a) Which one is the inner city area and which one is the suburb?

   b) Describe the main differences between the two areas.

4 Visual 1 shows a part of each area covered by the maps in Visual 2.

   a) Which photograph was taken in Hackney and which one was taken in Chislehurst?

   b) Using evidence from the maps and photographs, explain why the quality of life is probably higher in Chislehurst.

5 Read Visual 3.

   a) Why does the article refer to the 'gulf' between rich and poor?

   b) Who are London's rich and poor inhabitants? Where are they most likely to live?

   c) What could be the long-term effects of this widening poverty gap?

Poverty gap widening most quickly in London

by Helen Hague
Labour Reporter

THE GULF between rich and poor in London is widening more rapidly than in any other part of Britain, according to a study on living standards in the capital.

Poverty and Labour, published today by the Low Pay Unit, paints a picture of rapid social polarisation.

One of its authors, Paul Corrigan, has warned of the 'Yuppie invasion' of areas with high levels of deprivation, such as Docklands. "Having rich and poor living next to one another is bound to give rise to something – and it's most likely to be anger."

According to the study, the disposable income of London's poorest 10 per cent of households fell by more than 23 per cent between 1983 and 1985. In contrast, the 'new rich' spawned by the City are enjoying unprecedented affluence.

The findings are based partly on Government statistics, backed up by interviews with a representative sample of 2,700 Londoners.

Between 1971 and 1985 the capital lost nearly half a million jobs as rapid expansion of the financial sector followed the decline in manufacturing. Using government data, at least 1.8 million Londoners are estimated to be living on the poverty margin, on incomes at or below supplementary benefit level.

The report links deprivation to mortality: it found that the death rates among males aged between 40 and 44 and 50 and 54 who live in Hackney and Tower Hamlets are twice as high as those living in the relatively prosperous borough of Bromley.

3 An extract from an article in *The Independent*, 4 June 1987

47

ASSIGNMENT FIVE
Housing Contrasts: Birmingham

In any city, the land is used in many different ways. Take housing as one example. People tend to talk about two distinctly different housing zones: the inner city and the outer city or suburbs.

The media, politicians, charities and others frequently remind us of the great differences that exist within a city – the contrasts between the better-off people in the suburbs and the less well-off in the inner cities.

In some places, the inner–outer differences are very great and the evidence is there for anyone to see. Yet we must be careful not always to assume that all the inner city areas, or all outer city areas, are the same. Before coming to conclusions about differences in any city, we need to consider the facts and examine the evidence.

Your Assignment
◦ To consider the contrasts between different housing areas in the city of Birmingham.
◦ To use data from Birmingham given here, to map and compare different housing areas in the city.

Resources
1 The photographs.
2 DATA FILE.
3 The map of Birmingham's wards.

Work Programme A

1 Using the photos on this page and the information from some of the previous pages, make a list of what people might think of as the 'typical' characteristics of:

   a) Inner city areas and housing.

   b) Outer city areas and housing.

2 The inner city zone in Birmingham extends in a circle of 5 km radius from the city centre.

   a) On a copy of the Birmingham wards map given on this page, draw and shade a circle to show the location of Birmingham's inner city.

   b) Which Birmingham wards are completely or partly in the inner city?

Map of Birmingham's wards: Sutton Four Oaks, Oscott, Sutton Vesey, Sutton New Hall, Kingstanding, Perry Bar, Stockland Green, Erdington, Kingsbury, Sandwell, Handsworth, Soho, Aston, Washwood Heath, Hodge Hill, Nechells, Shard End, city centre, Ladywood, Yardley, Small Heath, Sheldon, Sparkbrook, Acock's Green, Quinton, Harborne, Edgbaston, Sparkhill, Fox Hollies, Bartley Green, Selly Oak, Moseley, Weoley, Bournville, Hall Green, Northfield, Brandwood, Billesley, Longbridge, King's Norton

N

0   5 km

	1	2	3	4	5	6
	BIRMINGHAM WARDS	% UNEMPLOYED	% OWNING 2 OR MORE CARS	% HOMES OWNER OCCUPIED	% HOMES WITH MORE THAN 1 PERSON PER ROOM	% HOMES WITHOUT INSIDE WCs
	ACOCKS GREEN	20.6	7.4	55.9	5.6	4.9
	ASTON	35.1	2.7	22.1	11.8	1.3
	BARTLEY GREEN	20.4	8.4	31.7	3.7	0.2
	BILLESLEY	17.1	11.1	48.8	5.1	6.3
	BOURNVILLE	14.3	10.8	57.3	3.0	3.5
	BRANDWOOD	17.2	12.1	50.1	3.7	0.6
	EDGBASTON	22.3	16.8	40.5	3.7	0.4
	ERDINGTON	17.9	10.7	59.1	3.5	1.6
	FOX HOLLIES	20.5	7.0	42.9	5.6	4.9
	HALL GREEN	13.6	15.9	80.0	2.7	2.6
	HANDSWORTH	36.5	5.8	51.7	12.3	1.4
	HARBORNE	14.5	13.1	53.3	2.3	1.5
	HODGE HILL	18.4	10.0	53.2	4.0	1.5
	KINGSBURY	23.7	6.6	27.9	5.4	3.3
	KING'S NORTON	20.8	11.1	36.7	4.6	0.2
	KINGSTANDING	24.7	5.8	30.2	7.5	20.1
	LADYWOOD	30.6	4.4	26.0	7.0	0.5
	LONGBRIDGE	19.7	8.1	44.7	5.2	2.1
	MOSELEY	20.5	15.3	61.2	4.9	1.1
	NECHELLS	36.7	2.4	31.6	12.7	3.2
	NORTHFIELD	14.2	11.2	59.9	2.5	1.1
	OSCOTT	12.7	10.4	73.3	3.8	3.6
	PERRY BAR	11.6	11.3	85.7	3.5	0.6
	QUINTON	13.8	14.7	61.9	3.2	1.0
	SANDWELL	21.4	14.3	73.9	8.6	1.0
	SELLY OAK	14.9	11.0	68.1	3.4	1.3
	SHARD END	21.4	6.5	28.9	5.2	0.8
	SHELDON	12.8	10.7	65.9	3.1	0.1
	SMALL HEATH	30.6	5.0	58.5	13.4	3.6
	SOHO	35.2	3.8	50.9	18.3	2.5
	SPARKBROOK	40.7	2.9	26.4	17.2	1.7
	SPARKHILL	30.1	7.6	55.6	12.0	2.2
	STOCKLAND GREEN	22.9	7.4	55.9	5.4	5.4
	SUTTON FOUR OAKS	8.7	37.6	82.6	0.8	0.1
	SUTTON NEW HALL	11.0	23.0	67.8	2.4	0.3
	SUTTON VESEY	9.2	29.9	85.6	0.9	0.5
	WASHWOOD HEATH	26.9	4.4	49.2	9.4	9.5
	WEOLEY	18.5	10.2	35.5	4.8	3.7
	YARDLEY	18.2	10.4	55.2	5.0	1.7

Work Programme C

STATEMENT

In the inner city, most people live in council (local authority) or private rented housing. In the suburbs, almost everyone owns their homes.

1 To test whether this statement is true or false, you can use the information in column 4 of the DATA FILE. Shade in a copy of the Birmingham wards map using this system of colour coding:

Colour 1 Less than 45% houses are owner occupied.

Colour 2 46-65% houses are owner occupied.

Colour 3 More than 66% houses are owner occupied.

2 What conclusions can you draw from the information you have mapped? You will need to compare this map with your map of the location of Birmingham's inner city.

a) What is the pattern of home ownership in Birmingham?

b) Does the evidence on the map support the statement about home ownership and rented housing?

c) Are there any 'untypical' housing areas? How could you explain these 'untypical' areas?

d) What further information would you want to make a fuller analysis of this question?

Work Programme D

STATEMENT

Living conditions and housing standards are poorest in the inner city areas and are best in the outer suburbs.

1 To test this statement, use the data from column 5 and/or column 6 of the DATA FILE. Decide on a good method of showing the data in map form. Carry out your method, using a copy of the Birmingham wards map.

2 To what extent does your map information support or reject the statement?

3 In testing this statement, how useful was the data you had available?

a) To what extent do you think that these two sets of data – on overcrowding and inside WCs – are good and reliable indicators of living conditions and housing standards?

b) What other information would you wish to have to test this statement properly?

Work Programme B

STATEMENT

People who live in the inner city are poorer than people who live in the suburbs.

1 Describe three different ways of testing this statement to see if it is true or false for Birmingham.

2 Look at columns 2 and 3 of the DATA FILE. The columns have two sets of information which gives us some idea of how poor or wealthy people living in different parts of Birmingham are.

a) On a copy of the Birmingham wards map, use a colour to shade in those wards whose unemployment levels are over 25%.

b) On the same map, use another colour to shade in those wards where over 10% of households own two or more cars.

3 Describe the pattern shown by your finished map. How useful is this information in helping to show whether the statement is correct, partly correct or false?

18 THE MULTI-ETHNIC CITY

People have been coming to settle in Britain for thousands of years. Some of the earliest *immigrants* were the Celts, Romans, Saxons and Vikings. In the centuries that followed, many other immigrants, from all over the world, have come to Britain. At the same time, many Britons have become emigrants and moved to live in other places.

In recent years immigrant groups have tended to settle in Britain's largest urban areas. Most immigrant groups, in their early years in Britain, settle in particular areas, and form closely linked communities. Often they want to carry on doing things in ways that are traditional in their culture – wearing particular clothes, eating certain foods, speaking their own language. People who share a similar culture are called an ethnic group. Britain's larger cities, like most others the world over, contain people from a multitude of ethnic groups.

The first large influx of immigrants into Britain's urban areas came from Ireland between 1800 and 1850. The Irish were trying to escape from rural poverty in their own country. They found unskilled work – either in building Britain's canals and railways, or in the growing number of factories. Many Irish settled in London, Birmingham and the industrial cities of the north such as Liverpool and Manchester. Between 1870 and 1910 large numbers of Jewish people came to Britain to escape religious persecution in Eastern Europe. Most Jewish people settled in London, Manchester and Leeds, finding work in the clothing trade and commerce. Afro-Caribbean people and Asian people were encouraged by the British government to come to Britain in the 1950s and this influx continued until the 1970s. The majority of these immigrants filled labour shortages in public transport, the health services and the textile factories of northern England, doing jobs that the white population was less and less willing to do. Most black immigrants settled in London, Birmingham, Leicester, Manchester, Bradford and Leeds.

Britain's immigrant and ethnic groups are more urban than the rest of the population. About 35% of Britain's total population live in London and the other seven major conurbations. Sixty-five per cent of the black population live in these areas and 75% of the Afro-Caribbean population. Traditionally, the major urban areas have provided most housing and jobs for immigrants.

Many immigrants have concentrated in particular parts of the city. In London, for example, Jamaicans are largely found in Brixton, Sikhs in Southall and Bangladeshis in Tower Hamlets. This type of *residential segregation* is an important feature of British cities.

Out in the City

When you're out in the city
Shuffling down the street,
A bouncy city rhythm
Starts to boogie in your feet.

It jumps off the pavement,
There's a snare drum in your brain,
It pumps through your heart
Like a diesel train.

There's Harry on the corner,
Sings, 'How she goin' boy?'
To loose and easy Winston
With his brother Leroy.

Shout, 'Hello!' to Billy Brisket
With his tripes and cows heels,
Blood-stained rabbits
And trays of live eels.

Maltese Tony
Smoking in the shade
Keeping one good eye
On the amusement arcade.

And everybody's talking:

Move along
Step this way
Here's a bargain
What you say?
Mind your backs
Here's your stop
More fares?
Room on top.

Neon lights and take-aways
Gangs of boys and girls
Football crowds and market stalls
Taxi cabs and noise.

From the city cafes
On the smoky breeze
Smells of Indian cooking
Greek and Cantonese.

Well, some people like suburban life
Some people like the sea
Others like the countryside
But it's the city
Yes it's the city
It's the city life
For me.

By Gareth Owen

Borough	Percentage of Jewish people	Borough	Percentage of Jewish people
Barnet	over 15	Islington	1–3
Hackney	10–15	Kingston Upon Thames	(contd)
		Merton	
Brent	5–10	Richmond Upon Thames	
Camden		Sutton	
Harrow		Waltham Forest	
Redbridge		Wandsworth	
Tower Hamlets			
Westminster		Bexley	under 1
		Bromley	
Kensington and Chelsea	3–5	Croydon	
		Ealing	
Barking	1–3	Greenwich	
Enfield		Havering	
Hammersmith		Lambeth	
Haringey		Lewisham	
Hillingdon		Newham	
Hounslow		Southwark	

1 London's Jewish population. Like other ethnic groups, Jewish people are more numerous in certain parts of the city than others

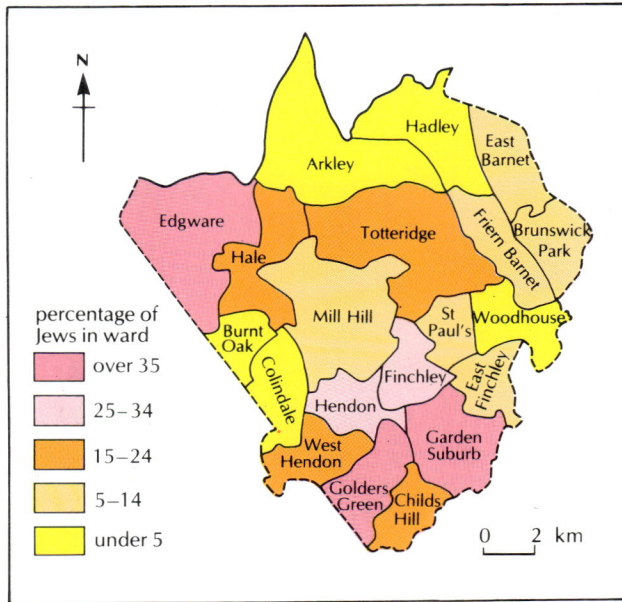

percentage of Jews in ward

- over 35
- 25–34
- 15–24
- 5–14
- under 5

2 The London Borough of Barnet has more Jewish people than any other part of London but they are not evenly spread across the borough

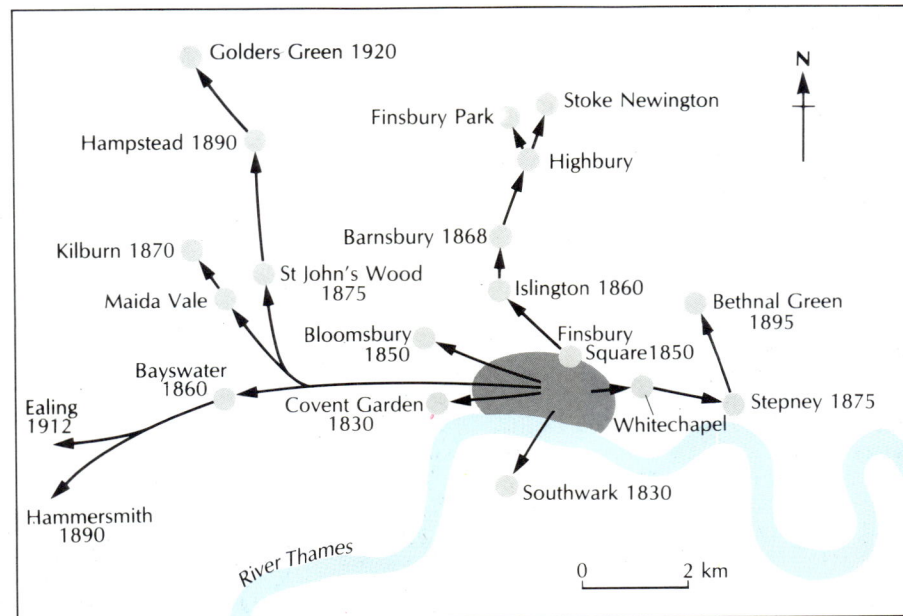

3 The spread of London's Jewish population from its point of origin

The people who have come to live in Britain have not come empty-handed. They have brought their skills and new ideas with them. These have affected life in Britain for everyone. For instance, British eating habits and tastes in music have changed because of our contact with other cultures. Life in Britain in the 1980s is richer and more varied because of multicultural influences.

Generally, people from different ethnic groups manage to live in harmony in most parts of Britain. But there is still cause for concern. Black people living in British cities are more likely to be unemployed, to live in poor housing areas and to suffer from racial attack and abuse. The problem of hostility between people of different ethnic groups is not unique to Britain. Immigrants and their descendents have met with hostility and discrimination in most countries. Racial discord is usually worst in the big cities, where most of the immigrants live.

1 Draw up a table like the one below and fill it in, using information given on page 50.

Immigrant group	Period of immigration	Cities where immigrants settled

2 Read the poem on page 50.

   a) What evidence is there in the poem that this is a multi-ethnic city?

   b) What picture of city life is the poet trying to give?

3 Look at Visual 1 which shows the percentage of Jews in each of the London boroughs.

   a) On an outline map of the London boroughs (like the one in Visual 2 on page 36) use different colours to show the distribution of Jews across London.

   b) Write a few sentences to describe the pattern shown by your map.

4 Visual 2 shows the distribution of Jews within the London Borough of Barnet.

   a) Write a few sentences to describe the pattern shown by this map.

   b) Explain how this map and your map show that Jews, like other ethnic groups, are residentially segregated.

5 Visual 3 shows how London's Jews have moved within the city.

   a) Mark on your map for question 3 the point of origin of London's Jews.

   b) Add arrows to indicate the main direction of movement up to 1920.

   c) London's Jewish population has continued to move outwards since 1920. Use different coloured arrows to indicate on your map more recent population movements.

So far, the 1980s have been a time of crisis for Britain's inner cities. Riots, rising crime and racial attacks are just a few of the things which keep these areas in the news. What is not reported is the fact that nearly four million people have to cope with the misery of everyday life in Britain's inner city areas.

High-density housing areas, which grew up around city centres in Victorian times, can be found in all of Britain's older and larger urban areas. These inner city areas, as they are known, suffer from environmental, economic and social problems. Visual 2 summarizes the main problems facing today's inner city residents. The inner city is a deprived urban area because many of the people who live there are deprived of basic needs such as decent housing, jobs and recreational facilities. Areas can easily fall into a cycle of decline because of a combination of environmental, economic and social problems. Such areas are said to be suffering from multiple deprivation.

According to a recent study, carried out by the Department of the Environment, Hackney is the most deprived urban area in England. This East London borough has the highest proportion of single-parent families, the second highest level of overcrowding and the third highest concentration of black immigrants. Within Greater London, Hackney has the lowest average income and the highest proportion of decaying housing. Two out of every five houses in Hackney are either unfit for human habitation or need major repairs. Hackney's adult male unemployment rate is nearly 30% and the figures are even worse for the young, black people and the unskilled. Hackney also has the second highest level of violent theft in the Metropolitan Police area.

During 1982–83, the journalist Paul Harrison lived in Hackney for 18 months to study its multiple deprivation. In the *Sunday Times* for 21 August 1983, he reported:

The bad state of housing and the environment in the inner city drives away the more fortunate. The able-bodied, the educated, those with higher incomes or savings tend to move out, leaving the old and less fortunate behind. The low rents draw in people on low pay and low incomes – the unskilled, immigrants, single mothers, the mentally and physically ill and handicapped.

This sifting process creates a local labour force which is low on skills and qualifications and has little to offer employers in expanding industries. The local economy of inner city areas is usually weak. Most are dominated by outdated industries or services, or outmoded premises,

1 Notice how this decaying terrace of houses is surrounded by debris and derelict land

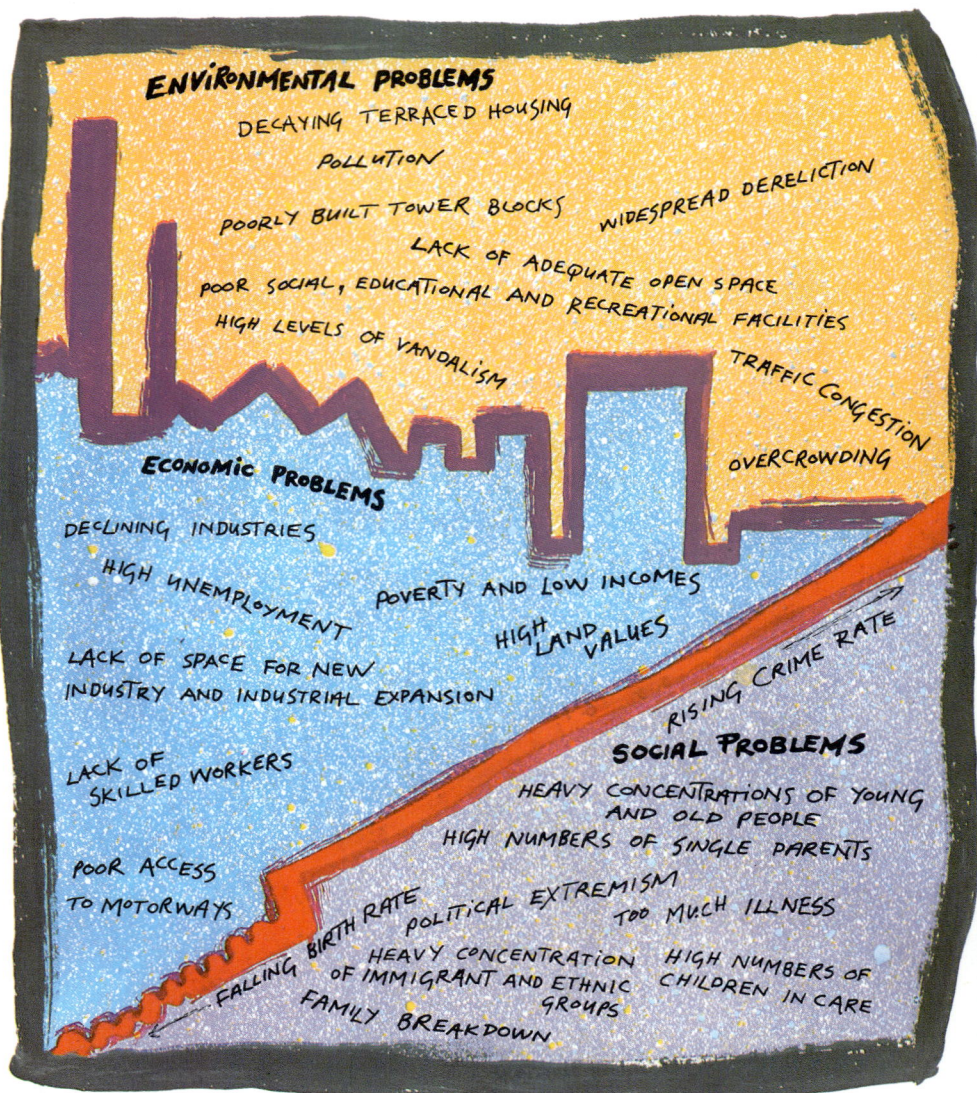

ENVIRONMENTAL PROBLEMS
DECAYING TERRACED HOUSING
POLLUTION
POORLY BUILT TOWER BLOCKS   WIDESPREAD DERELICTION
LACK OF ADEQUATE OPEN SPACE
POOR SOCIAL, EDUCATIONAL AND RECREATIONAL FACILITIES
HIGH LEVELS OF VANDALISM
TRAFFIC CONGESTION
OVERCROWDING

ECONOMIC PROBLEMS
DECLINING INDUSTRIES
HIGH UNEMPLOYMENT   POVERTY AND LOW INCOMES
HIGH LAND VALUES
LACK OF SPACE FOR NEW INDUSTRY AND INDUSTRIAL EXPANSION
RISING CRIME RATE
LACK OF SKILLED WORKERS
SOCIAL PROBLEMS
HEAVY CONCENTRATIONS OF YOUNG AND OLD PEOPLE
HIGH NUMBERS OF SINGLE PARENTS
POOR ACCESS TO MOTORWAYS
POLITICAL EXTREMISM   TOO MUCH ILLNESS
FALLING BIRTH RATE   HEAVY CONCENTRATION OF IMMIGRANT AND ETHNIC GROUPS   HIGH NUMBERS OF CHILDREN IN CARE
FAMILY BREAKDOWN

2 Today's inner city areas are faced with many serious environmental, economic and social problems

costly to adapt, with poor access to motorways. This makes the inner cities particularly vulnerable to recession.

All the ingredients for serious social unrest can be found in Britain's inner city areas. For years there were warnings that the inner cities were living on a short fuse that could start an explosion at any time. In the summer of 1981 the explosion occurred – several of Britain's biggest cities were hit by riots. The worst affected were London, Manchester and Liverpool, where hundreds of people were injured and damage to property ran into millions of pounds. Since then major riots have occurred in Birmingham and Bristol and again in London. It is obvious that the problems have not been solved. If conditions remain unchanged in our inner city areas, serious social unrest is likely to return from time to time.

1 Write short definitions for the following terms:

   inner city area   deprived urban area
   multiple deprivation.

2 Look again at Visual 2. Working in pairs:

   a) Discuss what effect these inner city problems might have on the following people:

      i)   A doctor
      ii)   A school teacher
      iii) A police officer
      iv)   A social worker
      v)   A housing officer
      vi)   An industrialist.

   b) Make a note of what you discussed for each person.

3 Visuals 1 and 3 show the two main types of housing found in inner city areas. Again, working in pairs:

   a) Discuss what problems each type of housing might cause for the following groups of people:

      i)   Old age pensioners
      ii)   Disabled people
      iii) Single people
      iv)   Families with young children.

   b) Imagine that you are designing a new inner city housing area. Make a list of those features which you would include in order to improve the quality of life for the groups of people listed in part a) of this question.

4 Visual 4 shows the location of minor riots in inner city areas in the 1980s.

   a) Make your own copy of the map from Visual 4.

   b) Using an atlas and the information in the table below, mark on your map the location of the major inner city riots of the 1980s.

   c) Write a paragraph to describe what your finished map shows. Which are the worst affected cities?

INNER CITY AREA	CITY	DATE
Brixton	London	Apr 1981 Nov 1985
Southall	London	July 1981
Toxteth	Liverpool	July 1981
Moss Side	Manchester	July 1981
Tottenham	London	Oct 1985
Handsworth	Birmingham	Sep 1985

3 Faulty Towers! Such tower blocks were built in the 1960s to solve the inner-city housing needs. This one, Ronan Point in London's East End, collapsed like a pack of cards after a gas explosion.

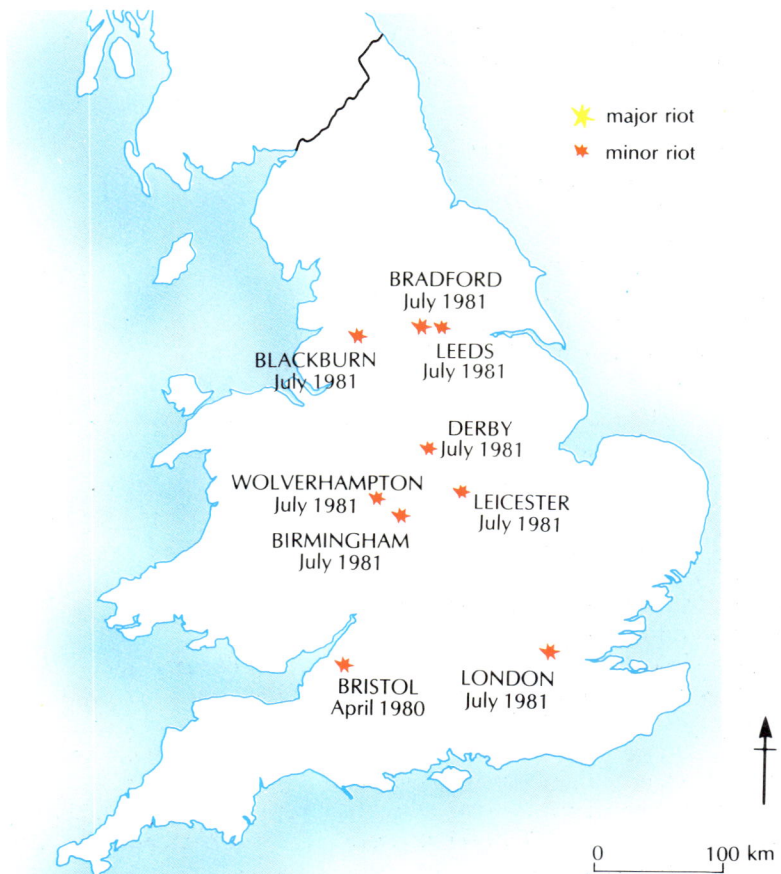

★ major riot
✳ minor riot

BRADFORD
July 1981

BLACKBURN
July 1981

LEEDS
July 1981

DERBY
July 1981

WOLVERHAMPTON
July 1981

LEICESTER
July 1981

BIRMINGHAM
July 1981

BRISTOL
April 1980

LONDON
July 1981

0   100 km

4 Inner city riots in the 1980s

THE OBSERVER

Established 1791   No. 9894

BLOODY CLASHES AS RIOTERS RAMPAGE ON STREETS OF LONDON

The night Brixton burned

Report by PATRICK BISHOP, GEORGE BROCK, DAVID CLARK, JONATHAN HUNT, GEOFFREY LEAN and HENRY PORTER.
Pictures by JOHN HODDER, NEIL LIBBERT and TONY McGRATH.

HUNDREDS of black youths, joined by some whites, rampaged through Brixton, South London, last night in a violent explosion of anger.

More than 50 police and an unknown number of civilians were injured, some seriously, during several hours of running battles. Dozens of shops were wrecked and burned out by petrol-bombs and there was widespread looting.

The rioters rained bricks, iron bars and bottles on the police lines. Two officers were badly burned by petrol-bombs and a third was undergoing surgery after being hit on the head by a brick. Another was treated for stab wounds.

Homes, a school and a pub were set alight. Firemen were unable to get into the area for several hours and some buildings collapsed in piles of rubble, blocking streets.

Police with riot shields arrested 20 people, and at one stage there was a baton charge by 200 officers. Burnt-out police and civilian vehicles littered the area. Rioters also wrecked a fire engine and a bus.

For most of the early rioting police stood helpless – waiting for reinforcements that only began to arrive 90 minutes after serious trouble first broke out.

Red flames towered high over the area in a scene closer to the blitz or Belfast than London. As dusk fell, the police began a new advance. The bricks flew and Molotov cocktails landed among them. The clothes of one police-

man caught fire and he was thrown to the ground by colleagues who doused the flames.

The atmosphere in Brixton had been heavy with impending trouble all day after an incident on Friday night when black youths attacked a policeman who went to question a youth who had been stabbed.

Scores of uniformed and plain-clothed police officers, many from outside the district, were in the area throughout yesterday. By mid-afternoon the battle lines were forming in Railton Road, scene of the Friday night flare-up.

Policemen patrolled under the eyes of large groups of black youths waiting on street corners. Other policemen stood by in vans.

An incident seemed inevitable: it came at 4.45 pm when two plain-clothed detectives arrested a young black outside a super-market in Atlantic Road.

Eye-witness, Maureen Boyle, who works at the Brixton Advice Centre, said, "One of the plain-clothed guys started saying 'you're nicked'. He punched the black in the stomach. Everyone was saying that he'd done nothing. They dragged him into a police van. People smashed on the door on the Transit and a window got broken."

The street quickly filled with police and young blacks. As further arrests were made the crowd began to pelt policemen and women with missiles. We saw one policeman reeling away after being struck on the head by a

flying bottle.

Then at 5.25 pm the troubles began in earnest. A police charge to clear Atlantic Road was driven back and a crowd of black youths raced after them, hurling smashed paving stones. At the junction of Mayall Road and Railton Road the rioters overturned a police van and car and set them ablaze. Mobs of jubilant young blacks took control of the streets, smashing cars and setting them alight.

A large mob gathered in Railton Road. They seized a number 37 bus and drove towards the police, now grouped in Mayall

Road. But their path was blocked by an over-turned vehicle. One gleeful rioter carried off the ticket machine as a trophy.

For nearly an hour the police waited in Mayall Road, retreating whenever the rioters launched another attack, and occasionally mounting a half-hearted counter charge.

Late last night sporadic fighting was still going on. Gangs of looters walked through the streets carrying clothes and radios, stolen from scores of shattered shop windows.

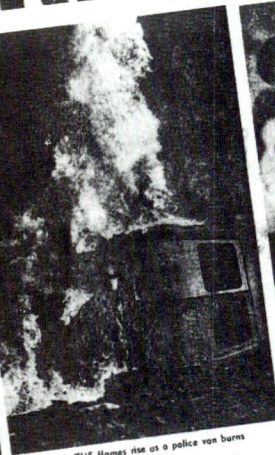

On the afternoon of Friday, 10 April 1981, and then again on the following Saturday and Sunday, there were serious disturbances in Brixton, an inner-city area of London.

The scale of the Brixton 'riot' was a shock to many people. They felt that, although such things had happened in other parts of the world, notably in some American cities, they would never happen in Britain.

Clearly, something as serious as what happened in Brixton over that April weekend did not happen without a reason. What caused the Brixton 'riot' and similar incidents in the inner-city areas of Liverpool and Manchester later that summer? The first answer is that there are *no* simple answers.

Your Assignment
○ To look at how the events were reported in the press immediately after they happened.
○ To consider some of the longer term factors that contributed to the events in Brixton in April 1981.

Resources
1 The Sunday newspaper extracts on this spread.
2 The summary of Lord Scarman's findings on page 56.
3 The extract from *The Economist* on page 57.
4 The photographs shown here.

Work Programme A

Work in pairs or small groups.

1 Read the two newspaper accounts fully and carefully, and in your own group discuss what you have read.

   a) Make a list of any ways in which the two newspaper accounts *differ* in their reports of what happened.

   b) Why are there differences?

2 What sparked off all the trouble in Brixton on Saturday, 11 April?

   a) Using just the two newspaper reports, piece together your own account of what the press, at the time, thought were the immediate causes of the trouble.

   b) Which of the two newspaper accounts do you consider to be more reliable in its reporting of the events? Discuss this in your group and then write your answer and explain your reasons fully.

   c) To write a *full* and *balanced* account of what sparked off the trouble on that Saturday in Brixton, what other information would you want to have? Which people would you want to talk to?

SUMMARY OF SOME OF LORD SCARMAN'S FINDINGS

HOUSING

The Borough of Lambeth (in which Brixton is located) suffers from very serious housing problems.

*There is a shortage of about 20 000 homes in the Borough.
*The council house waiting list contains the names of 18 000 families.
*If you are black you are twice as likely to be homeless than if you are white.
*20% of all the housing in the Borough is substandard - much of the worst housing is in Brixton.

LEISURE & RECREATION FACILITIES

There is a lack of leisure and recreational facilities in Lambeth, and in Brixton in particular, especially for young people. Opportunities do not at present exist in Brixton to the extent that they ought, particularly given the enforced idleness of many youths through unemployment.

EMPLOYMENT

Unemployment in Brixton, for whites and blacks, is high, above the national average. Partly this is because of the recession, and partly because of the decline in industry in inner city areas.

*In Brixton unemployment is rising faster among younger age groups.
*55% of blacks under 19 are out of work.
*There are many reasons for the higher level of unemployment among young blacks, including a lack of qualifications - however, discrimination by employers and at places of work certainly occurs.

POLICING

A considerable number of local people who talked to the inquiry said that a major cause of the riot was the harassment of young people by a racially prejudiced police force, who often abused their powers. It was claimed that police officers picked on black people, especially youths, and that they tended to think of all young blacks as potential criminals. These are some of Lord Scarman's findings:

*The policy of the Metropolitan Police as a whole is not racist.
*Racial prejudice does occur at street level, due to the immature and racially prejudiced actions of a small minority of police officers.
*There is no doubt that some harassment of young blacks does occur.
*Every instance of racial prejudice or harassment by the police has an immense effect on the local community.
*Some of the criticisms of the police are the result of gossip and rumour.

• Economic recession, becoming rapidly worse at the end of the 1970s, harshly affected young people, and especially those with little education.

• The decline of the inner cities, brought about by industrial change and by government policies to disperse employment, had left the low-paid and the unemployed concentrated in run-down districts near the centres of many large towns.

• Immigration into Britain in the years of relative prosperity from the 1950s to the 1970s attracted a significant number of non-white people from former imperial territories. They took jobs that the British-born preferred not to do, and settled in the outworn urban areas where British-born people preferred not to live.

• Racial prejudice combined with educational disadvantage kept the black immigrants, and their British-born black children, out of the better jobs and better homes. Verbal and physical abuse of black people heightened their discontent.

• Crime, particularly crime involving personal violence, increased in the inner cities. The crime-control methods of the police focused particularly on young black people, and offended all black people, including the law-abiding majority.

By the spring of 1981 the police were seriously alarmed at the level of street crime in Brixton – especially thefts from the person with actual or threatened violence, called 'mugging'. The police acted in secret, by putting large numbers of plain-clothed men on the street to stop and search suspects. The most highly suspect were black.

The operation, tactlessly named 'Swamp '81', began on Monday, April 6th. By Friday the police had stopped, searched and questioned 943 people, half of them black. 93 of them were charged with minor offences, just one with robbery. 850 people had been needlessly stopped. They, their friends and relations, and the black community at large, were furious.

Scores of newspaper and journal articles have been written about the Brixton and other riots which hit Britain in the spring and summer of 1981. Many, like this extract from the *Economist*, have been concerned with the social and economic circumstances in which Britain's riots began

Work Programme B

Immediately after the Brixton troubles, the government set up an enquiry to find out how and why it happened. That enquiry was carried out by a judge, Lord Scarman. In carrying out his enquiry, Lord Scarman had the cooperation of the police and local resident groups (including black groups). In his conclusion about the underlying causes of the riot, this is what Lord Scarman said:

While nothing can excuse the unlawful behaviour of the rioters, both the police and community leaders must carry some responsibility for the outbreak of disorder.

The social conditions in Brixton do not provide an excuse for disorder. But the disorders cannot be fully understood unless they are seen in the context of complex social and economic factors.

1 What did Lord Scarman mean when he said that what happened in Brixton could not be fully understood unless you take complicated social and economic factors into account? Discuss this in your group after you have read the summary of Lord Scarman's findings (page 56) and the extract from *The Economist* on the left.

2 Plan the outline for a television programme called 'What Caused the Riots?'. A programme outline shows how the programme will be organized. Your outline might include:

○ Ideas for the short *introductory sequence*, which sets the scene for the rest of the programme:
    What will the script say?
    What visuals will you show to match the script?

○ Ideas for the *main body* of the programme:
    What points do you want to make?
    What visuals do you want to include?
    Who do you want to interview?
    What are the main things you want to discuss with each of the people you interview?

○ Ideas for a short *concluding sequence*, which sums up what you think the programme will have been saying:
    What conclusions have you come to about the causes of the Brixton riots?

Urban Renewal Schemes

After the Second World War many city authorities started slum clearance schemes to tackle the problem of bomb damage and decaying housing in inner city areas. But it was not until the 1960s that comprehensive redevelopment schemes were introduced. These involved completely clearing large areas of the inner cities and building high-rise flats in tower blocks. Both of these types of scheme created new housing but many old communities were destroyed in the process. To make matters worse, the new housing was often poorly designed and badly built. From the late 1960s onwards the emphasis shifted to urban conservation schemes. Public money was spent on conserving older houses, but improving them so that they had modern facilities.

Between the late 1940s and the late 1970s, local authorities tried to remake the inner city areas through these various urban renewal schemes. But throughout the same period central government was encouraging people and industry to move out of the large cities to the new towns and to housing and industrial estates on the edges of towns and cities. This conflict of aims only made the problems of the inner city worse.

The Inner Urban Areas Act

In 1978 the Inner Urban Areas Act was passed by Parliament. It emphasized the need for a new joint approach between:

◦ Central government
◦ Local authorities
◦ Community organizations and local firms.

Forty-eight inner city areas (Visual 1) were chosen to receive help under this new law. The act set up several bodies to deal with administration. The *Urban Development Corporations* are organizing large-scale schemes to redevelop the run-down dockland areas of London and Merseyside. *Partnerships* and *Programme Authorities* organize the reclamation of derelict land, improve housing, transport and open space, help to create jobs, and encourage community involvement. *Designated Districts* receive grants for industrial and economic projects.

Despite the many changes which are taking place, some people say that still too little is being done to overcome the massive problems which exist in inner city areas. The social unrest in these areas, which sometimes erupts into violence and disorder, seems to support this view.

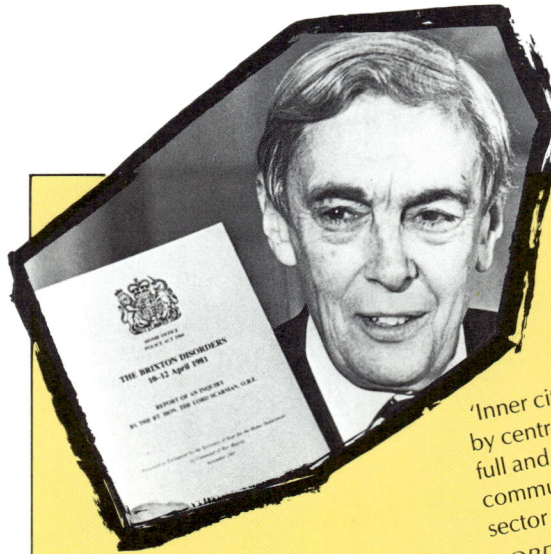

'Inner city problems must be attacked by central and local government with the full and effective involvement of local communities, including the private sector and the police.'
LORD SCARMAN
THE JUDGE WHO REPORTED ON THE BRIXTON RIOTS
1981

'The inner cities are the biggest complex of economic, social and physical problems that we face.'
PETER SHORE
ENVIRONMENT SECRETARY
1977

'Each generation brings a major social challenge and to my mind solving the problems of the inner cities is the challenge for late twentieth century Britain.'
DOUGLAS HURD
HOME SECRETARY
1986

'There is no single cause of inner city decay and there can be no master plan to provide a simple solution.'
MICHAEL HESELTINE
ENVIRONMENT SECRETARY
1982

1 Read the statements shown on page 58. In what ways are these people saying similar or different things?

2 a) List the three main types of urban renewal scheme.

b) Write a brief description of each one.

c) What do you think of each of these schemes? Give reasons for your answer.

3 a) On your own blank outline map of Britain, mark the location of the inner city areas which get urban aid.

b) Use your atlas and the information in the table below to match up the names of the Programme Authorities and Designated Districts with the symbols on the map. Use a number or a letter key.

PROGRAMME AUTHORITIES: Blackburn, Bolton, Bradford, Brent, Coventry, Hammersmith, Hull, Knowsley, Leeds, Leicester, Middlesbrough, Oldham, North Tyneside, Nottingham, Rochdale, Sandwell, Sheffield, South Tyneside, Sunderland, Tower Hamlets, Wandsworth, Wirral, Wolverhampton.

OTHER DESIGNATED DISTRICTS: Barnsley, Burnley, Doncaster, Ealing, Greenwich, Haringey, Hartlepool, Langbaurgh, Lewisham, Newham, Rotherham, St. Helens, Sefton, Southwark, Walsall, Wigan.

---

c) Write a paragraph to explain the differences between Urban Development Corporations, Partnerships, Programme Authorities and Designated Districts.

4 Read the newspaper extract on the right.

a) Where is Handsworth?

b) What is David Wright trying to do with his Image of Handsworth Project?

c) Why does he think that the present image of the area is misleading?

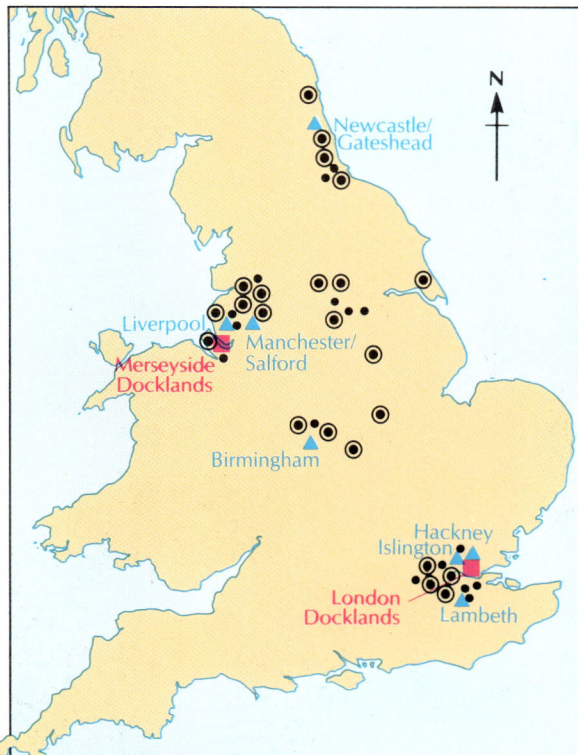

urban development corporation
partnership
programme authority
other designated district

1 The urban renewal map. Forty-eight inner city areas in England receive help of various kinds for urban renewal projects

Paul Hoyland reports on attempt to spread the good news about a one-time trouble spot in Birmingham

The harmony of Handsworth

EIGHTEEN months ago a deputy head teacher, Mr David Wright, stood on his patio listening to the crackle of the flames in the Handsworth riot that was happening a few hundred yards from his house.

Today he is in charge of the Image of Handsworth Project, whose aim is to make known the many positive aspects of education in the district and to counter the 'misleading and often incorrect portrayals of the area.'

At first sight it may appear a daunting task, but Mr Wright is relishing the chance to point to Handsworth's achievements and, he hopes, help to create an atmosphere in which 'our young people will be listened to instead of being ignored.'

More than 40 schools in the Handsworth district are participating in the project. Mr Wright passionately believes that while the district may be generally poor in terms of jobs and housing, the community is immeasurably richer for being multiracial.

"I am hoping to make people aware that our children cannot only read and write well but that they have something to say and need to be heard. If people can be aware of the children's abilities and the opportunities they offer we are beginning to get somewhere."

He is introducing a series of initiatives, including interschool exchanges throughout Birmingham and displays of the children's work in other parts of the city.

Locals refer to the riot as the uprising. Mr Wright describes them as the disturbances. "If I am going to call it a riot I will match it with Martin Luther King's words, 'A riot is the voice of the unheard.' You don't mobilise hundreds of people on the streets unless there is deep discontent, unless the people have not been heard."

3 An extract from The Guardian for 28 April 1987

FORMER TOWER BLOCK

OAK & ELDON GARDENS: OGDEN DEMOLITION

"WENT LIKE CLOCKWORK — WELL, ALMOST THE PLANNERS ESCAPED"

HAVE A NICE DAY AT URBAN DECAY THEME PARK

2 Liverpool's inner city problems – possible solutions?

FINANCIAL NEWS NEW LOOK FOR LIVERPOOL

THE GOVERNMENT HAS INTERVENED TO SOLVE THE FINANCIAL PROBLEMS OF LIVERPOOL. IT HAS SOLD THE CITY TO AN AMERICAN BUSINESSMAN, MR IVOR BIGWALLET.

HE WILL HAVE IT DISMANTLED AND SHIPPED BACK TO CALIFORNIA WHERE IT WILL BE OPENED AS AN URBAN DECAY THEME PARK.

P.S. LIVERPOOL JUMPED SIX POINTS ON THE STOCK EXCHANGE TODAY ....

REVIVING LONDON'S DOCKLANDS

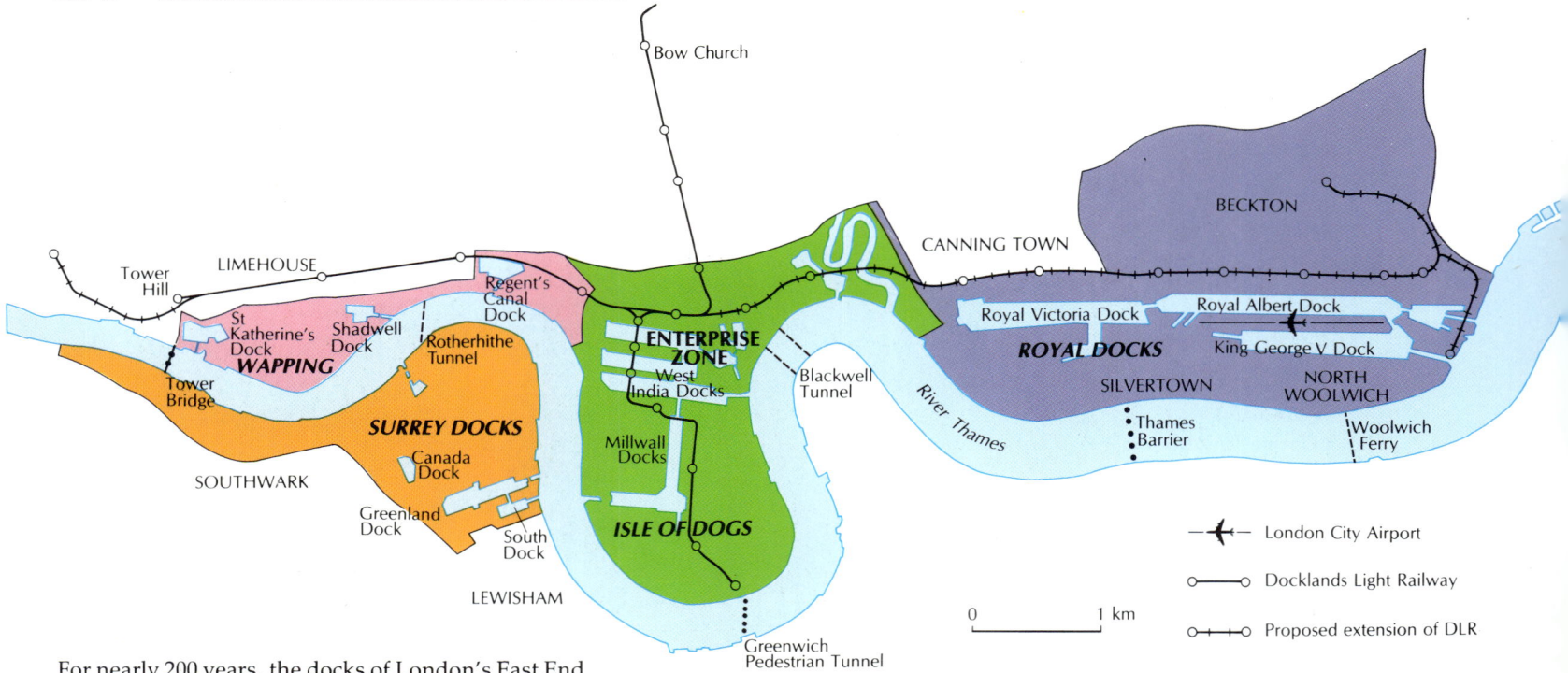

Bow Church

LIMEHOUSE

Tower Hill

CANNING TOWN

BECKTON

Regent's Canal Dock

St Katherine's Dock

Shadwell Dock

Rotherhithe Tunnel

ENTERPRISE ZONE

Royal Victoria Dock

Royal Albert Dock

ROYAL DOCKS

King George V Dock

WAPPING

West India Docks

Blackwell Tunnel

SILVERTOWN

NORTH WOOLWICH

Tower Bridge

River Thames

Thames Barrier

Woolwich Ferry

SURREY DOCKS

Canada Dock

Millwall Docks

SOUTHWARK

Greenland Dock

South Dock

ISLE OF DOGS

LEWISHAM

Greenwich Pedestrian Tunnel

0   1 km

London City Airport

Docklands Light Railway

Proposed extension of DLR

For nearly 200 years, the docks of London's East End were the commercial heart of the world's largest empire. At the beginning of the 1960s, one-third of all Britain's trade passed through the Port of London and there were jobs for 28 000 dockers. However, the use of larger ships and the advent of container vessels in the 1960s led to the closure of many of the docks. Today, only 2000 dockers are employed – mainly at Tilbury, London's new container port near the mouth of the River Thames.

Visual 1 shows the area covered by London's docklands. St Katherine's Dock, near Tower Bridge, was the first to close in 1967. Other closures followed in quick succession, the last three (Royal Docks) closing in 1981. What had once been the busiest port in the world suddenly became a vast area of rusting cranes, rotting warehouses and disused waterways. The impact on local residential communities, such as Wapping, the Isle of Dogs and Silvertown, was grim. It has been estimated that for every job lost in the docks, three other local jobs disappeared in related manufacturing, ship repair and transport industries. In 1985 male unemployment in London's docklands reached 32%. Throughout the 1960s and 1970s the young, the better educated and the better-off moved out of the area. By the mid-1970s the docklands were showing all the signs of multiple deprivation typical of inner city areas.

The London Docklands Development Corporation (LDDC) was set up by the government in 1981 and given the job of bringing about the economic, social and physical renewal of the docklands. To begin with, the LDDC concentrated on buying up vacant and derelict land and building new sewers and roads to make the area attractive to developers. The Docklands Light Railway has been built to connect the area to the city of London. The London City Airport (a short take off and landing airport) has been built in the Royal Docks. The government has also

made the Isle of Dogs an enterprise zone. This is an area free from normal planning restrictions, where no rates are payable on industrial and commercial property for ten years.

All these developments have transformed the decaying docklands landscape. New industries have started up, such as printing, media and communications, retailing, leisure and tourism, commercial and financial services. Many of these industries have relocated from other parts of London. Since 1981 about 6000 new houses have been built in Wapping, the Surrey Docks, the Isle of Dogs and Beckton. Another 9000 houses are expected by 1991.

1 London's docklands cover 22 square kilometres of the capital from Tower Bridge to North Woolwich. There are four main areas: Wapping and Limehouse, Surrey Docks, the Isle of Dogs and the Royal Docks

2 The new Eastenders. These data show the very rapid social and economic changes which are taking place in London's docklands

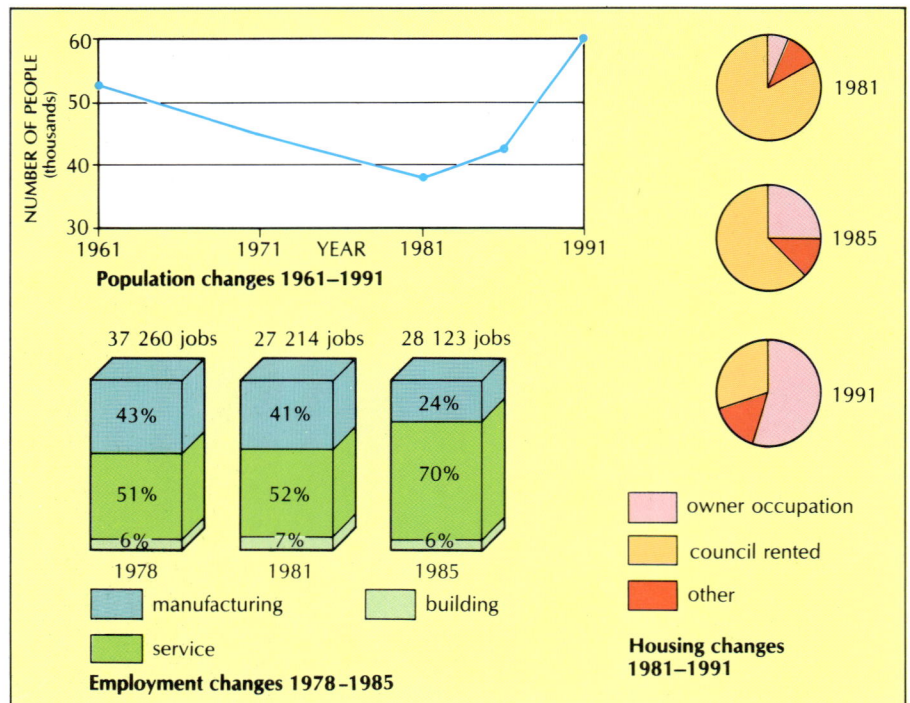

Population changes 1961–1991

NUMBER OF PEOPLE (thousands)

60
50
40
30

1961   1971   YEAR   1981   1991

1981
1985
1991

Employment changes 1978–1985

37 260 jobs

43% manufacturing
51% service
6% building

1978

27 214 jobs

41%
52%
7%

1981

28 123 jobs

24%
70%
6%

1985

manufacturing   building
service

owner occupation
council rented
other

Housing changes 1981–1991

Land and house prices have rocketed and increasingly people from outside the area are moving in. They tend to be young, owner-occupiers with well-paid non-manual jobs. Many commute to work in the City of London. These young, urban professional people are sometimes called yuppies.

There are still many arguments between the LDDC and the local authorities over the best schemes for the docklands. Local authorities and community groups would like to see renewal based on the needs of local people. They want better council housing, public open spaces, community facilities and small industries using local skills. The LDDC is building houses for sale rather than rent, is encouraging the building of office blocks, and is developing the area as an eastward extension of the City of London.

1 Visual 2 shows some of the changes affecting the people of London's docklands. Using this and other information from this chapter:

a) Describe the main changes which are taking place.

b) Explain why the number of jobs in manufacturing has fallen, while the number of service jobs has increased.

c) Explain why the share of rented council housing is falling while the share of owner-occupied housing is increasing.

2 Look at the photograph in Visual 3.

a) Working in pairs, try to pinpoint the area shown in the photograph on the map of London's docklands in Visual 1.

b) Make a simplified sketch of the area shown in Visual 3. Draw a frame for your sketch and then add each of the following: River Thames   docks   roads and

elevated railway   vacant land   warehouses and industrial units   areas of flats   areas of housing.

c) Identify the numbered buildings, services and sites in Visual 3 from this list:

West India Docks   new private housing estate new industrial units   Docklands Light Railway blocks of council flats   vacant land for development newspaper offices under construction.

3 The community wall poster shown in Visual 4 presents a different view of what the LDDC is doing to the docklands.

a) In your own words summarize the message which this poster is trying to get across.

b) How do you think that the LDDC would answer the objections of local people?

c) Imagine that you work for the publicity department of the LDDC. Design a poster, to be used in a publicity campaign, to show how the LDDC is changing the face of the docklands.

3 Looking from the Isle of Dogs' Enterprise Zone (in the foreground) towards the City of London. The immense size of London's docklands makes them one of the most important urban renewal sites in Europe

4 Not everyone is happy with the way in which London's docklands are being redeveloped, as this community poster points out

ASSIGNMENT SEVEN

Renewal of Beaubourg–Les Halles, Paris

1 A market had existed at Les Halles for several centuries. The great wrought-iron market halls were built in the 1850s to house the growing wholesale markets of Paris. The halls became a familiar landmark of central Paris and conservationists fought hard to save them before they were demolished in 1969.

2 The Forum des Halles now occupies the site of the old market halls. The 'futuristic' look is achieved largely by the daring use of glass, plastics and steel. The Forum has three levels which contain a range of shops and entertainment facilities, appealing particularly to middle-class Parisians and foreign tourists.

Beaubourg and Les Halles are located north of the River Seine, close to the business and retailing centre of Paris. By the 1950s, these areas had many of the classic problems of inner-city decline. When the decision was taken in 1960 to move the capital's wholesale markets from Beaubourg–Les Halles, an opportunity arose for a major urban renewal programme in a key city centre location.

The renewal of Beaubourg–Les Halles has been controversial. Conflicts have arisen between those who wish to conserve the city's historic core and those who wish to promote Paris as an international centre for commerce and tourism. In the past 20 years, plans for the area have changed rapidly and there has been considerable wrangling taking place over the different schemes for the area.

In 1960 the area was dominated by wholesale markets and housed a poor, working-class population. Thirty years later the area has been transformed into a fashionable part of Paris with its up-market shopping complex, leisure and cultural facilities and green, open spaces.

Your Assignment

Study carefully all the information given here. Then:
- Consider some of the issues involved in city centre renewal schemes.
- Identify the different interest groups involved.
- Think about how decisions are made.

Resources
1 Visuals 1 and 2.
2 Extracts from a newspaper article.
3 Map of the Beaubourg–Les Halles area.
4 DATA FILE.

Work Programme A

1 Using Visuals 1 and 2, describe the area of Les Halles a) before its renewal and b) after it.
2 a) What are the main land uses of Les Halles today?
   b) What were they originally?

DATA FILE

**BEAUBOURG–LES HALLES
COUNTDOWN TO URBAN RENEWAL**

1960	Decision made to move Paris's fruit and vegetable market from Les Halles to Rungis, a motorway site on the edge of the city.
1963	Studies start on how best to redevelop the area.
1969	Market moves to Rungis.
1969	President Georges Pompidou agrees to a plan which includes a central interchange for the new express metro, a museum and cultural centre, an international centre of commerce, a shopping and entertainments complex, offices, some housing and open space.
1971	Decision made to redevelop a 35 hectare site stretching from Les Halles in the west to the Beaubourg area in the east.
1971	Demolition work starts on the area after much opposition from conservation groups.
1974	President Giscard d'Estaing suggests that the Les Halles area should be changed into a garden. All building work stops for two years and plans for an international centre of commerce are dropped.
1977	Pompidou National Centre for Art and Culture opens at Beaubourg.
1977	Châtelet–Les Halles underground station opens. This is the central interchange for Paris's express metro system.
1979	First part of Forum des Halles shopping complex opens.
1986	Final part of Forum des Halles shopping complex opens.

Upmarket move for an historic city centre

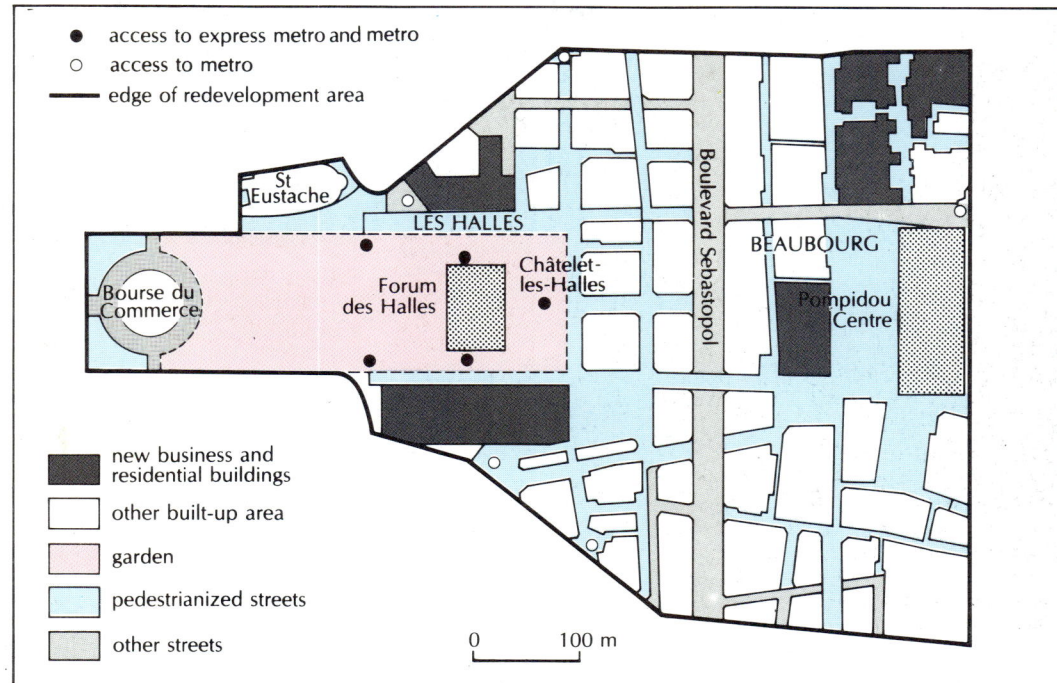

PARIS, which is always fascinated by its own charm, is beginning to rediscover one of its favourite haunts. Fifteen years after the fruit and vegetable market of Les Halles was pulled down amid controversy, the new *quartier* of the *Forum des Halles* is nearing completion.

This month the final wing – over 60 fashion boutiques, gift and gadget shops – of the giant underground shopping complex was opened. Next year the last shrubs and turfs of grass will be planted in the gardens above, revealing views of the handsome gothic church of Saint Eustache and of the Bourse de Commerce.

The redevelopment of Les Halles is the largest inner city development project Paris has undertaken since the war. It also marks a shift in the focus of the city towards the east – away from the flashy Champs Elysée and back towards the popular roots of Paris in the districts surrounding Les Halles.

Two ideas lie behind the project. The first was to maintain the historic character of Les Halles as one of the capital's major market places – which it has been since the twelfth century.

This has been achieved by locating the shopping complex, the cinemas and restaurants largely underground. The originality of architecture of Mr Claude Vasconi and Mr Georges Pencreach was to bring light to the three tiers of streets and shops through a system of glassed arcades that tumble downwards like a waterfall.

Espace Expansion, promoters of the shopping complex, now claim that the first part opened in 1979 does more business than any other complex in the world – with an average annual turnover of FFr 47,000 (£4,600) a square metre.

The other main idea was to provide an open space in the heart of a city that is desperately short of parks and gardens. The centre's landscape gardening includes sunken walks, children's playgrounds, banks of shrubs, flower beds and tree-lined alleys.

For much of the past 15 years Les Halles has been a building site and an ugly hole in the ground. The history of the construction has been one of continual political pressure and jostling.

President Georges Pompidou – who had a taste for monumental architecture – wanted to build a giant international chamber of commerce on the site that would have obscured the view of Saint Eustache. President Giscard d'Estaing, taking over as President in 1974, scrapped this idea in favour of transforming Les Halles into a garden. Work stopped on the western part of the project for two years.

Mr Jacques Chirac, arriving as Mayor of Paris in 1977, pulled down a building designed by Boffil that was beginning to rise on the north side.

In commercial terms the advantage of the Forum is that it is one of the natural meeting places of Paris. Five

metro lines converge on the area and the new express metro links nearby Chatelet by faster commuter train to the suburbs. On top of that the Beaubourg Centre, commissioned by President Pompidou as a modernistic art centre, has proved one of Paris's most successful museums. Some 20 million people a year visit the Forum – equivalent to the combined total of visitors to Paris's five most popular tourist spots.

When the first part of the shopping complex opened in 1979, the aim had been to attract some of the smarter shops that line the Faubourg St Honoré. But the goal was rapidly abandoned in favour of drawing in stylish boutiques which took their lead from the nearby Beaubourg centre.

With over 300 shops and 23 cinema halls, the Forum, says Mr Michel Guidet, the President of Espace Expansion, is for a clientele

that sees itself as avant-garde and "in search of a life-style."

The Forum has had problems with the drug trade and petty crime – but now seems to be keeping away the loafers, drug addicts, buskers and pavement artists who loiter around the Beaubourg.

The complex has involved an investment of over FFr 900 million since 1973, with the wing opened this month costing FFr 190 million. The money has been put up by banks, property groups and insurance companies.

Linked to the Forum are a series of entertainment, cultural and sports centres, including a swimming pool, gymnasium, an auditorium, a photographic centre and a discotheque. The final project to be opened will be a mock-up of the ocean bed dedicated to Mr Jacques Cousteau, the French underwater explorer.

Work Programme B

Read the *Financial Times* article above and look carefully at the DATA FILE.

1 Why do you think that this area was chosen for renewal?

2 Make a list of all the individuals and groups who were involved in the area and its redevelopment. For each individual or group:

a) Note their interest in the area.

b) Say whether they were likely to gain or lose from the development.

3 Which other groups or individuals, not mentioned here, would have been interested or involved in this project? Say whether they would have been in favour. Explain your answer.

Work Programme C

1 Why do you think there was so much disagreement and controversy over how Beaubourg–Les Halles should be redeveloped? Write a paragraph to explain your ideas.

2 a) How do you think such areas should best be redeveloped?

b) Is there a need to limit and control changes in our towns and cities?

c) Who should make the final decision?

1 The development of the planned environment:
A Robert Owen's New Lanark
B Ebenezer Howard's Letchworth Garden City
C Harlow – a new town started in 1947
D Milton Keynes – a new town started in 1971

Some countries have tried an alternative to renewing the worn out parts of old towns and cities. They have built completely new settlements. In Britain today more than two million people live in these new towns. The idea of building towns from scratch, to provide a better urban environment, has been around for a long time. From early experiments in Britain in the 1800s, the new town idea has spread to other countries in Western Europe, to North America and to some countries of the South.

The Industrial Revolution, which affected so much of Europe in the 1800s, created many new social and environmental problems. In the industrial towns poorly built and overcrowded housing grew up around dirty and noisy mills, factories and mines. Living conditions for the workers and their families were disgraceful, disease was common, infant mortality was high and life expectancy was low. Some well-meaning industrialists built new settlements for their workers. They thought that lower density housing with improved facilities would produce healthier, happier workers for their factories. Robert Owen's New Lanark in Scotland, Titus Salt's Saltaire in West Yorkshire and George Cadbury's Bournville near Birmingham are examples of these early *model towns*.

One man who had a great influence on town planning was Ebenezer Howard. He had been brought up in the squalor of London's East End in the last century. This made him think a great deal about how to develop better towns and cities for the future. In 1898 Howard published his ideas in a book now called 'Garden Cities of Tomorrow'. Howard wanted to bring together all the advantages of town and countryside into a new type of settlement known as a garden city. These garden cities would have the following important features:

- A population limit of 32 000
- A surrounding green belt of agricultural land and open space
- Houses with gardens as well as public parks and gardens
- Separate land uses so that, for example, housing and industry were located in different areas
- Wide, open, tree-lined roads and avenues

The building of the first garden city at Letchworth, in Hertfordshire, started in 1903. A second garden city was started by Howard in 1919 at Welwyn, also in Hertfordshire. Following the translation of Howard's book into Italian, German and French, garden cities were built throughout Western Europe. Milanino was built outside Milan (Italy) in 1910, Staaken near Berlin (Germany) in 1913, and Floréal near Brussels (Belgium) was founded in 1925.

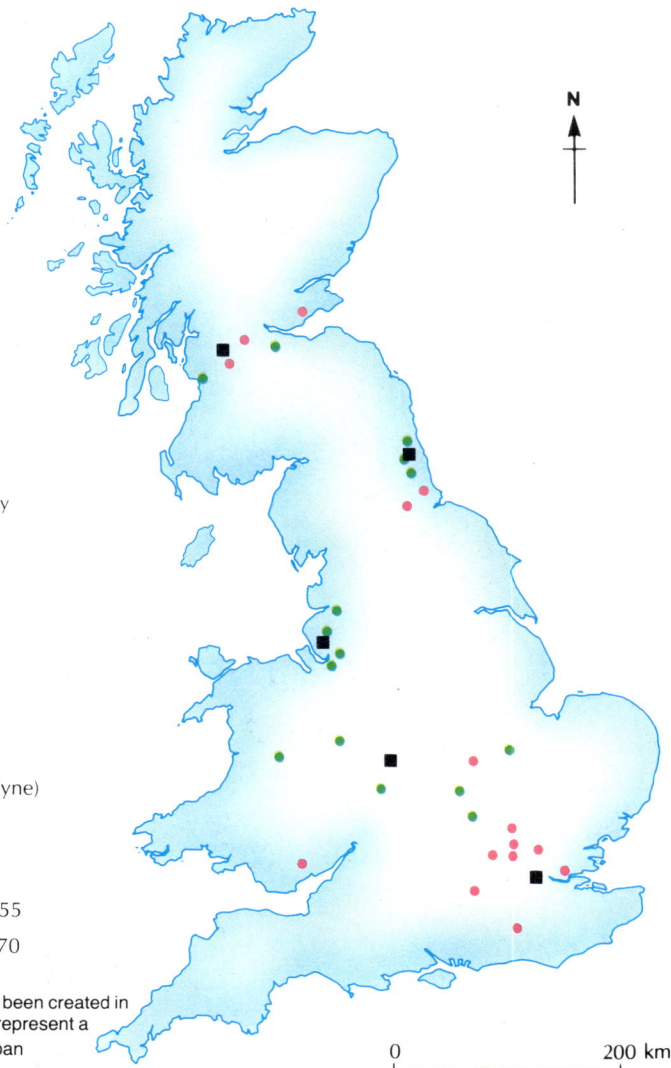

New towns

1 Glenrothes
2 Livingston
3 Cumbernauld
4 East Kilbride
5 Irvine
6 Newtown
7 Cwmbran
8 Cramlington
9 Killingworth
10 Washington
11 Peterlee
12 Aycliffe
13 Central Lancashire
14 Skelmersdale
15 Warrington
16 Runcorn
17 Telford
18 Redditch
19 Peterborough
20 Corby
21 Northampton
22 Milton Keynes
23 Stevenage
24 Welwyn Garden City
25 Harlow
26 Hatfield
27 Hemel Hempstead
28 Basildon
29 Bracknell
30 Crawley

Major cities

Lo (London)
B (Birmingham)
G (Glasgow)
L (Liverpool)
N (Newcastle upon Tyne)

● designated 1946-1955
● designated 1961-1970

2 Thirty new towns have been created in Britain since 1946. They represent a major achievement in urban planning

0 ⊢———————⊣ 200 km

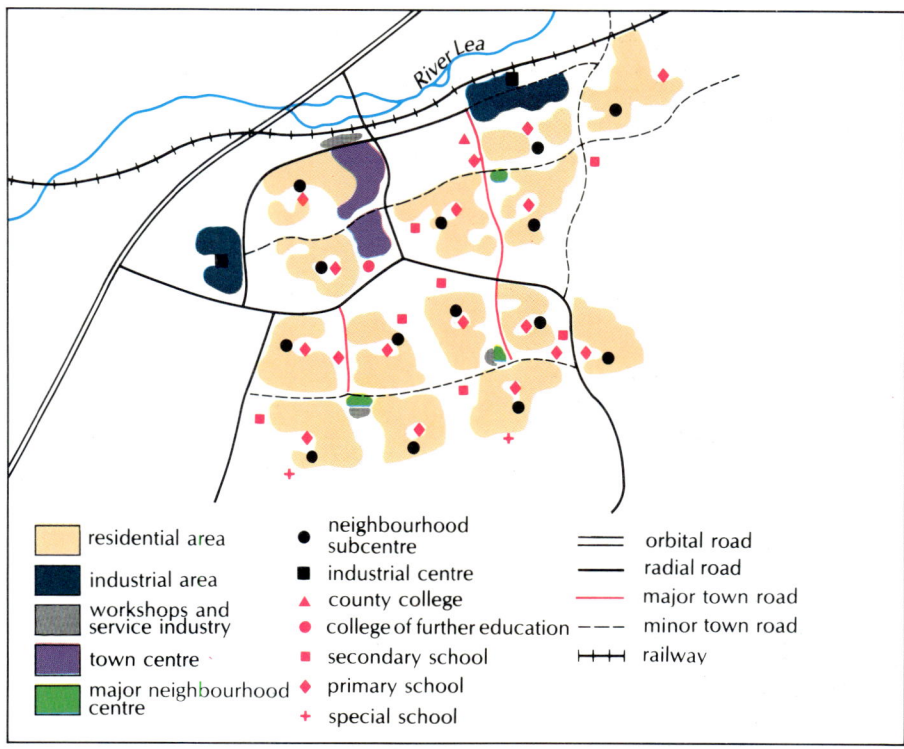

residential area
industrial area
workshops and service industry
town centre
major neighbourhood centre

● neighbourhood subcentre
■ industrial centre
▲ county college
● college of further education
■ secondary school
♦ primary school
✛ special school

══ orbital road
── radial road
── major town road
--- minor town road
╫╫ railway

3 The plan for Harlow New Town. Harlow was one of the original new towns around London

The Great Depression of the 1930s and the Second World War caused a temporary halt in urban planning. By 1945, when the Second World War ended, interest in new types of settlement was still strong but society had changed a great deal from the early years of the century. With the development of the motor car people were becoming more mobile and there was an increasing demand for leisure and recreation. During the late 1940s and throughout the 1950s there was a chronic housing shortage caused by bomb damage and the rapid increase in population. The first new towns, created by the 1946 New Towns Act, tried to tackle these problems. They were planned to relieve overcrowding in large cities, to control the spread of large cities and preserve open land, and to provide a better environment for their residents. Later, new towns also acted as centres for the development of new industry. The form of British new towns has been heavily influenced by the original garden city idea – small populations, houses rather than blocks of flats, carefully planned roads, lots of green space, compactness, and industrial areas which are separate from other land uses.

1 The terms 'model town', 'garden city' and 'new town' mean different things. Look back through this chapter to find out exactly what they mean. Write a few sentences to explain each term.

2 Look at Visual 1 which shows some of Britain's planned towns. Working in pairs:

a) Discuss what evidence exists in the pictures to show that these towns were developed at different times during the last 200 years.

b) Discuss what evidence exists in the pictures to show that these towns were planned.

c) Make a note of the main points which have arisen from your discussion.

3 Visual 2 shows the new towns which have been developed in Great Britain over the past 40 years. On your own blank outline map of Britain and using your atlas:

a) Mark the location of the following major cities: London, Birmingham, Liverpool, Newcastle upon Tyne and Glasgow. Use the letter key as shown on the map.

b) Mark the location of the new towns. Use the number key as shown on the map.

4 a) Describe, in your own words, the distribution of new towns in Britain.

b) Can you see any relationship between the location of the new towns and when they were built?

5 Harlow, in Essex, was one of Britain's first new towns. A plan of the town is shown in Visual 3.

a) In what ways do you think that garden city ideas influenced the plan for Harlow?

b) What other evidence is there on the plan for Harlow to suggest that it is a planned new town?

c) What advantages and disadvantages does this type of planned environment have for its residents?

d) Would you like to live in a new town? Give reasons for your answer.

1 Cergy-Pontoise

The massive experiment in new town development has not only taken place in Britain. The new town idea caught on in a big way in the rest of Western Europe. More than 100 planned communities have been developed since the end of the Second World War. For example, the Netherlands, West Germany, Italy, Spain and Switzerland have new towns similar to those in Britain.

France, also, has turned to the new town idea as a way of solving some of its urban problems. It now has nine new towns, the majority of them situated around the capital city of Paris (Visual 2). The Greater Paris area contains ten million people, or about 20% of the total population of France. The city completely dominates the political, social, economic and cultural life of France. Such a dominant centre is known as a primate city.

Central Paris is very overcrowded. The suburbs have sprawled outwards with little planning or organization and the city faces:

- Congestion
- Inner city decline
- Overloading of commuting and other transport facilities
- Not enough housing
- Inadequate shopping and leisure facilities

Since 1960, plans have been put forward to combat these problems. The latest master plan for Paris was drawn up in 1975. It aims to channel new urban growth along two growth axes (Visual 3) in an attempt to meet the needs of the area by the year 2000. The development of five new towns (Cergy-Pontoise, Marne-la-Vallée, St Quentin-en-Yvelines, Evry and Melun-Sénart) is an important part of the overall plan. Visual 3 shows where these new towns and the suburban growth centres are located.

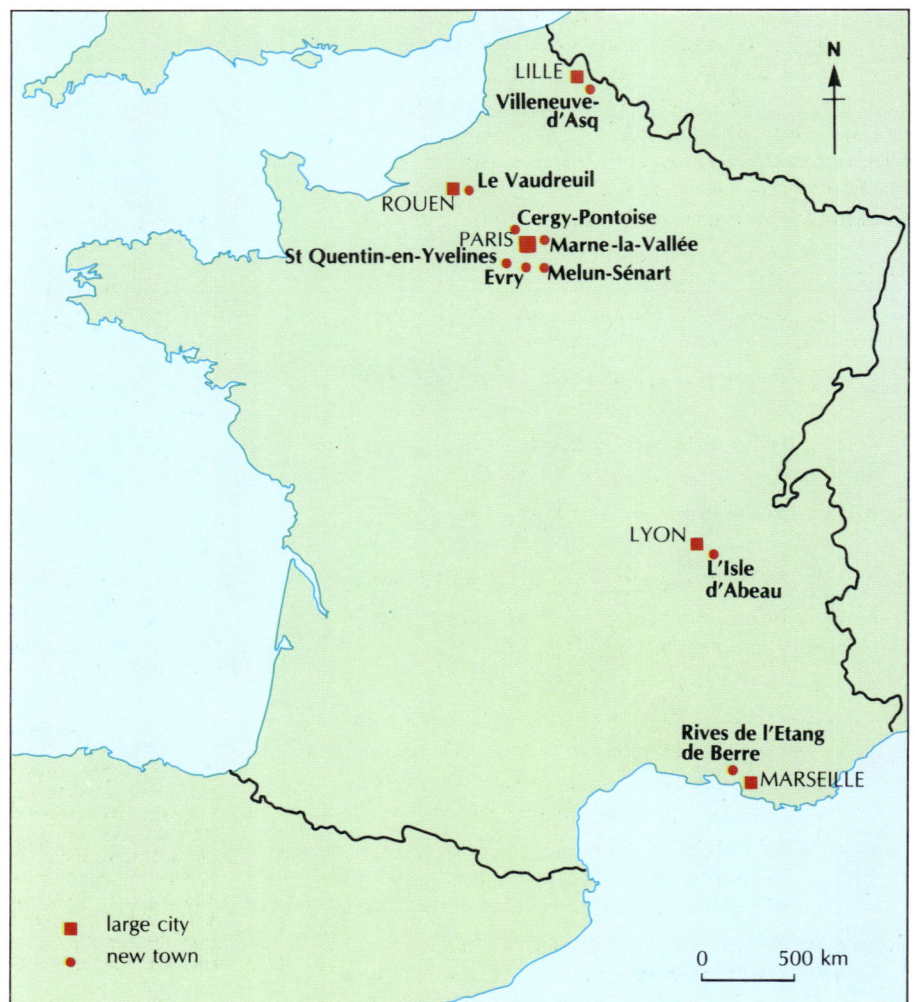

2 France has nine new towns. Five are located in the Paris region and the other four are in the provinces

3 Since 1960 there have been several plans for urban development in the Paris region. This map shows the 1975 plan

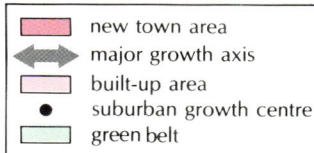

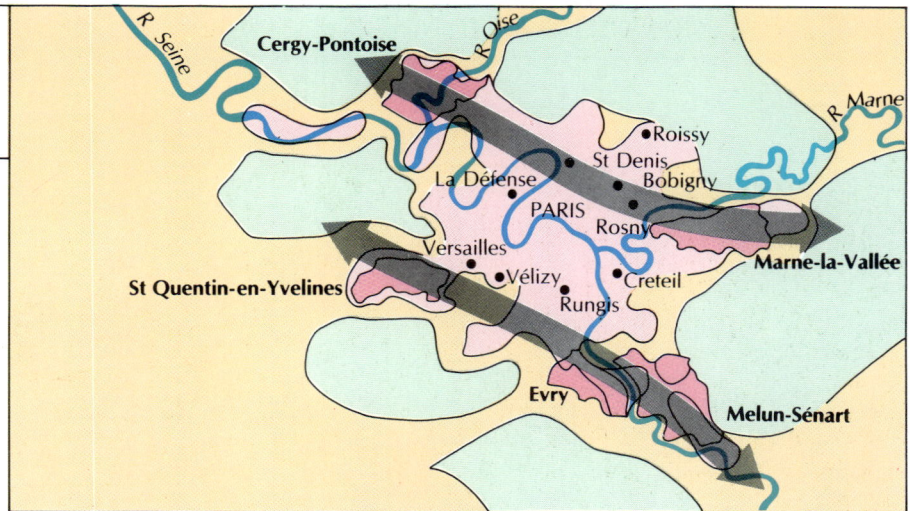

In the 1960s the population of the Paris region was growing very rapidly. It was thought that between two and four million extra people would be added to the region's population before the year 2000. The five new towns were originally designed to accommodate up to 500 000 people each. However, population growth has since slackened and the new towns are now unlikely to reach their target populations in this century. Despite this, the new towns have been immensely useful. Pressures on housing and space in the capital have been eased by directing growth towards the new towns. Industry, and particularly office development, has also become less centred on Paris. This policy of *decentralization* has encouraged many new and relocating industries to set up either in the growth centres of the suburbs or in the new towns. Regional shopping centres and modern leisure facilities are also a feature of the new towns, bringing much needed public services to the outer suburbs of Paris. Urban motorways and a new express metro system have linked the new towns and the suburban growth centres with central Paris.

Although the new towns around Paris owe their origin to early thinkers such as Ebenezer Howard, they also reflect the French approach to town planning. Of all European new towns the ones around Paris have moved furthest away from the neatly ordered, garden city style of planning. New technology has resulted in very modern, futuristic-looking town centres and unusual building designs.

1 Using the information from Visual 2:

  a) Make a list of France's nine new towns. Indicate which large city is located near each.

  b) What do you notice about the distribution of French new towns?

2 Look back through the information on these pages and study the map shown in Visual 3.

  a) What problems was Paris suffering from in the 1960s?

  b) Describe the main points of the Paris 'master plan'.

  c) Why are the new towns and the suburban growth centres an important part of the plan?

3 Look at Visual 1 and the box on the right.

  a) In what ways is Cergy-Pontoise similar to the garden cities and early new towns of Britain? You might mention each of the following: i) size   ii) separate land uses   iii) type of housing and industry   iv) amount of open space   v) road layout.

  b) What evidence is there that Cergy-Pontoise is a 'technological' new town?

4 Imagine that you live in the new town of Cergy-Pontoise. You are about to write your first letter to a pen-friend in one of Cergy-Pontoise's twin towns. Write a letter in which you try to give an impression of what the new town is like. You can include a sketch map if you wish.

A Quick Guide to Cergy-Pontoise

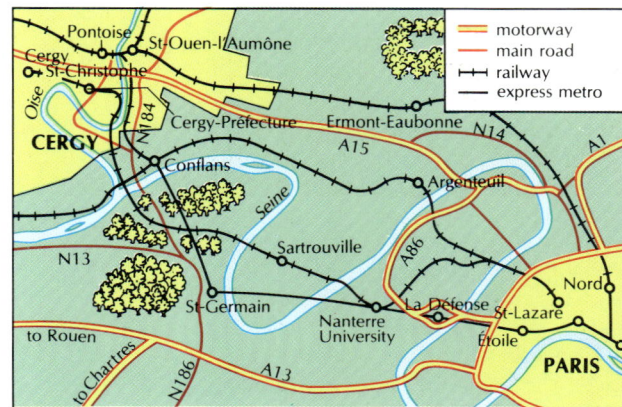

motorway
main road
railway
express metro

135 000 inhabitants

Cergy-Pontoise, as chief town of the Val d'Oise département, is built on 8000 hectares of land and has a population of 135 000 people. 65 000 live in the newly built districts of Cergy-Préfecture, Eragny, Cergy-Saint-Christophe, Cergy-le-Haut and Versants de l'Hautil. 31 000 new dwellings have already been built and when building is complete in the 1990s the total population should rise to 200 000 people.

Cable TV

Cergy-Pontoise is also the French town covered by the best TV network – all dwellings are connected by cable. Since 1986 it has been possible to choose from 15 different channels.

Fast communications

Located 30 km north-west of Paris, Cergy-Pontoise is linked to the city by the A15 motorway and 3 railway lines. In 1985 the Paris–St-Lazare to Cergy-Préfecture railway line was extended into the newly developed district of Cergy-Saint-Christophe. In 1987 the RER (express metro) was extended from St-Germain to Cergy-Pontoise, giving the new town a rapid link with the capital.

Employment: 55 000 jobs

New jobs have been created recently at the rate of 2000 per year. Today there are about 8000 new factories and 55 000 jobs in Cergy-Pontoise. The town is becoming a powerful economic centre and big companies, such as Scania and Johnson-France, have located factories here. More than 60% of local workers find employment in Cergy-Pontoise and only 15% commute to Paris.

Leisure park of Mirapolis

Mirapolis, the largest leisure park in Europe, opened in 1987. This park uses a high level of technology, like American ones. Mirapolis should attract 2.5 million visitors each year.

Downtown

Cergy downtown (town centre) was completed in 1984. It was built over the Cergy-Préfecture railway station and contains pedestrian streets, squares, cafés, a cultural centre and a regional shopping centre.

International links

Cergy-Pontoise is twinned with new towns in other countries: Colombia (USA) near Washington, Erkrath (West Germany) near Düsseldorf and Skelmersdale (GB) near Liverpool.

Siting and Planning a New Town

Imagine a small county in West Germany, which we shall call Halbheim. It is located to the south of a major conurbation which contains six million people. Much of Halbheim is rural and the main land use is agriculture. However, it has a large and increasing population, and there are several growing urban areas within Halbheim, the majority being located along north–south transport routes.

The greatest pressure of urban expansion is felt in the north of Halbheim. It is this part of the county which also contains the highest grade farmland. To help plan for, and control, future urban growth, the Halbheim County Council has decided to build a new town which will eventually accommodate 75 000 people. Most people moving to Halbheim from the nearby conurbation will be encouraged to move to the new town.

Your Assignment

- Select a suitable site for the development of a new town in Halbheim.
- Plan the layout of the new town.

Resources

1 The three maps given here.
2 Role outlines.

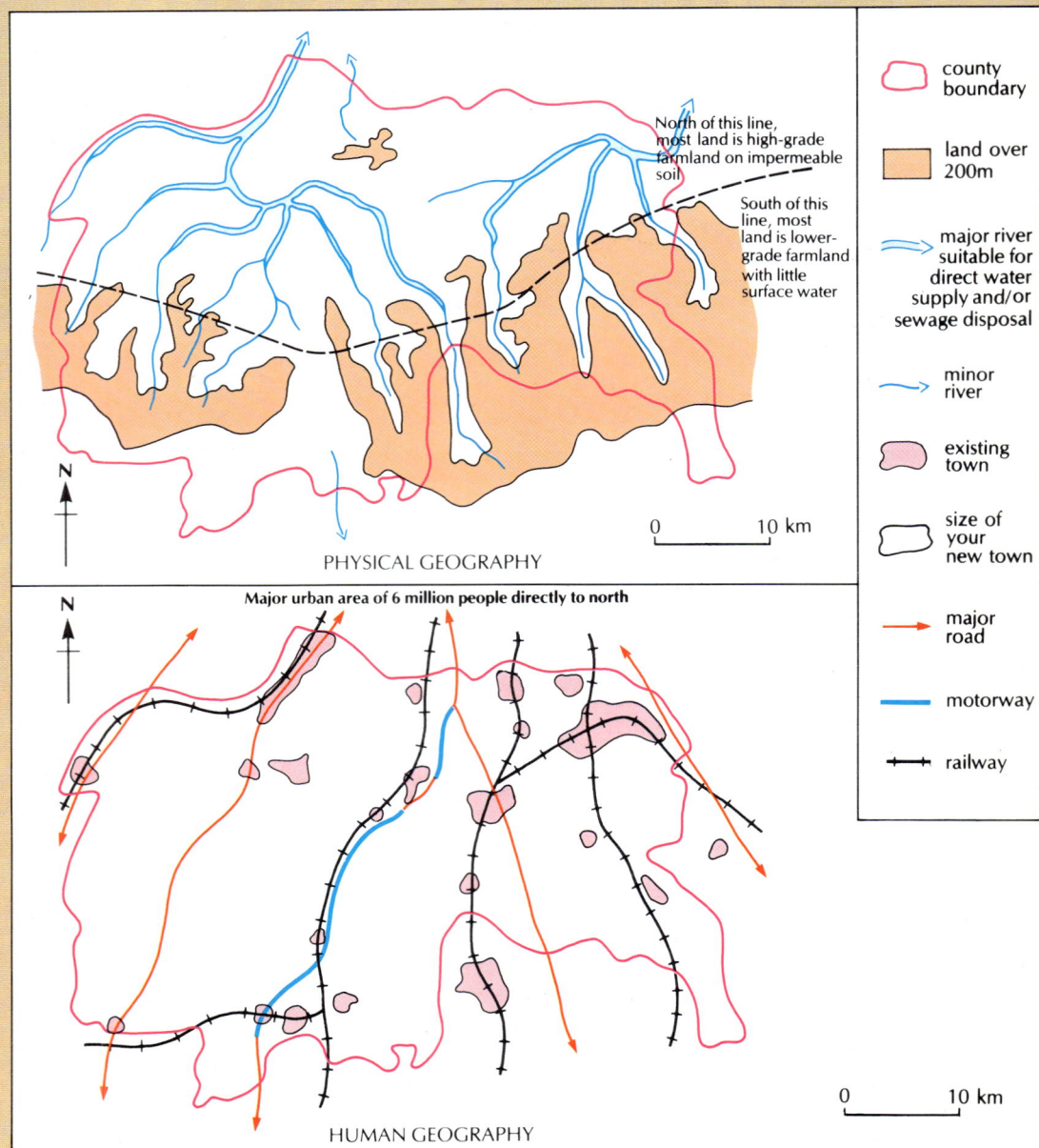

North of this line, most land is high-grade farmland on impermeable soil

South of this line, most land is lower-grade farmland with little surface water

PHYSICAL GEOGRAPHY

0   10 km

Major urban area of 6 million people directly to north

HUMAN GEOGRAPHY

0   10 km

county boundary

land over 200m

major river suitable for direct water supply and/or sewage disposal

minor river

existing town

size of your new town

major road

motorway

railway

Work Programme A

Work in groups of four.

1 a) Study the two maps on this page, which show details of Halbheim's physical and human geography.

b) Read through the role outlines.

2 Each person in your group must choose one of the roles. Together you form a Planning Committee that has to select a site for the new town.

3 Using his or her role outline as a guide, each member of the committee must prepare and write up his or her ideas on where to locate the new town.

4 The Planning Committee, chaired by the County Planner, then meets to discuss the site selection. Each person presents his or her case to the committee. When all viewpoints have been

heard, the committee makes a final decision on the new town location.

5 After the meeting, write up the committee's decision. Include a summary of all the views expressed and the reasons for the final choice of site. Include a sketch map to show the location of the sites considered.

WALTRAUD MAIER
County Planner

You are concerned with what is happening in the county as a whole. You want to prevent the growth of unplanned urban sprawl across Halbheim. You think a small existing town should be expanded to form the new town. You think that the new town would develop its own identity and be less of a commuter town if it were located in the south of the county away from the major urban area. As chairperson, you have the casting vote.

HANS SCHNICK
Industrial Development Officer

The success of the new town will depend largely on its ability to attract new industry. Industrialists will be attracted by fast, modern communications. A site must be chosen, in your view, which has both good road and rail links. The conurbation to the north is likely to be a major market for industries and the site needs to be as close as possible to this area.

OTTO SCHMIDT
County Surveyor and Engineer

A major concern for you is transport. There is likely to be little money to build extra roads and railways. A site which makes use of existing road and rail links would be a good choice in your view. You would also prefer a site which would enable the water supply to be drawn from major rivers. You would support any ideas that help to keep down costs.

LOTTE BAUM
Green Party

You want to preserve the rural character of Halbheim, prevent the loss of high-quality farmland in the north and protect the hilly scenery to the south. In your view, a site in the south makes sense as most of the present urban centres are in the north. You think environmental arguments are more important than economic ones.

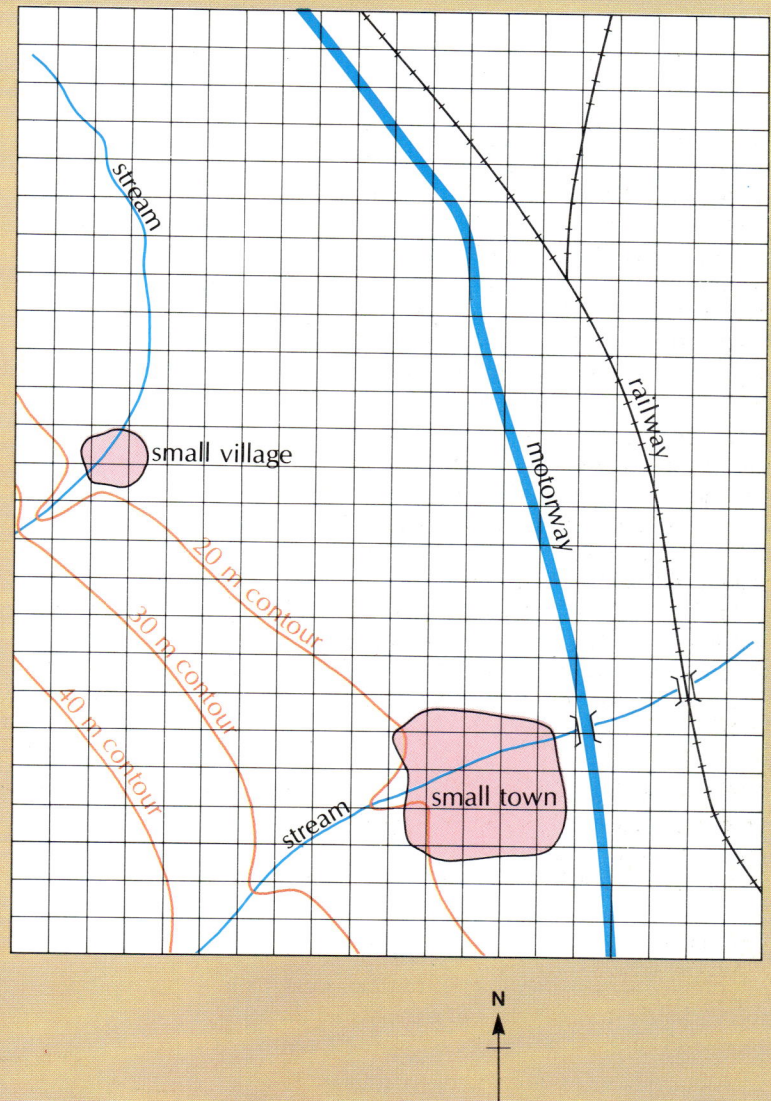

Work Programme B

1 Imagine that the site chosen for the new town in Halbheim looks like the one shown above. On a copy of the base map prepare a master plan for the new town, showing the layout of major land uses.

2 Your plan is for the whole new town, which is designed for 75 000 people. The plan should include the following:

Housing	200 units
Industry	50 units
Recreation	25 units
Central business district	5 units
Local shopping and community centres	5 × 1 units
Education campuses (including schools, sports centres and libraries)	5 × 1 units

The plan should also include the new town's transport network. The town's internal road system and other transport facilities should be shown on your plan. Some matters will need careful thought, for example: the position of the central business district; whether to separate certain land uses; whether to group housing into neighbourhood areas.

3 Compare your finished plan with those produced by others in the class.

RANDSTAD: PLANNING THE CITY REGION

The Netherlands is one of the smallest countries in Europe and the most densely populated. Land is needed for farming, industry and urban growth and so great is this need that the Dutch have to reclaim land from the sea. In fact, 16% of the total area of the Netherlands has been reclaimed in this way since the 1400s. The Dutch take great care to make the best use of every square kilometre of land. During the past 100 years many towns and cities have grown up and the Dutch have planned carefully to lessen the impact of urban growth in their small country.

Unlike Britain and France, the Netherlands has no single dominant city. However, there is a giant city region. This is in the western Netherlands where four large conurbations and many small and medium-sized towns and cities have developed close to each other. Visual 1 shows how this city region has developed since 1850. Today, an almost continuous band of urban areas curves round through Dordrecht, Rotterdam, The Hague, Leiden, Haarlem, Amsterdam, Hilversum and Utrecht. The Dutch call this region Randstad ('rim city') because it resembles the rim of a saucer. On the inside of this rim is a 'green heart' of land given over to agriculture, recreation and open space and dotted with villages and a few small towns.

Although the towns and cities of Randstad have grown closer together, they have kept their own functions and identity. Of the four main conurbations Amsterdam is the country's capital; The Hague is the seat of national government; Rotterdam is the main port and industrial centre; and Utrecht, situated in the middle of the country, is a major route centre.

Randstad has a population of six million. This means that 42% of the Dutch people are clustered in 20% of the country's land area. The western Netherlands has always been at the centre of economic life and until about 1970 the population of Randstad increased quite fast. During the 1970s, however, the populations of the four main conurbations and of some of the major cities showed a marked decrease. People were moving to the smaller settlements in the 'green heart'. More recently, renewal and redevelopment of areas in the conurbations and cities are encouraging more people to set up home within Randstad again.

The growth of Randstad, population movements, and changes in society have kept planners in the Netherlands busy in recent years. Visual 3 shows how the planners have had to change their plans over time. In the 1960s planners tried to slow down and redirect the growth of Randstad. Today the planners are trying to concentrate development within the northern and southern wings of the Randstad area.

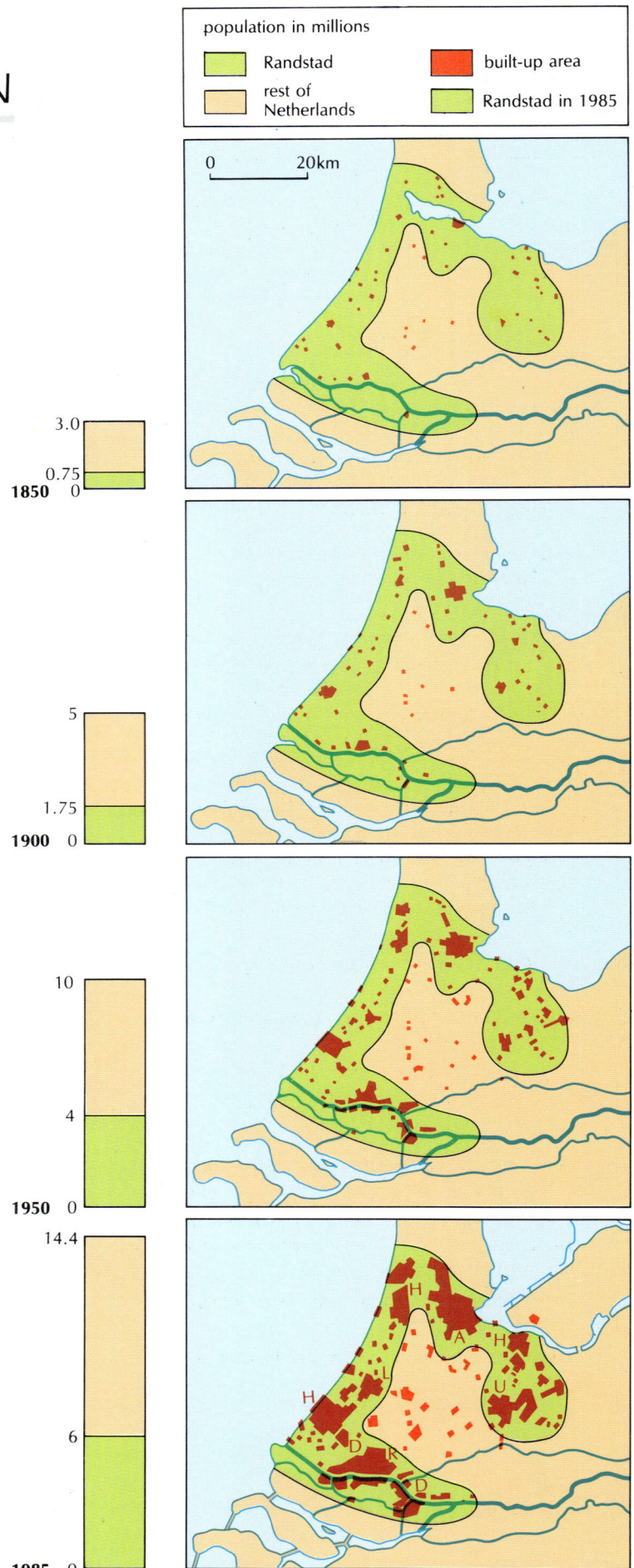

1 The development of Randstad since 1850. Although the towns and cities have grown closer together, they have not merged completely

1 In your atlas find a map which shows the countries of Western Europe.

a) Find the Netherlands and compare its size with other countries in Europe.

b) Draw up a table like the one shown below.

COUNTRY	POPULATION *thousands*	AREA *000 km²*	POPULATION DENSITY *persons/km²*
NETHERLANDS	14 400	41	
WEST GERMANY	61 400	249	
BRITAIN	56 300	245	
FRANCE	54 700	547	

c) Complete your table by working out the population density for each country using the following formula:

$$population\ density = \frac{population}{area}$$

d) Why are the population density figures a useful addition to the population figures?

2 Study the information shown in Visual 1.

a) Draw your own bar charts to show the population of Randstad and the Netherlands in 1850, 1900, 1950 and 1985.

b) Work out what percentage of the Netherlands' total population lived within the Randstad area for each date. Write the figures at the side of your bar charts.

c) What do these figures tell you about the importance of the Randstad city region?

d) Make your own sketch map of Randstad based on the map for 1985. Use your atlas to help you name the nine most important cities (marked with their first letter on Visual 1).

3 Visual 2 shows the overall plan for the development of Randstad up to the year 2000.

a) What is the purpose of the 'green heart' and 'green corridors'?

b) What is the purpose of the buffer zones?

c) Where will most development take place in the 1990s?

d) How might Randstad develop if there were no plans?

4 Look back through the information on these pages and then at Visual 3.

a) Choose two or three of these planning policies and write a short paragraph for each to explain how they propose to solve particular problems.

b) In what ways are plans for the 1980s different from plans of the 1960s?

c) Why have planners tried to change their policies over the years?

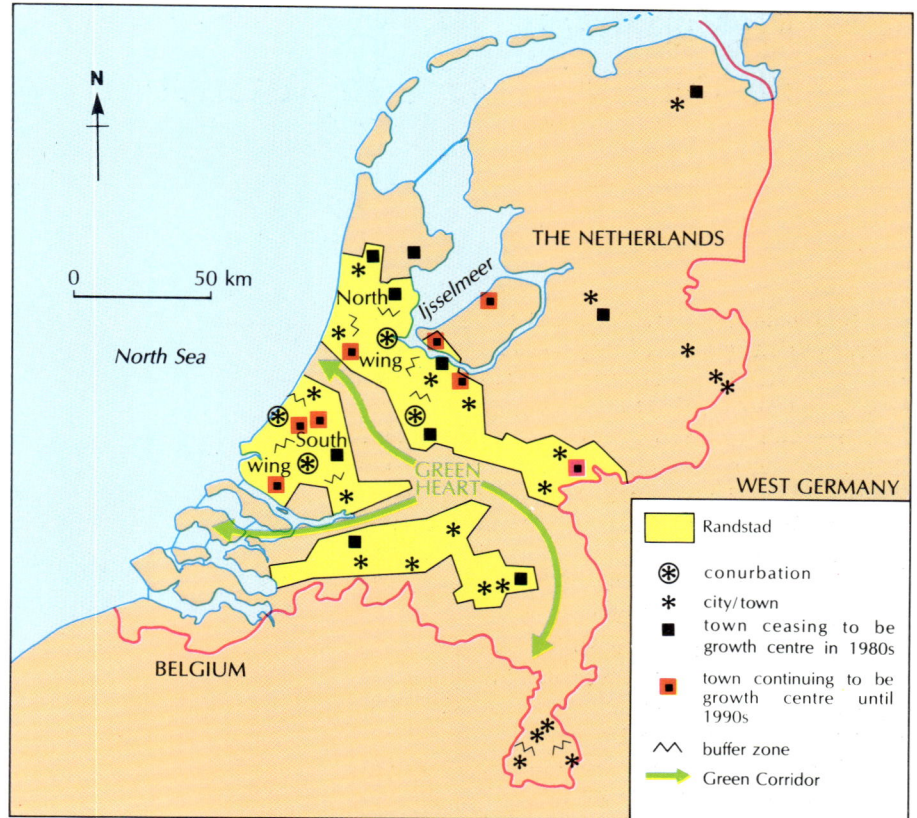

2 Plans for Randstad in the 1980s and 1990s

PLANNING POLICIES FOR RANDSTAD

1960s
* Prevented the separate towns and cities from growing together physically and filling up the Green Heart.

* Any population growth within Randstad limited to urban growth centres on the outer edge of the city region.

* Dispersal policy of directing people and jobs towards underdeveloped regions in the north, east and south of the country.

1970s
* Continued attempts to prevent the filling up of the Green Heart but allowing some new development in urban growth centres on the inner edge of the city region.

* Abandoned dispersal policy because of the high level of natural emigration from Randstad.

1980s
* Most future development to be encouraged in growth centres in the northern wing (Amsterdam–Utrecht) and the southern wing (The Hague–Rotterdam) of Randstad.

* Reduction in the total number of growth centres within and outside Randstad.

* Redevelopment of old sites within existing cities and towns of Randstad.

3 The Dutch planners have tried at different times to slow down, direct and concentrate the development of Randstad

1 Europe's urban geography. The map on the left shows the large cities in the urban regions. The map on the right shows population movement towards Europe's urban core

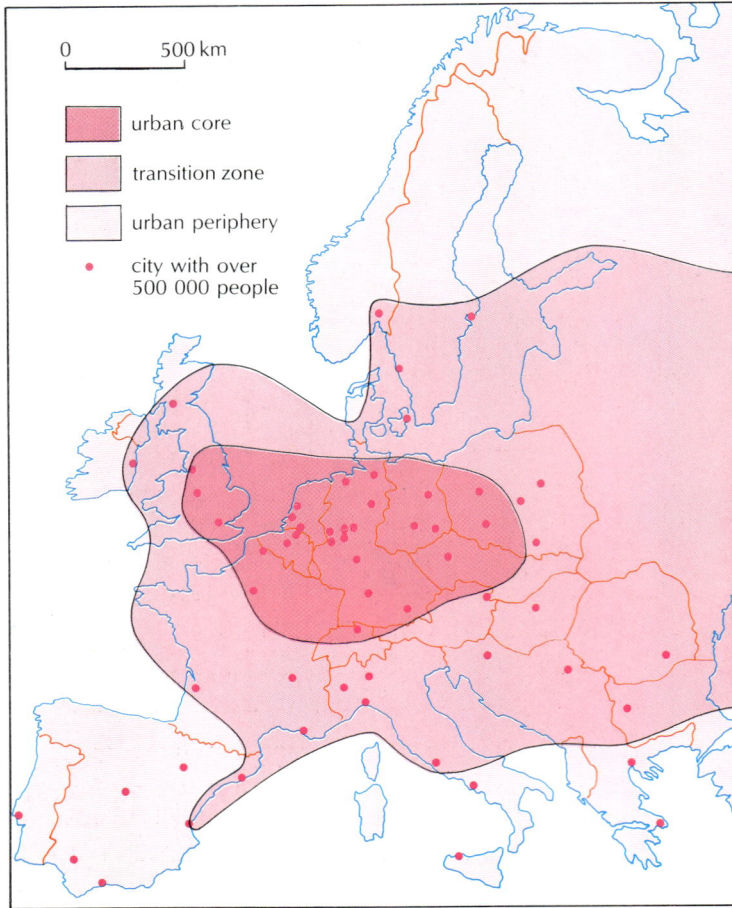

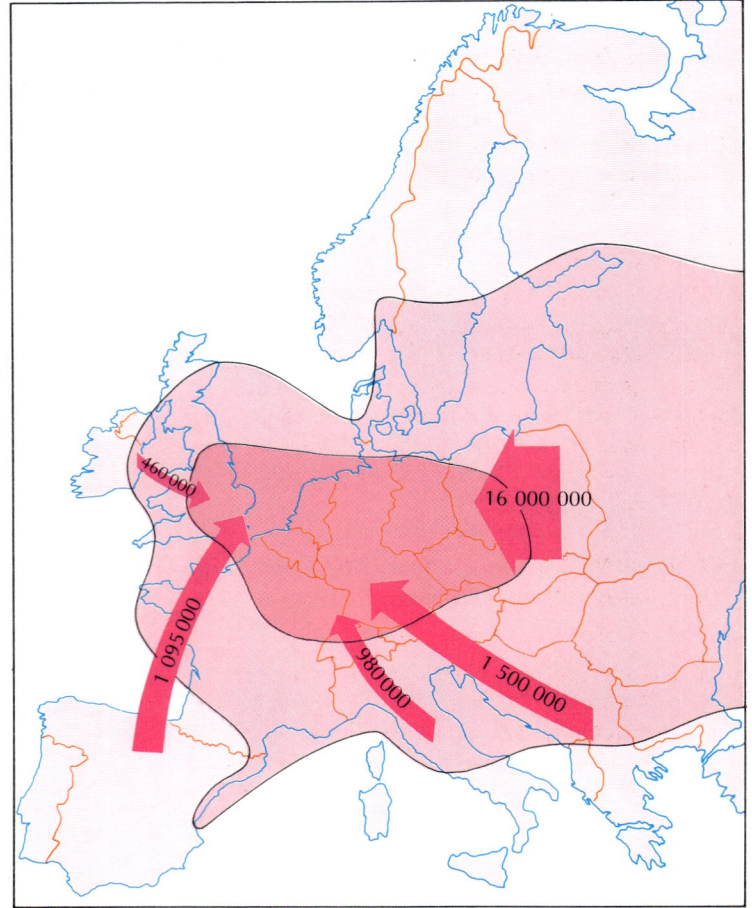

London, Paris, Berlin, Rome – Europe contains many of the world's oldest, largest and most important cities. Europe is one of the most highly urbanized regions in the world and 65% of its population lives in urban areas. In Western Europe this figure rises to 74%. Planning Europe's future will largely be a question of planning its towns and cities.

Visual 1 shows that three distinct regions can be identified in Europe:

○ URBAN CORE An area of dense population with many large cities and several city regions. This core area is highly industrialized and agriculture is intensive.

○ TRANSITION ZONE An area of medium population density with moderate urban development. This area is less industrialized and agriculture is less intensive.

○ URBAN PERIPHERY An area of sparse population with few large cities. Primary industries dominate the economy of the periphery.

During the last 200 years the dominant movement of people in Europe has been towards the cities, especially those in the urban core. The core region, with its higher level of industrialization and greater job opportunities, attracts or 'pulls' people who are 'pushed' from peripheral areas. The European

Community (EC) allows workers to move freely within member countries and many have migrated towards the cities of the urban core – often emigrating to do so.

There are many urban patterns between and within European countries. In some countries, especially in the peripheral region, urbanization is still taking place as people move from rural areas to towns and cities. In the 1970s a new trend was noticed in the urban core region. Many people were migrating from the large cities to the nearby rural areas or small towns further away. This process is known as counter-urbanization. Urban renewal, involving the creation of new housing and job opportunities in the central areas of cities, has produced some population increase in the cities of the urban core in the 1980s. This process is re-urbanization.

It is only during the last half century that countries in Europe have tried to direct the future growth and shape of any major city. Before the Second World War there was little urban planning and cities were sprawling outwards into the surrounding countryside. Since the mid-1940s, however, urban planning has had a great influence on cities, large and small. The main types of urban planning have been:

- ° PLANNING WITH GROWTH AXES New growth is channelled along preferred lines or axes, usually a river valley or motorway.
- ° PLANNING WITH GROWTH CENTRES New growth is restricted to preferred points or locations. These are sometimes in the suburbs, sometimes on the edge of or beyond the city.
- ° PLANNING WITH A HIERARCHY OF GROWTH CENTRES New growth is concentrated in a number of centres within the city, some being more important than others.
- ° PLANNING WITH NEW TOWNS New growth is directed to a number of new or satellite towns around the city.
- ° PLANNING INVOLVING A COMBINATION OF SEVERAL OF THESE METHODS.

The problems facing planners in Europe in the 1980s are very different from those that faced planners in the 1940s. Plans for moving people away from large cities, for example Britain's new towns policy, have given way to plans for revitalizing the central areas of large cities. In most cases plans are for city regions so that urban and nearby rural areas can be planned together.

1 Write short definitions for the following terms:

urbanization counter-urbanization re-urbanization.

2 Look at Visual 1.

a) Draw up a table like the one shown below and, using your atlas, list the countries which are found either entirely or mainly in each urban region.

COUNTRIES OF THE URBAN CORE	COUNTRIES OF THE TRANSITION ZONE	COUNTRIES OF THE URBAN PERIPHERY

b) Count up the number of large cities in each of the three regions and add this information in a note at the bottom of each column in your table.

c) Work out the total number of people who have migrated to the urban core since 1945. Make a note of the figure.

3 Visual 2 shows the level of urbanization for European countries in 1960 and 1980. Working in pairs:

a) Use a calculator to work out the percentage change in urban population for each country between 1960 and 1980.

b) Make a list of the six countries which have increased their urban populations the most and the six countries which have increased them the least.

c) What do you notice about the location of each group of countries? What does this tell us about the pattern of urbanization in Europe?

4 Five types of city plan are described here. Draw a diagram to illustrate each type of city plan. Give each one a title and add labels to explain your diagrams. An example illustrating the first type of city plan is shown in Visual 3.

5 Using information from Visuals 1 and 2 and your table, write a summary of Europe's urban geography. Use the heading 'The Development of Urban Regions in Europe'.

COUNTRY	URBAN POPULATION AS % OF TOTAL POPULATION		% CHANGE IN URBAN POPULATION 1960–1980
	1960	1980	
Austria	50	54	
Belgium	66	72	
Bulgaria	39	64	
Czechoslovakia	47	63	
Denmark	74	84	
Finland	38	62	
France	62	78	
Germany, East	72	77	
Germany, West	77	85	
Greece	43	62	
Hungary	40	54	
Ireland	46	58	
Italy	59	69	
Luxembourg	23	21	
Netherlands	80	76	
Norway	32	53	
Poland	48	57	
Portugal	23	31	
Romania	32	50	
Spain	57	74	
Sweden	73	87	
Switzerland	51	58	
United Kingdom	86	91	
Yugoslavia	28	42	

2 Urbanization in Europe, 1960–1980

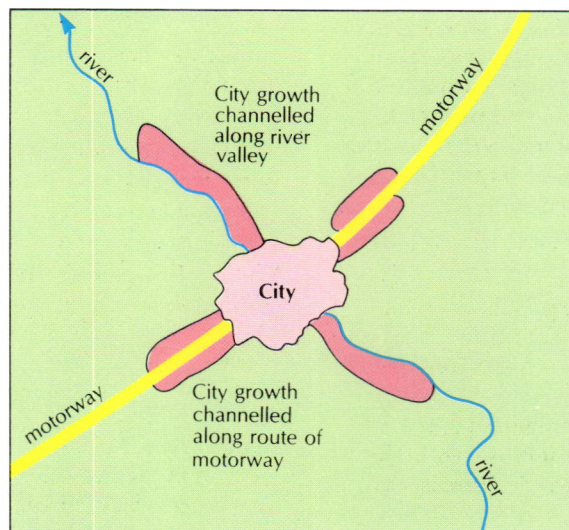

3 A city plan with growth axes

THE WORLD'S SWELLING CITIES

1 Calcutta, New York and Shanghai are just three of the world's fastest growing cities. Their combined populations could be more than 60 million by the year 2000

By the year 2000, for the first time in human history, the majority of people will be urban dwellers. Within the lifetime of children born today, almost two-thirds of the world's population will be living in towns and cities.

Urbanization has affected both the richer countries of the North and the poorer countries of the South. As we have seen earlier (pages 32 and 33) Britain became largely urban in the 1800s during the Industrial Revolution. In 1801 Manchester, for example, had a population of 75 000. By 1851 it had grown to 303 000. The growth of industrial cities in other countries of the North, where industrialization came later, was even faster. The German city of Essen increased its population from 9000 in 1850 to 439 000 in 1920. Chicago, in the United States, grew from 300 000 in 1870 to 2 700 000 in 1920. Many countries in the North now have largely urban populations.

In the South, every day an estimated 75 000 people are leaving rural areas to migrate to the towns and cities. This type of migration is called rural-to-urban migration. Migrants from the surrounding countryside arrive on the outskirts of the Brazilian city of Rio de Janeiro at the rate of 5000 every week. The city acts as a magnet for the rural poor. As with Britain in the last century, the big attraction is the possibility of a better job. Today, the cities of the South have even more attractions for people living in the countryside. Visual 2 gives some idea of what is tempting vast numbers of rural people to uproot themselves from their villages and farms and head for the swelling cities.

1 Look at Visual 3, which divides the world's population into urban and rural:

a) What will have happened to the world's population, as a whole, between 1900 and the year 2000?

b) Work out the number of people living in urban and rural areas for the years 1900, 1950 and 2000.

c) What will have happened to the urban and rural share of the world's population between 1900 and the year 2000?

2 Working in pairs:

a) Discuss the changes that have occurred in the countryside and in cities during the last 100 years.

b) Draw up a list of the main changes under two headings:
   i) Changes in the countryside.
   ii) Changes in the city.

3 a) Five thousand newcomers arrive in Rio de Janeiro each week. Work out how many arrive each year. How many people would be added to this city's population in ten years, just by rural-to-urban migration?

b) Using Visual 2 as a guide, write a paragraph to explain the attractions of cities for the rural poor in countries of the South.

c) Which of these attractions would not have existed for someone moving to a city in Britain in the early 1800s?

4 Look at the map opposite.

a) Describe the general pattern of urbanization across the world.

b) Do you think there is any connection between level of urbanization and level of development?

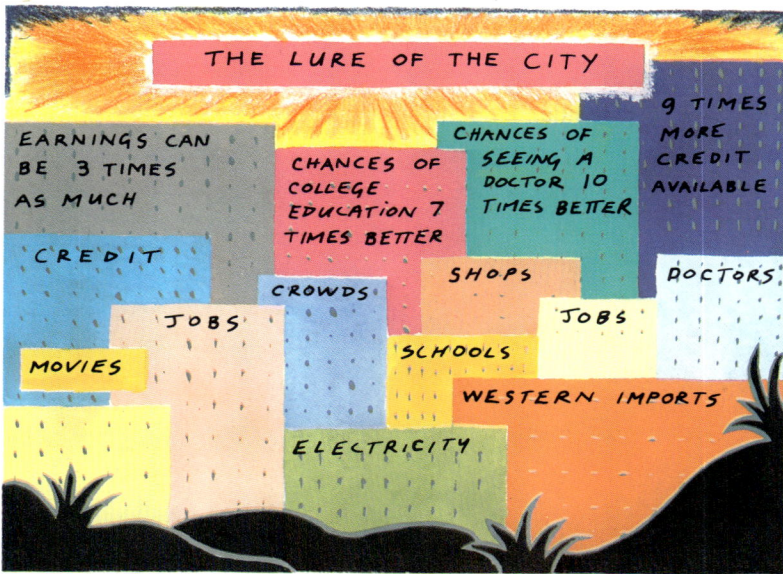

2 Cities in the South offer a tempting alternative to the poverty and hardship of the countryside

Text in illustration:
THE LURE OF THE CITY
EARNINGS CAN BE 3 TIMES AS MUCH
CHANCES OF COLLEGE EDUCATION 7 TIMES BETTER
CHANCES OF SEEING A DOCTOR 10 TIMES BETTER
9 TIMES MORE CREDIT AVAILABLE
CREDIT
CROWDS
SHOPS
DOCTORS
MOVIES
JOBS
SCHOOLS
JOBS
WESTERN IMPORTS
ELECTRICITY

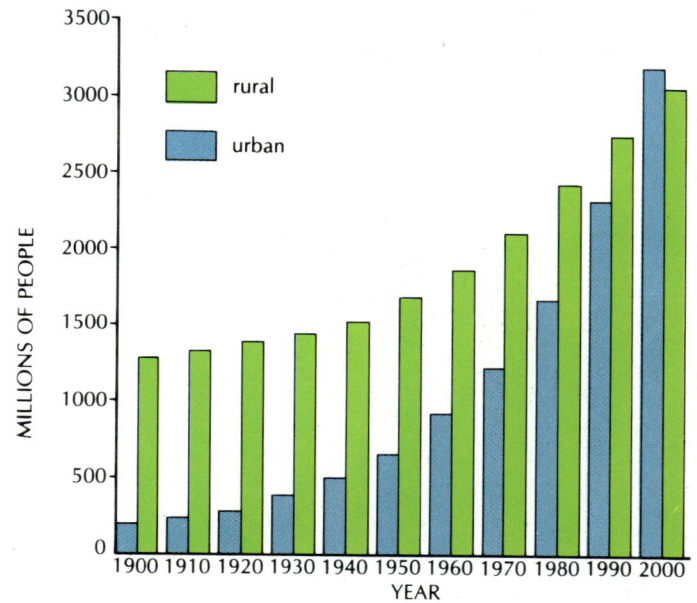

3 The changing share of urban and rural population in the world

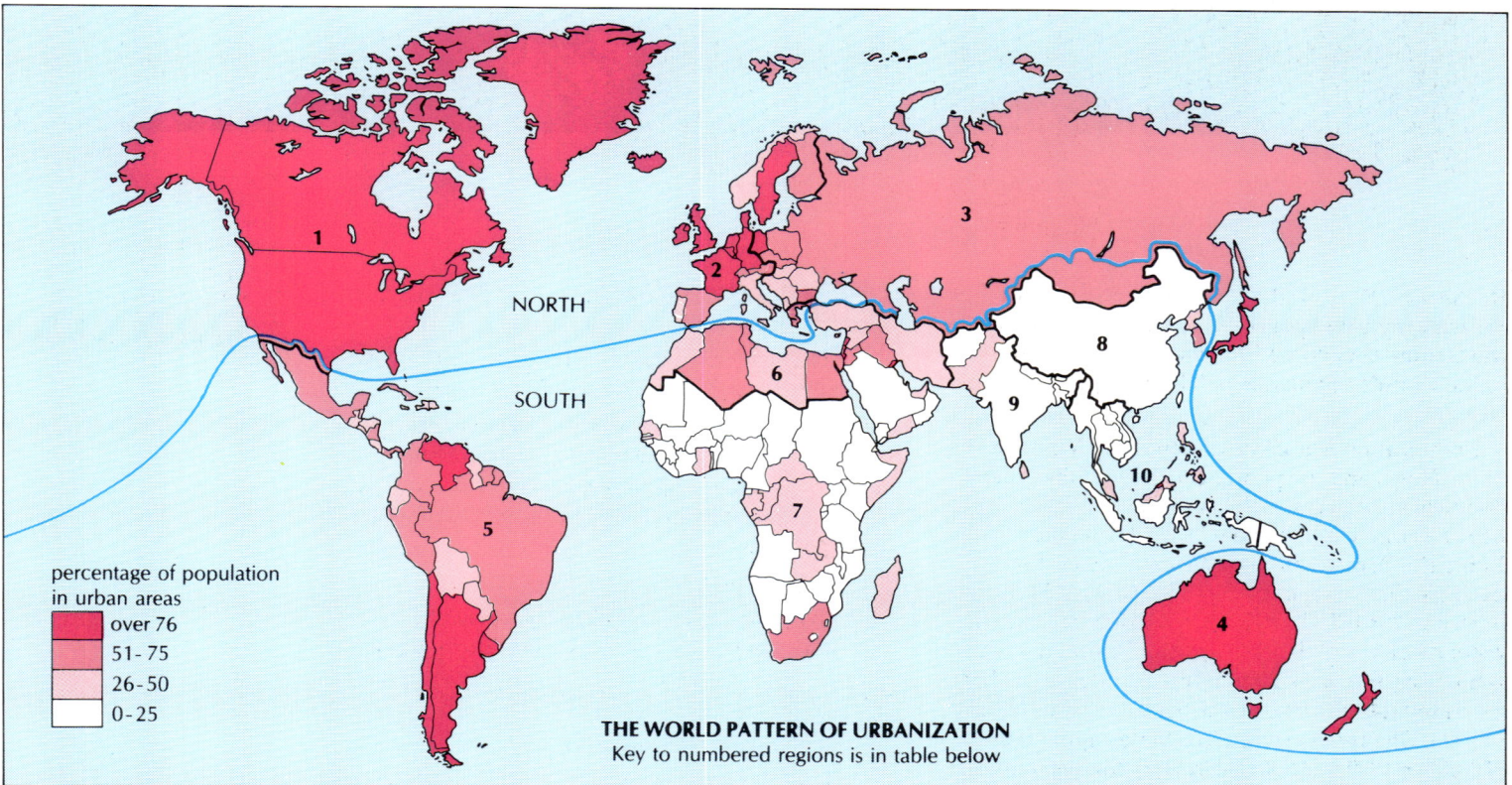

THE WORLD PATTERN OF URBANIZATION
Key to numbered regions is in table below

NORTH

SOUTH

percentage of population in urban areas
- over 76
- 51- 75
- 26- 50
- 0- 25

WORLD REGION	URBAN POPULATION (MILLIONS)		
	1950	1980	2000 (ESTIMATE)
1 North America	105	196	256
2 Western Europe	177	260	321
3 Eastern Europe/USSR	108	243	344
4 Australasia	8	17	26
5 Latin America	67	237	464
6 North Africa/Middle East	26	112	243
7 Subsaharan Africa	17	80	210
8 East Asia	112	358	591
9 South Asia	69	199	441
10 Southeast Asia	23	90	207
The North	457	842	1107
The South	257	950	1996
World	714	1792	3103

5 The figures in the table on the left tell you about changes in the pattern of world urbanization.

a) Draw bar charts to show the increasing number of urban dwellers in each of the world regions.

b) Which regions are experiencing the largest increases?

c) Now study both the map above and the bar charts carefully. What do the bar charts tell you about how the pattern on the map will change in the future?

6 Imagine that you are a journalist working for a national newspaper. The editor has asked you to write a major article about world urbanization entitled 'Half the World in Cities'. Your article should be lively, interesting to read, and should include relevant facts, figures and illustrations. Use any of the information in this chapter but try to find some of your own information as well.

75

1 Mexico City will probably be the largest city in the world by the year 2000. Its size is likely to cause many problems for people living there

1 *Think for a moment about the world's largest cities.*

a) *Quickly write down which you think are the ten largest cities in the world.*

b) *Compare what you have written with a neighbour. Do you agree?*

c) *Now look at Visual 2 and check the section for 1980. Which are the ten largest cities in the world? How many did you get right?*

2 *Read Visual 3, which is an extract from an article about the world's largest cities.*

a) *What do all these cities have in common?*

b) *Why are New York and Tokyo different from all the other cities?*

3 *Referring to Visual 2:*

a) *Use your atlas to find out where these cities are located.*

b) *Mark the position of these 20 cities on a blank outline map of the world. Use two types of symbol – one for cities in the North and one for cities in the South.*

4 *The figures in the table below show how the number of millionaire cities and supercities is growing.*

a) *Draw a line graph to show the growth of millionaire cities and supercities in the world as a whole. Use two different coloured lines – one for the millionaire cities and the other for the supercities.*

b) *Write a paragraph to describe the patterns shown by the table and your graph. Mention what is happening in the world as a whole, but try also to mention some of the differences between North and South.*

The number of large cities in the world is increasing rapidly. Those cities with more than one million people are known as millionaire cities. Cities with more than five million people are sometimes called supercities. At the moment there are more than 200 millionaire cities in the world and more than 25 supercities.

Not very long ago, most of the world's largest cities were found in the more developed countries of the North. Today, most of the largest cities are found in the poorer countries of the South. With one or two exceptions, the rate of growth of large cities in the North is slowing down. In the South the opposite seems to be the case, and the number of millionaire cities and supercities is increasing. The table in question 4 shows this pattern in greater detail.

In countries of the South, the bigger the urban area, the faster it grows. Towns are growing faster than villages, cities faster than towns, millionaire cities faster than cities with less than a million people and supercities fastest of all. Some of the supercities are becoming 'giants'. By the year 2000, Mexico City could have more than 31 million people and São Paulo could have more than 26 million people. Together, these two cities could contain more people than the number currently living in the whole of Britain.

CITY SIZE	1950			1980			2000 (ESTIMATE)		
	NORTH	SOUTH	WORLD	NORTH	SOUTH	WORLD	NORTH	SOUTH	WORLD
Over 5 million	5	1	6	11	15	26	16	43	59
1–5 million	43	22	65	99	101	200	134	221	355

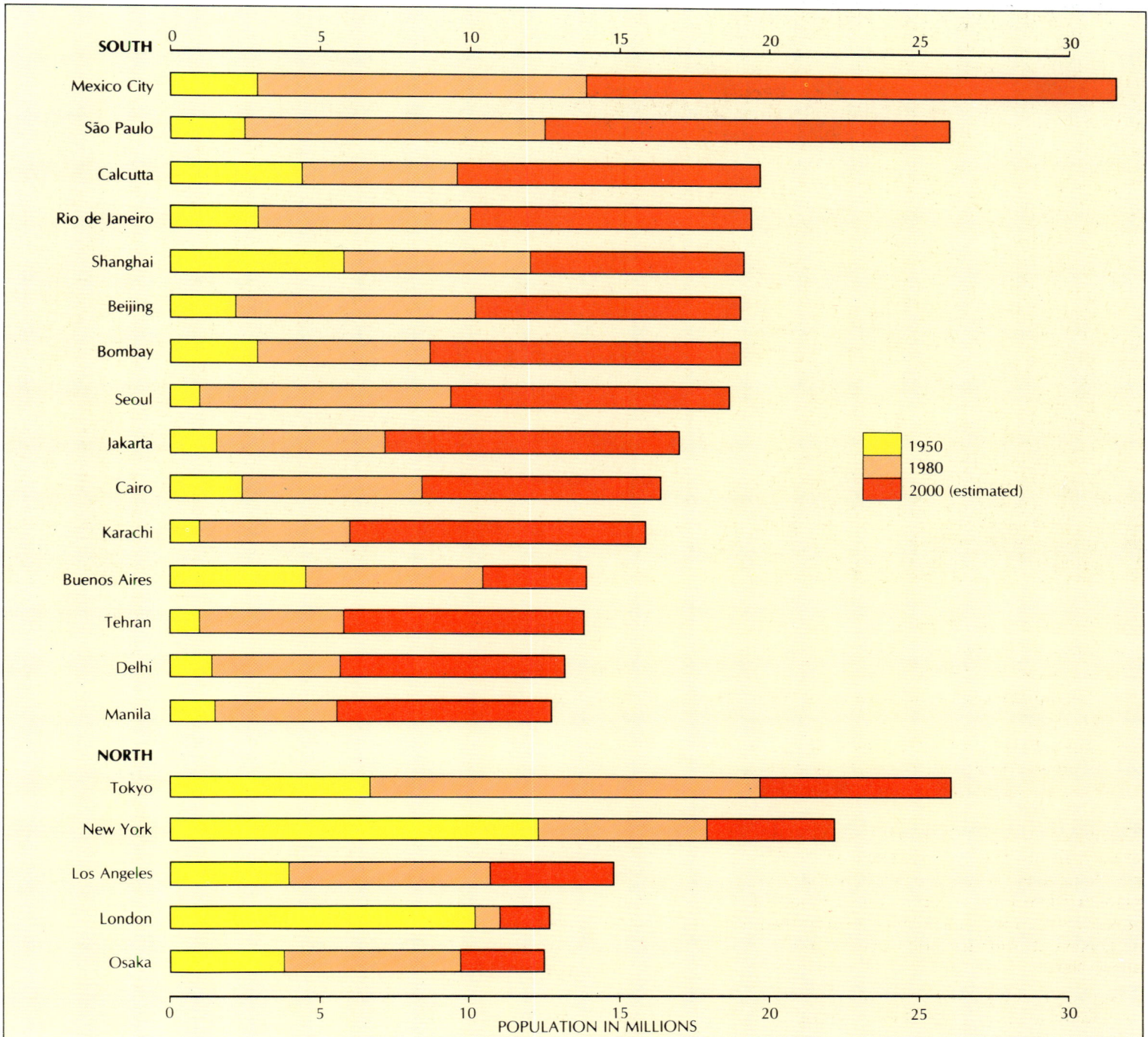

Chart axes: POPULATION IN MILLIONS (0 to 30)

SOUTH
- Mexico City
- São Paulo
- Calcutta
- Rio de Janeiro
- Shanghai
- Beijing
- Bombay
- Seoul
- Jakarta
- Cairo
- Karachi
- Buenos Aires
- Tehran
- Delhi
- Manila

NORTH
- Tokyo
- New York
- Los Angeles
- London
- Osaka

Legend:
- 1950
- 1980
- 2000 (estimated)

2 The population expansion of major cities. A large part of the increase in the world's urban population will be taken up by just 20 supercities, 15 of them in the South

5 Look at Visual 1. Working in pairs, make a list of some of the problems facing people living in large cities in countries of the South (pages 74 and 78 may help you).

6 Write an essay about the world's urban giants. Include in your account relevant maps, graphs, tables, etc. Divide your account into these sections:

◦ Introduction

◦ What is happening in the world as a whole

◦ Millionaire cities and supercities in the North

◦ Millionaire cities and supercities in the South

◦ Conclusion.

In 1950 Mexico City, with a population of just under three million, was a mere stripling amongst urban giants. By the end of the century it will be the largest metropolis in the world. More than 30 million people will live there. Brazil's São Paulo is undergoing a similar process of dramatic growth. Its population was two and a half million in 1950; ten million in 1975; and is not likely to be less than 26 million in the year 2000. The list is a long one: Bombay, Calcutta, Karachi, Beijing, Shanghai, Seoul, Cairo, Rio de Janeiro all are in the 15-30 million megacity line-up for the end of the century. Only New York and Tokyo in the developed world will be in the same league.

3 One writer's view about the world's largest cities

1 Different parts of São Paulo and some of the problems created by rapid urban growth

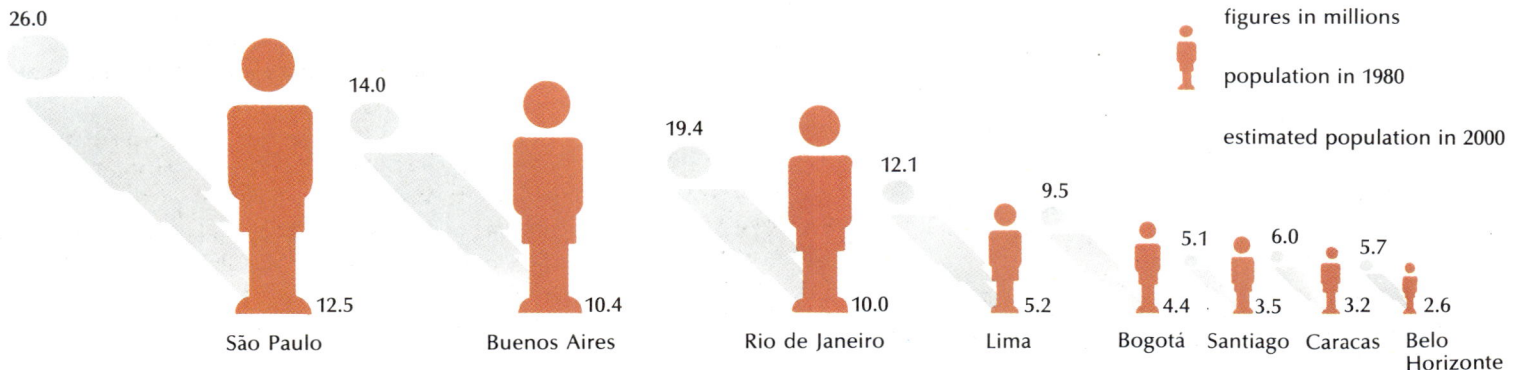

São Paulo, in Brazil, is one of the world's supercities. It is already the largest city in South America and by the year 2000 is likely to be the second largest city in the world. The story of its growth and development is typical of large cities in other countries of the South.

São Paulo was founded in 1554 but remained a small town of only 25 000 people until the 1870s. The coffee boom changed things completely. By 1890 its population had risen to just under 65 000 and went on increasing rapidly to reach just over 579 000 by 1920. In 1924 it overtook Rio de Janeiro (the former capital city of Brazil) as the most important industrial area in South America. By 1960 São Paulo had a population of nearly six million – more people than Rio de Janeiro. Today, there are more than 12 million people living in São Paulo and its population continues to increase at the incredible rate of 350 000 a year. By the year 2000 there could be 26 million people living in the city.

The dramatic growth of São Paulo can be explained by three factors:

○ The migration of Brazilians from the surrounding countryside, in search of better jobs and housing.
○ A high birth rate and a low death rate resulting in a rapid natural increase in the urban population.
○ Immigrants to Brazil usually head for the bigger cities.

To some extent São Paulo is a successful city. The area which surrounds it is the most important in Brazil for both agriculture and industry. (Ninety per cent of Brazilian-made cars are manufactured there.) The city centre looks like the centre of a North American city with giant skyscrapers and all the facilities of a modern city.

There is, however, another side to São Paulo. The city is encircled by vast areas of slum housing, largely occupied by migrants who flood in from the surrounding countryside. Basic services, such as sanitation and water supply, are often lacking in these poorer parts of the city. São Paulo is growing so quickly that the number of jobs cannot keep pace with the number of people and unemployment is high. The sheer size of the city creates enormous problems of traffic congestion and pollution. These problems of urban growth are shared by many other large cities of the South.

2 How South America's supercities will have grown by the end of this century

figures in millions

population in 1980

estimated population in 2000

City	2000 estimate	1980 population
São Paulo	26.0	12.5
Buenos Aires	14.0	10.4
Rio de Janeiro	19.4	10.0
Lima	9.5	5.2
Bogotá	5.1	4.4
Santiago	6.0	3.5
Caracas	5.7	3.2
Belo Horizonte	12.1	2.6

SÃO PAULO

A CITY FOR TOURISTS?

São Paulo is the capital of the state of São Paulo. It is Brazil's most prosperous city, where salaries are high by Brazilian standards and where people on the whole enjoy a good standard of living. About 40% of the total industrial production for all Brazil is accounted for by the city of São Paulo, the most dynamic of all Latin American urban centres ...

It is a city of skyscrapers, some of astounding architectural beauty, for example the very luxurious Maksoud Plaza Hotel ...

In the well-known Avenida Paulista there are still some grand old houses which were built at the beginning of this century by the coffee barons, contrasting with modern skyscrapers and banking offices. Rua Augusta is the street of fashion. The Viaduto do Chá, a landmark of the city bridging the central avenue, leads to the splendid Opera House, built in the 19th century. The residential districts of the city of São Paulo are remarkable for the beauty of their houses and gardens ...

The restaurants in São Paulo are perhaps the best in Brazil with a great variety of dishes both Brazilian and international ...

SÃO PAULO

A CITY FOR...?

São Paulo is much admired but little loved. It combines the disadvantages common to most large cities – noise, rush, stink, danger – with some specific to Brazil. Public services lag far behind the boom in industrial and commercial development. The telephone service, if you can find a telephone, is uncertain. In sudden rainstorms, sewers block and children drown in their beds. The motor car factories choke the broken streets with their products. São Paulo cannot stop, say the Paulistanos (citizens of São Paulo). They might add, cannot stop to think. Health, education, street lighting and paving – the city rushes ahead without them.

1 Use your atlas to find out where the cities mentioned in this chapter are located.

2 Look at Visual 2.

   a) Using the information in the diagram, draw up a table which shows the size of each city's population for 1980 and the year 2000. Put the cities in order of their population size for the year 2000.

   b) Add an extra column to your table and, using your atlas to help you, make a note of the country in which each city is located.

   c) Which country has most cities? How big will São Paulo be in the year 2000 compared with other cities?

3 Working in pairs, study the photographs in Visual 1.

   a) Decide which problems of urban growth are shown by the photographs.

   b) Make a list of problems affecting cities in countries of the South. Use the photographs and other information in this chapter as a guide.

   c) Make a list of problems affecting cities in countries of the North.

   d) Look at your two lists. Are urban problems the same in all countries or are they different in the North from the South?

4 Read through the two extracts in Visual 3. The first is from an information leaflet published by the Brazilian Embassy in London. The second is from a geography book which looks at life in urban and rural areas.

   a) Who do you think the information leaflet was written for? What evidence is there in the article to support your answer? Why does the second extract differ so much from the first extract?

   b) Try to make a list of positive words from the first extract, eg 'most prosperous', and a list of negative words from the second extract, eg 'stink'.

5 Write your own article on São Paulo, using no more than 200 words. Make the article as balanced as possible by referring to some of the good things about São Paulo as well as some of the bad things.

3 São Paulo – a city fit for whom?

1 Waiting for disaster? These slums are on a ravine in Lima, an earthquake-prone part of Peru. It was housing like this that was destroyed in the Guatemala earthquake in 1976

In 1976 Guatemala, a small country in Central America, was rocked by a violent earthquake. Some 25 000 people were killed, 75 000 were injured, and about 250 000 houses were destroyed leaving one million people homeless. The capital, Guatemala City, was right in the middle of the affected area. The city is built on a high plain which is cut by deep ravines. The cost of building safe houses in Guatemala City was too high and the poor built their shacks in any available space.

The earthquake destroyed or seriously damaged one-third of the city's houses. Those living in the richer suburbs, where houses were built of cement and brick, were not badly affected – only 5% of these houses were seriously damaged. In the poor neighbourhoods, the ruins were everywhere and many of the mud-built houses were seriously damaged or destroyed. Along the ravines, the slopes had caved in, carrying whole settlements with them.

The situation in Guatemala City is not unique. All over the world poor people are fighting the extremes of nature and poverty in order to survive. They have only a limited choice of where to live because of their poverty. Most of the poor people in the cities of the South live in slums and squatter settlements.

Slums are usually found near city centres. These are areas of older housing which are run down and overcrowded. Land is in short supply near the city centre and many of these slums are high-rise tenement blocks. As the housing is old, services are poor and many slums lack a proper water supply and electricity. Squatter settlements contain makeshift dwellings on land which the squatters do not own. These settlements are usually found on the edge of cities where land is available. The squatters build their shacks from any materials that they can find – cardboard, corrugated iron sheets, straw mats or sacks. The building of these squatter settlements is not controlled and they lack basic services such as sewerage, water and lighting. Often they are built outside the city boundary where the city authorities are not able to provide services.

South America has some of the largest cities in the world and some of the worst slums and squatter settlements. Forty per cent of São Paulo's 12.5 million inhabitants live in these conditions. People are migrating to the cities in such large numbers and the population is increasing so quickly that city authorities cannot build houses and provide services fast enough. That's if people could afford to buy a house anyway. A modern house is simply beyond the reach of most people. They earn too little and their income may be irregular.

At one time, many governments saw squatter

settlements as a threat – they were illegal, unhealthy and encouraged crime and political opposition. The solution was to bulldoze them down and move the people on. More recently, some governments have realized that self-built housing offers the best hope of easing the chronic housing shortage. Gradually, paved roads, street lights, water supply and sewage disposal are being added to these squatter areas by city authorities.

1 Look carefully at Visual 1 and re-read the first two paragraphs of this chapter.

   a) Imagine that you have a friend who has not seen this photograph. Write a brief but clear description of the area and the conditions in which people live.

   b) In your own words briefly explain the effects of the Guatemalan earthquake.

2 Make a sketch of the area shown in Visual 1. Draw a frame for your sketch and then add each of the following:

   the horizon   the steep-sided ravine and river   the bridge   the narrow road   the mudbrick houses   the wood/corrugated iron houses   the larger buildings   rubbish piles   pipes allowing raw sewage to drain into the river.

   Add labels to the features you have drawn.

3 On an outline map of South America and using Visual 2:

   a) Mark on the names of the countries shown.

   b) Locate, with a pencilled dot, the positions of the 15 millionaire cities.

   c) Look at Visual 3. Using your atlas match up the millionaire cities and supercities with the dots on your map. Give the cities a number key.

   d) Look at the third column in Visual 3. Enlarge the dots on your map for those cities with 40% and 60% of their populations living in slum and squatter settlements. You will need dots of different sizes to represent the two different percentages. Show what the dot size means in your key.

   e) Look at the fourth column in Visual 3. Produce a colour key to go with the five groups of numbers (the lowest group is under 20 and the highest is over 80). The lightest colour should go with the lowest number and the darkest colour should go with the highest number. Now colour the countries on your map to fit in with your colour key, which you should also add to your map.

4 Now look carefully at your completed map. Write a detailed description of what the map shows. You will need to refer to particular countries. Which countries seem to have the worst problems and which have the least serious problems?

2 South America's slum cities: millionaire cities where more than 20% of the people live in slums or squatter settlements

COUNTRY	MILLIONAIRE AND SUPERCITIES	% OF CITY POPULATION LIVING IN SLUMS AND SQUATTER SETTLEMENTS	% OF POPULATION WITHOUT A SAFE WATER SUPPLY
Argentina	Buenos Aires	20	21–40
Bolivia	—	—	61–80
Brazil	São Paulo	40	41–60
	Rio de Janeiro	40	
	Belo Horizonte	20	
	Recife	60	
	Brasilia	60	
	Pôrto Alegre	20	
Chile	Santiago	40	21–40
Colombia	Bogotá	60	21–40
	Cali	40	
Ecuador	Guayaquil	60	61–80
French Guiana	—	—	not available
Guayana	—	—	under 20
Paraguay	—	—	over 80
Peru	Lima	40	41–60
Surinam	—	—	not available
Uruguay	Montevideo	20	under 20
Venezuela	Caracas	60	21–40
	Maracaibo	60	

3 South America's slum cities: some idea of their welfare problems is given by the amount of slum and squatter settlements and by lack of access to a safe water supply

ASSIGNMENT NINE

Urbaid

The World Bank exists to provide financial and technical help for the poorer countries of the South. Most countries are members of the World Bank. Wealthier countries deposit money in the Bank, while poorer countries take out loans to help finance development projects.

The Bank's headquarters is in Washington DC, in the USA. Here, the staff of the Bank have to deal with a large number of requests for loans which come from the developing countries of the South. The World Bank provides billions of dollars every year to support projects which are designed to raise living standards, especially among the poor.

As more and more people are living in towns and cities, the World Bank is having to increase the funding of urban development projects.

Your Assignment

You work in the Urban Development Department at the World Bank headquarters. It is part of your job to analyse the requests for loans for urban development projects in Latin America. You have to decide which projects will get financial help from the World Bank.

Resources

1 The information provided on page 83.
2 DATA FILE.

DATA FILE

REQUESTS FROM LATIN AMERICA FOR URBAN AID IN 1987

City	Country	Project type	Project objectives	Loan requested US $ million
São Paulo	Brazil	Shelter	Upgrade squatter settlements to the east of the city by providing water supply, sewerage and electricity	48.6
Quito	Ecuador	Shelter	Extend several 'high-quality' housing areas including development of shopping and community facilities	62.0
Bogotá	Colombia	Integrated	Improve housing, road access and water supply in the ten poorest neighbourhoods in the city	186.0
Pôrto Alegre	Brazil	Transport	Extend bus services and road access to low-income neighbourhoods. Road improvements also intended to encourage industry to locate near these neighbourhoods	176.0
La Paz	Bolivia	Shelter	Build new housing areas to the west of the city for diplomats and other key foreign workers	34.0
San José	Costa Rica	Transport	Improve traffic flow in congested central areas. Separate bus lanes and expanded bus service are an important part of this scheme	33.0
Cali	Colombia	Transport	Renovate the main railway station and the surrounding area. Facilities for staff and waiting passengers would be much improved	53.8
San Salvador	El Salvador	Shelter	Build basic accommodation to house people left homeless by a recent earthquake	13.4
Curitiba	Brazil	Transport	Extend the urban motorway from the central area to the suburbs in the west, reducing congestion for car drivers	180.0
Lima	Peru	Shelter	Encourage homeless people to build their own houses on sites which have been provided with basic services such as water and electricity	43.2
Santiago	Chile	Integrated	Build sports complexes, conference halls and hotels to promote the city as an international centre for sport, conferences and other events	140.0
Kingston	Jamaica	Shelter	Upgrade the city's worst shanty town by providing mains water and electricity	30.0

Work Programme A

Your first job is to analyse the information available.

1 List the three types of project which may receive urban aid from the World Bank. Make a note of any special features which the Bank is looking for.

2 From the requests for urban aid in Latin America in 1987, draw a set of bar charts to show the number of projects in each project type.

3 Draw another set of bar charts to show the amount of money requested for the projects in each type. What is the total value of the loans requested?

4 On an outline map of Latin America, mark on the location of the cities listed in the DATA FILE. Use a colour key to indicate the project type for each city.

Work Programme B

Now you must decide which projects will get financial help from the World Bank and which ones will not. Work in groups of four.

1 Discuss each project in turn and decide whether it has the special features which the World Bank is looking for.

2 You have US$600 million to spend on urban aid in Latin America in 1987. Decide which of the 12 projects will receive World Bank support. You do not have to spend all of the money but you cannot spend more than $600 million.

3 Write a short report in which you outline your 'Urban Aid Policy for Latin America'. Include details of the types of project you are trying to encourage generally and details of particular projects receiving World Bank support in 1987.

SHELTER PROJECTS

The World Bank recognizes that shelter is a basic need in developing countries. The Bank will lend money to those projects which aim to satisfy this need for the urban poor. Projects which try to upgrade existing housing or encourage self-help solutions will attract Bank support.

TRANSPORT PROJECTS

The Bank is keen to lend money for low-cost public transport projects. Ideally these should give people greater access to job opportunities and also provide better facilities for cyclists, pedestrians, bus and rail services. Projects which are aimed at the needs of the urban poor are more likely to get Bank support.

INTEGRATED PROJECTS

The Bank will consider lending money for integrated projects which try to bring about broad, city-wide improvements. These projects may seek to improve shelter, transport, health and education services across entire urban areas. The Bank will need to be satisfied that the urban poor will benefit most from such projects.

All three people shown on the right are affected by South Africa's apartheid laws. Apartheid is an Afrikaans word meaning 'apartness'. By this the South African government means the 'separate development' of the 'races' in South Africa. To others, apartheid means the system of total racial discrimination between whites and non-whites.

The white Afrikaaners have ruled South Africa since 1948 and have passed hundreds of laws which control where people live, work and play. The apartheid laws are built on the beliefs of 'racial purity' and white supremacy. Black people are not allowed to vote or take part in the government of the country.

Many of these laws control where people live. For instance, the Group Areas Act has created separate housing areas within cities. Each area is for people in one of the four 'racial groups' officially recognized in South Africa (blacks, whites, coloureds and Asians). This *residential segregation* has meant that many non-whites have had to move to parts of towns and cities which have been set aside for them. Others, without jobs, have had to move hundreds of miles to *tribal homelands*. About three million enforced moves took place between 1960 and 1980. The result of all this has been the formation of *political cities*.

The effect of these movements has been to shift non-white people to the edges of towns and cities, leaving more central areas for the use of white people. Millions of non-whites must commute daily from their homes on the edge of the city to their place of work nearer the city centre. Every day 250 000 people commute from the black township of Soweto to the nearby city of Johannesburg. A further 750 000 people commute daily from the black homelands to nearby urban areas.

1 Look at the three people here and their captions, and read the first part of this chapter again. In your own words:

  a) *Define apartheid.*

  b) *Say how apartheid is affecting the lives of non-whites in South Africa.*

2 Visual 1 shows two faces of apartheid.

  a) *Make a list of the differences in living conditions shown by the two photographs.*

  b) *What do these two particular photographs suggest about the difference in lifestyles for blacks and whites in South Africa?*

  c) *What other information would you need in order to judge whether blacks and whites have different standards of living?*

Maria Sobukwe works as a maid for a white family in Johannesburg. Her working day lasts from 7 am to 6 pm. Because of South Africa's laws, which ban a black person from living in the same area as whites, she has to travel 32 km to work from the black township of Soweto. She gets up at 5 am every day.

Rajiv Chandra once ran a very successful menswear shop in the centre of Durban. His family lived in accommodation above the shop. A few years ago a law was passed in this area. As a result, Rajiv has had to move his family and business to another part of Durban where only Asians live. Business is not as good in this area.

Steve Majeke lives in Crossroads squatter settlement on the edge of Cape Town and works as a labourer in the docks. Fifteen years ago he lived in District Six, an area of coloureds within walking distance of the docks. A law was passed making District Six a 'whites only' area and all coloureds had to move out. Now the government wants to bulldoze Crossroads and move the coloureds to a new township called Mitchells Plain. This will mean that Steve will have to travel even further to work.

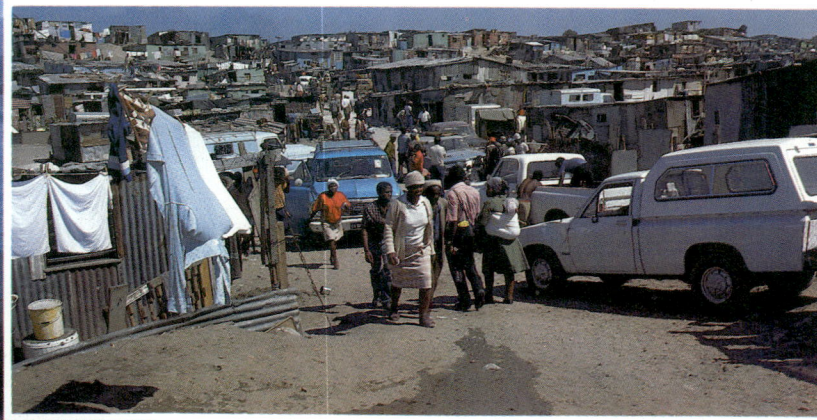

1 Two faces of apartheid: the urban rich and the urban poor. These photographs show a white suburb in Cape Town and part of the Crossroads squatter settlement

3 Look at Visual 2.

a) If you lived in Crossroads squatter settlement and had a job in the CBD, how far would you need to travel to work each day?

b) The South African government is trying to move as many coloured people as possible to Mitchells Plain. Why do you think they are trying to do this? What problems is this likely to cause for coloured people?

c) Using Visual 2 as a guide, draw a sketch map to show the separate housing areas in Cape Town. Give your finished map a title and a key. Indicate, by arrows, the direction in which the government is trying to move non-white people.

d) Write a few sentences to describe the pattern shown in Visual 2. Try to mention all of these: i) separate housing areas ii) CBD iii) workplaces iv) journey to work v) squatter settlements vi) city edge.

4 Study the information in Visual 3.

a) Use your atlas to locate South Africa's political cities.

b) Working in pairs, discuss how the information in Visual 3 could be put on to a blank outline map of South Africa. The finished map would need to show the location of the urban areas and the proportion of people in each of the different 'race' groups. Can you think of more than one way of doing this?

c) Put the information from Visual 3 on to an outline map of South Africa.

d) Write a few sentences to describe what your map shows.

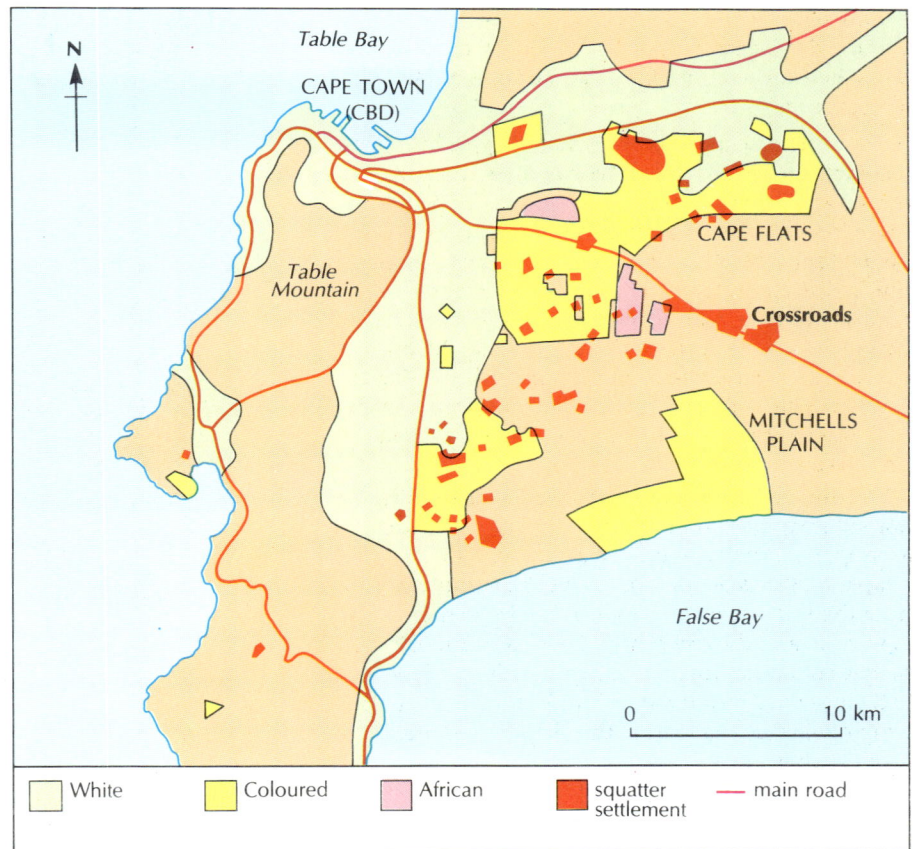

2 The separate housing areas in Cape Town. Forty years ago, many non-whites lived much nearer the city centre. Now they have been forced to live on the edge of the city

| URBAN AREA | RACE GROUP | | | | TOTAL |
	BLACKS	WHITES	COLOUREDS	ASIANS	thousands
Johannesburg	1885	992	136	72	3085
Cape Town	172	484	820	14	1490
Durban	117	320	56	468	961
Pretoria	322	386	14	14	736
Port Elizabeth	279	157	140	7	583

3 The populations of South Africa's main urban areas. The number of people in each of the four official ethnic groups is also given

1 Many socialist cities have a large central square for military parades and state events. This photograph shows Red Square in Moscow

People in Britain do not know much about city life in socialist countries such as the USSR. One common image might be the giant May Day Parade in Moscow's Red Square, when thousands of flag-waving workers march past government leaders in front of the Kremlin. But what about everyday life and what does the rest of Moscow look like? What is a socialist city?

In a socialist country the central government owns and controls land and industry. The planning of towns and cities is also the responsibility of this central government. Older cities have been redeveloped and new towns have been built using socialist ideas. This has created many differences between socialist cities and non-socialist or western-style cities.

In Moscow and other planned socialist cities, the centre of the city is dominated by a large square. This is used for military parades and other state events. Around the square are government buildings, museums, theatres, department stores and hotels for tourists. There are fewer offices and commercial establishments than would be found at the centre of a British city, for example.

A typical Soviet family lives in an apartment in a large block. These blocks are grouped together and provided with shops, schools and recreational areas to form a neighbourhood unit. These self-contained neighbourhoods are known as mikrorayons. The first mikrorayons were built around the city centre. Housing is found much nearer the city centre than in British cities. Many newer mikrorayons, however, have been built in the suburbs. Most people use public transport to get to work. A planned system of roads and railways has allowed Soviet cities to spread out. Soviet cities are planned with parks, sports stadiums and green belts in mind.

The socialist city is supposed to be a classless city because it has been planned and built to provide all of its inhabitants with a decent home, a place of work and opportunities for education and recreation. In reality, differences between people do exist. For example, Communist Party officials and top scientists have better quality housing, often in a segregated part of the city.

Socialist city planning has been occurring in the USSR since the Revolution of 1917. It developed much later in countries where socialism came later – after 1945 in the countries of Eastern Europe and from the 1950s onwards in socialist countries within Asia, Africa and Central America.

2 The world's socialist countries. The capital cities are shown in brackets

EASTERN EUROPE	ASIA
Albania (Tirana)	Cambodia (Phnom Penh)
Bulgaria (Sofia)	China (Beijing)
Czechoslovakia (Prague)	Laos (Vientiane)
East Germany (Berlin)	Mongolia (Ulan Bator)
Hungary (Budapest)	North Korea (Pyongyang)
Poland (Warsaw)	USSR (Moscow)
Romania (Bucharest)	Vietnam (Hanoi)
Yugoslavia (Belgrade)	
AFRICA	**CENTRAL AMERICA**
Angola (Luanda)	Cuba (Havana)
Mozambique (Maputo)	

3 A typical mikrorayon in Moscow. The eight-storey blocks were built in the 1960s. The higher blocks were built more recently and have more shops and more parking space

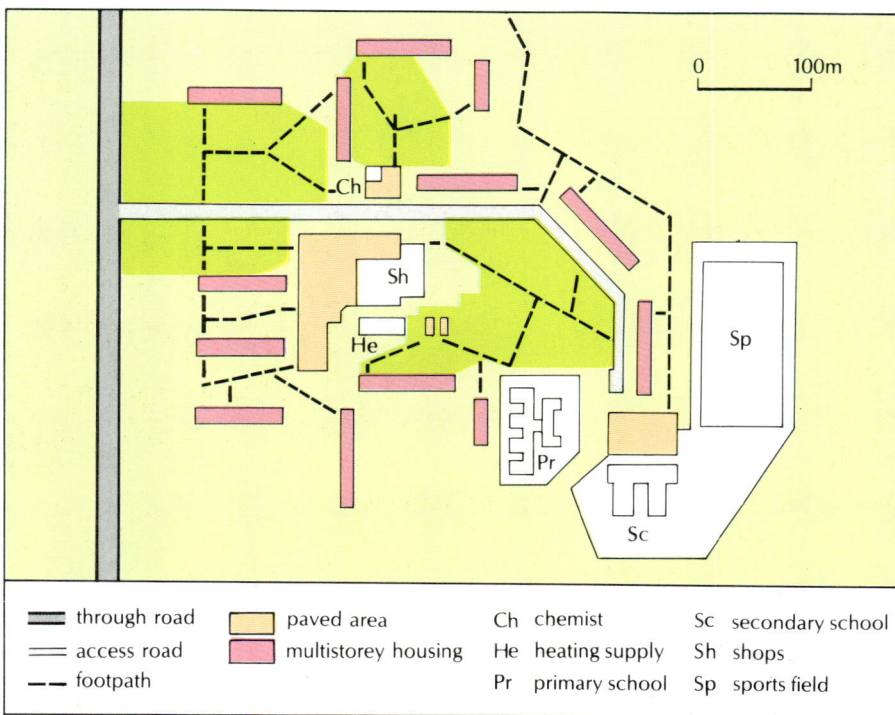

through road | paved area | Ch chemist | Sc secondary school
access road | multistorey housing | He heating supply | Sh shops
footpath | | Pr primary school | Sp sports field

4 A Soviet mikrorayon is a traffic-free residential neighbourhood with centrally located schools, shops and recreational facilities

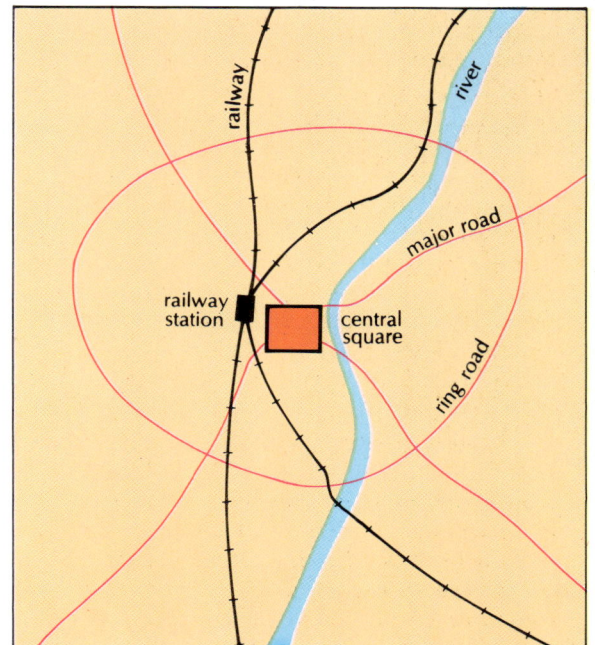

5 Model of a socialist city. The model is largely incomplete at this stage and is not drawn to scale

1 Look at Visual 2. Using your atlas to help you:

  a) Shade in the listed countries on a blank outline map of the world.

  b) Mark on the position of the capital cities.

  c) Choose a title for your map and give it a key.

2 Study the diagram shown in Visual 4. Working in pairs:

  a) Discuss the advantages and disadvantages of living in such a planned residential neighbourhood.

  b) Make a list of the main advantages and disadvantages.

3 Visuals 1 and 3 show two very different parts of Moscow. Working in small groups:

  a) Discuss what impression the photographs give about Moscow and its people.

  b) Imagine that you could send six photographs to someone in the Soviet Union to give them an impression of life in British cities. Discuss what the six photographs could show.

4 a) On your own copy of Visual 5, use a colour code to locate each of the following:

  i)   An area of government buildings, theatres, museums, department stores and tourist hotels.

  ii) Older mikrorayons near the city centre.

  iii) Newer mikrorayons in the suburbs.

  iv) Parks and sports stadiums.

  v)   A green belt surrounding the built up area.

  b) Give the finished diagram a title and put the items which you have included in a key.

The United States of America is a country on the move. The effects of the motor car are felt everywhere. There are drive-in cinemas, banks, fast food stores, dry-cleaners, chapels and even drive-in mortuaries where relatives can view the deceased without the inconvenience of leaving their car. The United States is also one of the world's most urbanized countries with more than 170 million city dwellers and more than 30 millionaire cities.

The American city has special features – a city centre dominated by skyscrapers, segregated housing areas based on class and race, sprawling suburbs, and huge areas given over to freeways and parking lots. Many of these features have developed only in this century. Until 1920, most cities were quite small and were located on the east coast. Since then, population growth and industrialization have led to a massive growth in cities across the whole country. Mass car ownership has allowed cities to develop sprawling suburbs. Cheap cars and petrol, a highway system, and the transfer of many industries to the suburbs, have enabled some people to live in rural areas beyond the city. These rural areas, too, are changing as city people move in. In some areas, cities are beginning to merge together.

Los Angeles is the second largest city in the United States, with a population of more than ten million. It is a young city which has grown up during the motor car age. The sprawl of Los Angeles extends 113 km from east to west and covers 1166 square kilometres. The city has 1050 km of freeway to carry over four million cars. Visual 1 gives an impression of what the city is like. Los Angeles has been described as the biggest car park in the United States.

The outward growth or *urban sprawl* of American cities has been a feature of the motor car age. It has brought with it many problems. For those living on the edge of cities, it has meant longer journeys to work and traffic congestion. For those living near the city centre, or downtown areas, it has meant poverty and hardship. These downtown areas are increasingly occupied by those who cannot afford to live in the suburbs – the old, the disabled and the poor. Downtown America and suburban America are becoming increasingly unequal. Yet again, the quality of life varies according to who you are and where you live.

1 A typical daily scene on any Los Angeles highway. The continual stream of vehicles and the many traffic jams are the result of widespread car ownership and poor public transport

1 Read the extract in Visual 2.

a) Make a list of the problems which the motor car has brought to Los Angeles.

b) Now look back through this chapter. What other effects, not mentioned in Visual 2, have motor cars had on American cities?

2 a) With the help of Visual 3 draw a sketch map to show how Los Angeles has grown.

b) Write a paragraph to describe the spread of the city. Refer to specific places from the map.

c) What has prevented Los Angeles from growing in certain directions? Why do you think that Los Angeles has grown so much to the east and south-east?

3 Look at Visual 4.

a) Write a few sentences to say what the map is trying to show.

b) Now write a paragraph to describe the pattern shown by the map. In which parts of the United States does the quality of life in cities seem to be highest/lowest?

c) Work out the average 'quality of city life' figure for each state. Add up the numbers in each state and divide the total by the number of cities. Round up or down to the nearest whole number.

d) On your own blank outline map of the United States, shade the states to show the average quality of life. Use a different colour for each of the numbers 1 to 5.

e) Look at your finished map. Does it show the pattern more clearly?

4 What would a city need to have for you to feel that the quality of life was very good? Think about those things you would want in a city and those things you would not want to find. Write a short essay to develop your ideas.

Americans regard their vehicles as a symbol of independence and rarely share rides. This means that, despite the fact that virtually all highways have at least four lanes, and many freeways can be as wide as ten or twelve lanes in total, there are frequently serious problems of traffic congestion which would make rush hour in London, Leeds or Newcastle seem mild by comparison. No one who has ever travelled in Los Angeles between 4 and 6 pm in the evening will forget the sight of hundreds of thousands of automobiles crawling nose-to-tail along every available road — not just away from the downtown area, but in every conceivable direction. The freeways vibrate to the sound of traffic late into the night, and the periodic chaos of over-use is such that a radio station exists whose only function is to relay traffic information and advice.

Los Angeles is, along perhaps with Houston, the archetypal product of the motor age. Even in the 1930s and 40s, it was a sprawling collection of communities. This sprawl originally developed because of street cars and railway links, but was encouraged with the building of the highway system, which began in 1941.

The results of this growth can be interpreted in several ways. To many observers, the urban sprawl is unpleasant. The pollution problem is in no sense aided by the carbon monoxide levels, although California does lead the country in automobile emissions control equipment, which had to be fitted to every vehicle. Fatalities and injuries from accidents are high.

2 One writer's view about the impact of the car on Los Angeles

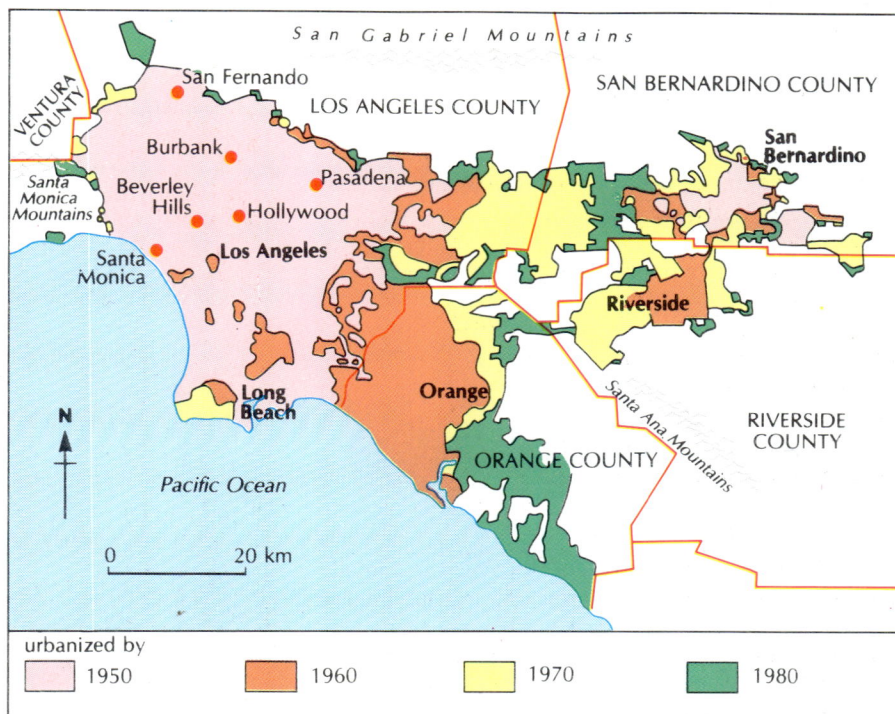

urbanized by 1950 | 1960 | 1970 | 1980

3 Urban sprawl in Los Angeles has developed during the last 40 years. The city now spreads across four counties and, with the addition of another four million people before the year 2000, it will spread still further

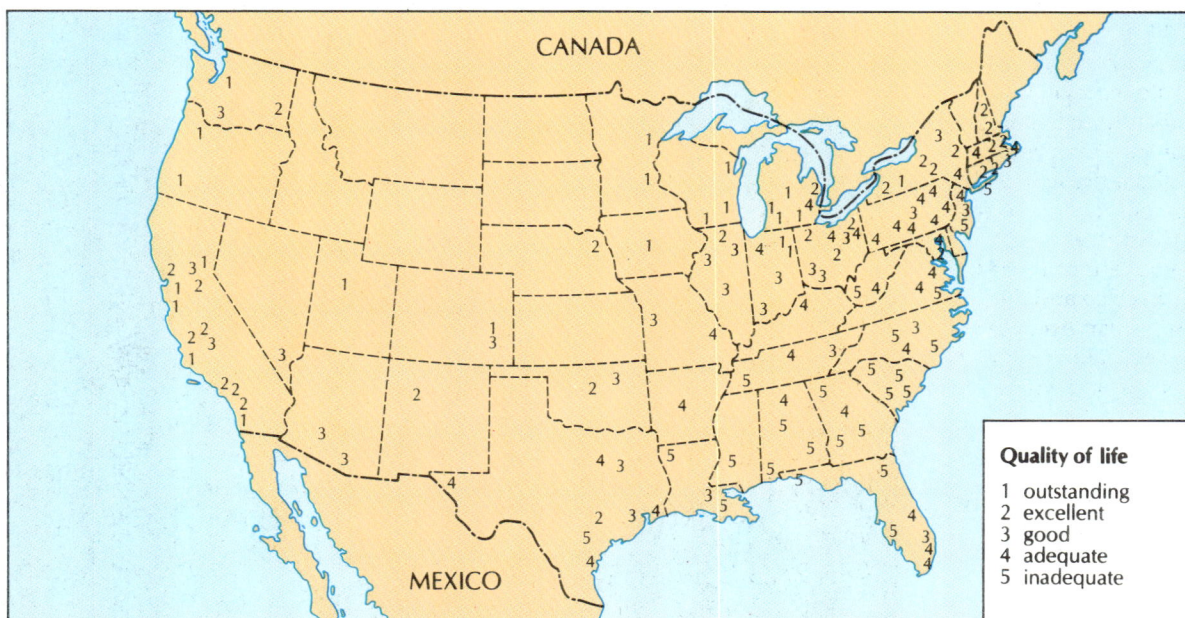

Quality of life
1 outstanding
2 excellent
3 good
4 adequate
5 inadequate

4 The quality of life in large and medium-sized cities in the United States. The figures are based on surveys which look at economic, social and environmental aspects of city life

33

WORLD CITY REGIONS

In some parts of the world, nearby cities have grown so much that they are merging together to form giant city regions. The Americans call this type of area a megalopolis.

A number of conditions are needed for a megalopolis to form:

- The presence of several millionaire or supercities.
- Fast transport routes between the urban centres.
- Urban growth with the built-up areas spreading outwards and along transport routes.
- Rapid population movement into the rural areas between the cities.

These conditions exist in a number of places in the world, especially in North America, Western Europe and Eastern Asia.

Perhaps the best example of a megalopolis is Bowash on the north-east coast of the United States (Visual 1). Bowash is a giant city region which extends more than 800 km between the city of Boston in the north and the city of Washington DC in the south. It is formed by a succession of large and small cities which are connected by a fast interstate highway system and by rail and air links. The main cities are Boston, New York, Philadelphia, Baltimore and Washington DC. Although its population is nearly 50 million, Bowash is not one continuous built up area. It contains millionaire cities, sprawling dormitory suburbs, industrial zones and areas of intensive agriculture.

Japan is another part of the world where the right conditions exist for the development of a megalopolis. For its size, Japan has a large population (119 million). Because of its mountainous nature, there is a shortage of flat land. Seventy-six per cent of the population live in urban areas and more than 40 million people live in the Tokaido megalopolis. This is a vast urban and industrial area linking the capital city, Tokyo, with the cities of Nagoya and Osaka. Surrounding rural areas are becoming more urbanized and smaller cities in the region are also growing rapidly. It is thought that the Tokaido megalopolis might grow in the future so that it stretches from Tokyo in the east to Nagasaki in the west. Few countries in the world show so much concentrated urbanization.

One planner has suggested that Bowash and Tokaido will be part of one worldwide city region by the next century (Visual 2). This will be formed when megalopolises join together across continents.

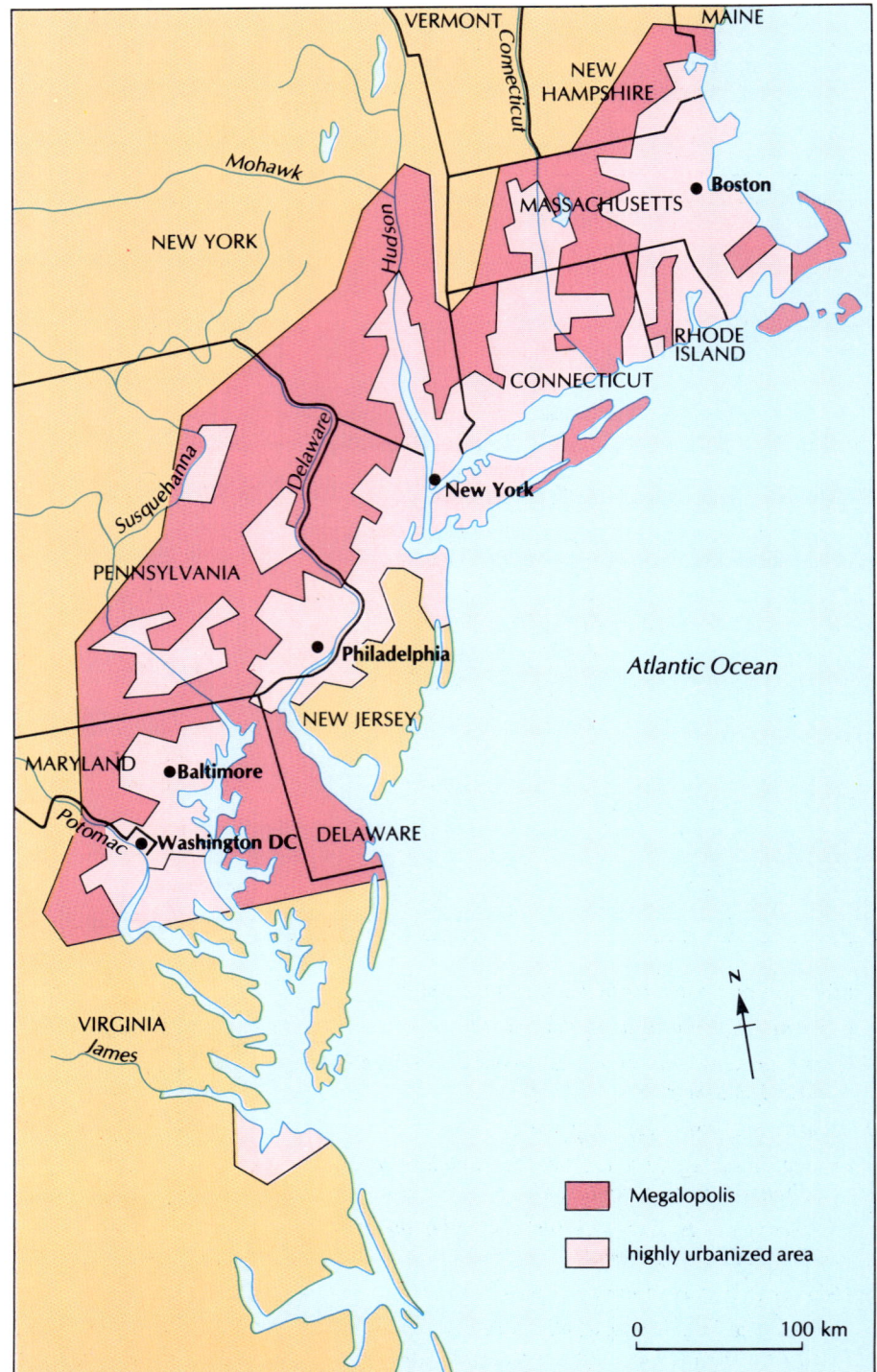

1 The Bowash megalopolis is one of the world's largest city regions, crossing ten states and containing nearly 50 million people

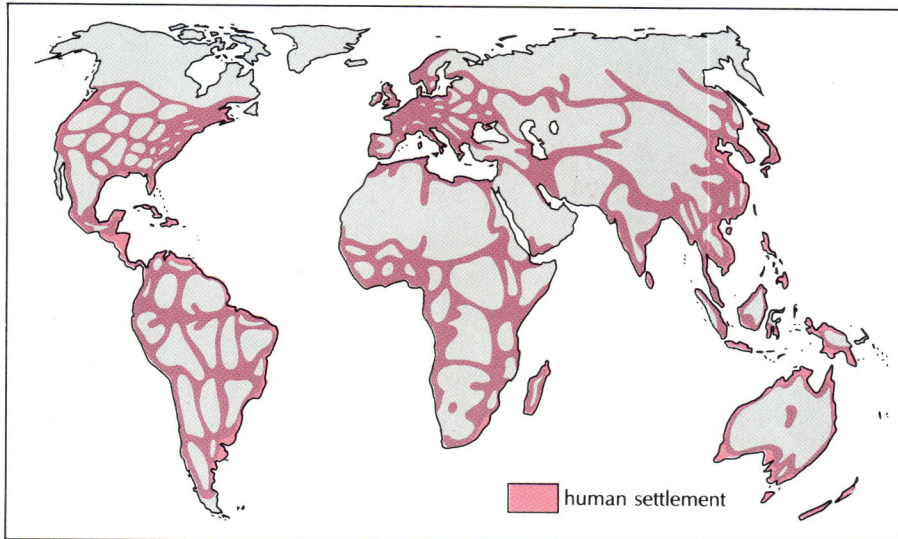

2 The ultimate form of human settlement: one worldwide city region covering six continents

human settlement

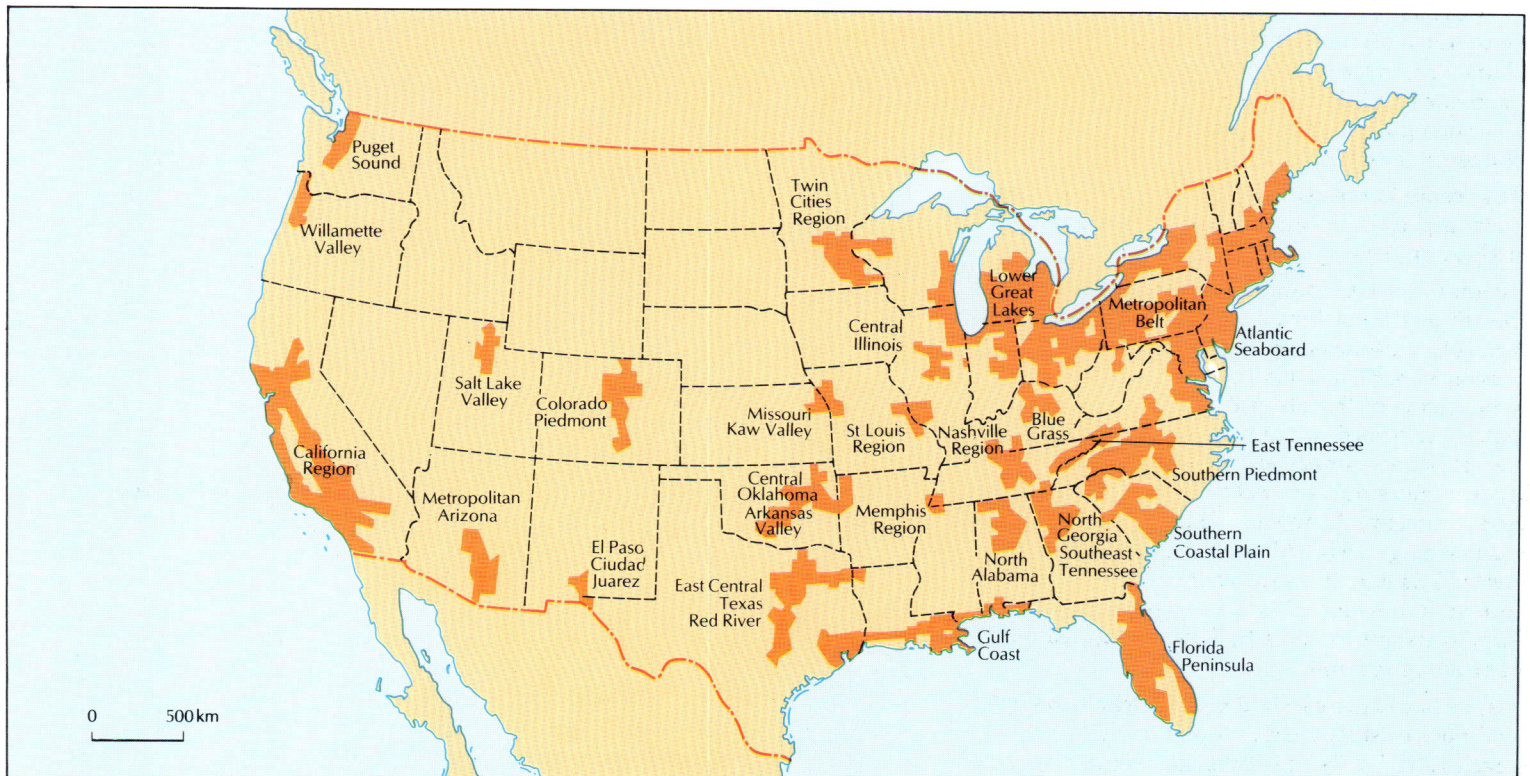

3 City regions in the United States in the year 2000. Within the city regions, most people and land will be urbanized

1 Looking back through the first part of this chapter:

a) Write a definition of a megalopolis.

b) In your own words, outline the conditions which are needed for a megalopolis to form.

2 On your own outline copy of Visual 1:

a) Locate the cities of Boston, New York, Philadelphia, Baltimore and Washington DC.

b) Add any smaller cities which are also within the area of the Bowash megalopolis.

3 Using your atlas and working in pairs:

a) Locate the Tokaido megalopolis. Notice how much bigger it might grow in the future. Use the scale to work out the distance from Tokyo to Nagasaki.

b) Try to find some other parts of the world where a megalopolis might develop. Look for areas where cities are grouped closely together.

4 Visual 3 gives you information about city regions in the USA.

a) Draw up a table with two columns, one headed 'Urban Regions of the USA', and the other headed 'Main City'. Under the first heading, make a list of the city regions.

b) Using your atlas and working in pairs, decide which is the main city in each city region. Under your second heading, make a list of the main cities.

c) Write a brief paragraph to say what the map shows.

5 Write a science fiction story called 'The Concentrated City', about a giant city which is so large that many people have never been outside it. Start the story like this: 'Lorna went up a thousand levels on the Blueline elevator and came out on 576th Street. The journey across the West Millions had been tiring and her mind turned to thoughts of what, if anything, was beyond the West Millions Zone ...'

34

THE URBAN FUTURE

If we were able to return in 100 years from now, what would we find in the world's towns and cities? Would they still be there? Would we recognize them? How much would still be familiar and how much would have changed? What will the city of the future be like?

Although looking into the future has never been an easy business, many people are concerned with what our future cities will look like. Dreamers and people with vision produce ideas and designs which have an influence on what the urban future ought to be like. Forecasters tell us what things will be like if present trends continue. Planners make decisions in the present which affect the way in which the urban future develops.

Just as there is great variety in towns and cities today, it is likely that great variety will exist in the future. Urban patterns and processes vary greatly between different parts of the world and even vary within countries.

As we approach the end of the 20th century, cities have emerged as the single most popular type of settlement throughout the world. More people are living in urban areas than ever before. One thing seems certain – the future for most people on this planet will be an urban future.

CITY OF THE FUTURE?

CONFLICT CITY	INTERNATIONAL CITY	NEIGHBOURHOOD CITY	CONSERVATION CITY	LEISURE CITY
A city of class and race hostility. Soaring crime rates and frequent social unrest in the form of riots and major distrubances. A widening gulf between the well-off suburban residents and the disadvantaged population of the inner city. Political inaction and crisis.	A city of worldwide importance brought about by the need for international centres in an increasingly international economy. A centre for international trade, finance and high technology. Linked to other centres by advanced telecommunication and air travel.	A city where people see the need for small-scale 'urban villages' so that residents develop a sense of community. New towns and purpose-built cities constructed around a series of separate neighbourhood units.	A city where environmental concern and action have developed to an important level. Appreciation of historic and special areas within the city, which are protected and conserved for future inhabitants as well as the present population.	A city for the 'leisure age'. Shorter working hours, longer holidays, growth in joblessness all increase the demand for widespread recreation and leisure facilities within the city.

'Coexistence'
A GARDEN CITY TO BUILD SKYWARDS

This huge skyscraper consists of alternate sections of homes and offices. It could rise to over 600 m and house some 30 000 people.

Each residential section consists of eight floors of apartments, housed in the cylindrical core of the skyscraper and surrounded by landscaped parklands, with individually-designed gardens and play areas. Each business section consists of eight floors of offices, arranged in an inverted cone which forms the platform for the parkland above. With this arrangement the offices are shielded from the sun.

A glazed lattice encloses each residential section and its parkland, to form a giant conservatory which protects the apartments and the plants from high winds. The apartments are shielded from direct sunlight by a moving shade which tracks round with the sun. This shade also carries solar energy converters to supply the energy needs of the skyscraper.

Is 'Coexistence' a solution to the problems of urban living in the 21st century, when over half the world's people will be living in cities? The designers, Jan Kaplicky and David Nixon, believe it will be. They claim their design has none of the disadvantages of present skyscrapers and tower blocks.

Brave new garden city

The postwar 'New Town' ideal may be in the doldrums but 12 families are about to risk their traditional lifestyle with a relaunch for the 21st century, complete with solar energy and goat yogurt. **David Nicholson-Lord** reports

On a freshly-mown Shropshire hayfield in early summer they are playing houses. A cabinet maker, a computer programmer and an unemployed engineer hover over a model soldier's terrain of plastic hills and woods, gesturing and positioning the odd small cardboard artefact. Slowly a settlement of houses, gardens and outbuildings takes shape.

This exercise has the feel of a board game for grown-ups. But the cardboard buildings represent what one day may be the players' homes, sheds and workshops. From the toyscape of paddock and smallholding they may, with good management, feed themselves. The participants are playing, if not for their lives, then for something scarcely less serious – their lifestyles and livelihoods.

At Lightmoor, an undistinguished patch of countryside on the southern borders of Telford New Town, oddly assorted organizations and individuals are attempting to create a new kind of community. It is an endeavour in the traditions of New Lanark and Saltaire, of Ebenezer Howard and the garden cities.

But while its roots may be in the nineteenth century, its sights are set on the twenty-first. On the 250 acres of Lightmoor, microprocessors and sewage digesters will sit alongside the vegetable patch. Solar panels and heat pumps will share space with sheep, goats and cattle. Traditional crafts like joinery and cabinet-making will vie with electronics and fibre optics. There is talk of fish-farming and coppicing woodland for fuel.

But the meeting of new and old technologies, while eye-catching, is far from the whole story. Lightmoor is about building neighbourhoods from the bottom up. Hence the board game – 'planning for real' as it is known – in which future residents design their own communities, co-operatively and with only limited advice from experts. This autumn, once they have decided where their homes are going, they will build them. Do-it-yourself may never by the same again.

1 Britain's newest settlement, as described in *The Times*, 4 July 1984. Is Lightmoor the shape of things to come?

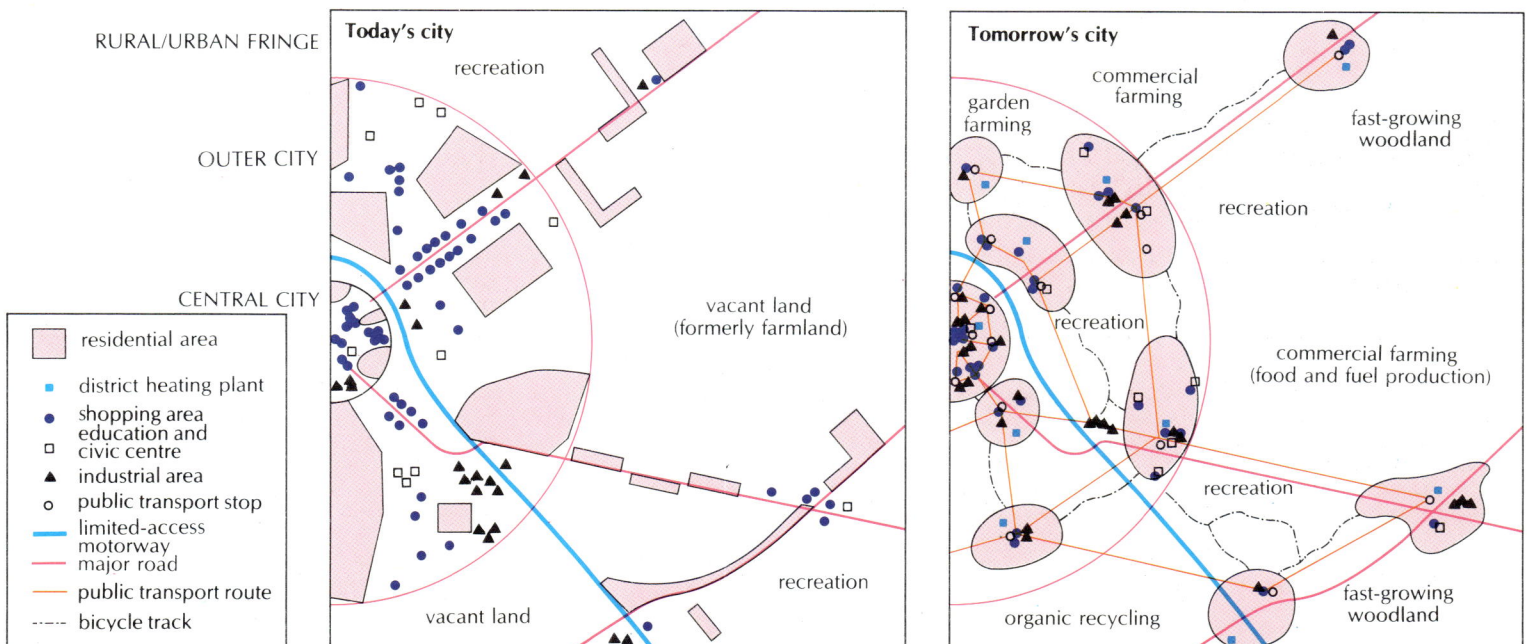

2 The contemporary and future urban landscape

Legend:
- residential area
- district heating plant
- shopping area
- education and civic centre
- industrial area
- public transport stop
- limited-access motorway
- major road
- public transport route
- bicycle track

Today's city — RURAL/URBAN FRINGE, recreation, OUTER CITY, CENTRAL CITY, vacant land (formerly farmland), vacant land, recreation

Tomorrow's city — garden farming, commercial farming, fast-growing woodland, recreation, commercial farming (food and fuel production), recreation, organic recycling, fast-growing woodland

GLOSSARY

Community area   A small area of housing which has its own special feeling or atmosphere, created by its location, by its amenities and by the people who live there. Also called a neighbourhood.

Commuting   Travelling each day to and from a city or town to work. Most commuters travel by train or car.

Conflict of land use   Sometimes different groups of people need the same area of land for different uses which do not go well together. The groups are then in conflict about how the land should be used.

Conurbation   The large urban area formed when several nearby cities and towns grow so big that they eventually merge.

Corner shop   A shop which serves a small neighbourhood and stocks basic foodstuffs, household goods and other things such as sweets and cigarettes. Most corner shops are family-owned businesses. This type of shop is slowly disappearing because of the competition from supermarkets and superstores, which can afford to cut their prices through buying very large stocks of goods.

Cottage industry   Traditional craft work, such as making clothes, mats and baskets, which is done on a small-scale and does not involve mechanization or mass production.

Decentralization   The movement of people and jobs away from a city centre to its suburbs and locations beyond the city. Sometimes a government will encourage decentralization.

Designated district   An area within a town or city for which government grants are available to help local industries and businesses to improve and grow, and thus provide more jobs.

Green Belt   An area of countryside around a city, which is protected by laws to stop people building on it and spreading the city still further.

Heavy industry   The manufacture of large machinery and plant, shipbuilding, iron and steelmaking.

Hypermarket   *See* Superstore.

Image   The idea or mental picture a person has of something, such as a place or another person. No two people will have exactly the same image of the same thing.

Immigrant   Someone who moves into, and settles down, in a country where he or she was not born.

Market   A place or area where goods or services are sold. It can also mean a group of people for which particular goods or services are produced.

Mental map   The image a person has of the layout of a place. No two people will have exactly the same mental map of the same place.

Migrant   Someone who moves from one place to live in another.

Model town   A carefully planned 'village' which was built near a factory to house the workers and their families. The houses were well-designed and superior to the usual workers' dwellings of the time, and were often set in gardens with extensive open space. Some model towns had educational and recreational amenities. They were built by the more caring factory owners to improve the living conditions of their workers.

Neighbourhood   *See* Community area.

Neighbourhood area   A purpose-built neighbourhood, designed by planners to help create a community spirit and a sense of belonging among the people who live there.

North (The)   Another term for the developed regions of the world, first used in the *Brandt Report*. The term is used because almost all the world's wealthier, more technologically advanced countries lie in the northern hemisphere (*see also* The South).

Partnership   A joint operation to fight inner city decay involving a local authority, local businesses and central government. The government provides the major share of the money needed and has a big say in the choice and development of projects.

Periphery   An area which is located away from an industrial core.

Planning permission   The permission that has to be given by a local council before any new building can be put up, or the existing use of a building changed. It may also apply to changes in the use of land.

Political city   A city controlled by the laws of central government which state where people must live. These laws thus establish residential segregation and the urban pattern.

Population density   The average number of people living in each square kilometre of land. It can be worked out for any type of area (for example, town, borough, region or whole country) by dividing the total number of people living there by the land area in square kilometres.

Programme Authority   An organization similar to a partnership but in which the local authority has more control over the redevelopment projects set up by the authority.

Racial discrimination   The unfair treatment of someone because of his or her ethnic or racial origin.

Residential segregation   The settlement of people in particular residential areas according to the social class or ethnic or religious group to which they belong. This may happen naturally where newcomers to a city tend to settle close to their 'own' people, as in the case of the Asian community in Bradford, England. Or it may be enforced by government policy as in the case of the black Africans in Johannesburg, South Africa.

Ribbon development   The building of housing and business premises in a line along a main road, extending outwards from a town or city. It was one of the main forms of suburban development in the 1920s and 1930s.

Shanty town   Another name for squatter settlement. Part of a large town or city, usually on its outskirts, where people live in low-cost housing which they have built themselves from any material around (often rubbish), and on land which they do not officially own. Shanty towns usually have a concentration of poor people. Some have a communal water supply but few have sewers or other amenities.

South (The)   Another term used for the developing regions of the world, first used in the *Brandt Report*. The term is used because almost all the world's poorer, less technologically advanced countries are located south of the Tropic of Cancer, and many of them in the southern hemisphere (*see also* The North).

Standard of living   How well off and comfortable people are. People's standard of living depends on how much they have to spend on food, clothes, housing, lighting, heating, travel to work, entertainment and holidays. It also depends on whether they have good schools and colleges, proper medical care, social security, welfare services, water supplies, electricity, sewage disposal and good transport and communication systems.

Suburbanization   The shift of people from the inner areas to suburbs.

Supermarket   A self-service store, often large and usually on a single level, selling most foods and some houshold goods. Most supermarkets provide trolleys to carry the shopper's purchases and have several checkouts for payment.

Superstore   A very large self-service store (total area over 2250 square metres), built on a single level and situated on the outskirts of a town or city. It has a big free car park, sometimes with a service station. A superstore (also called a hypermarket) sells a wide variety of food and non-food products, and may include a cafeteria or similar eating place. All superstores provide trolleys to carry the shopper's purchases and have several checkouts for payment.

Transport planning   Working out ways of making it easier for people and goods to be moved about. It includes such things as improving railway services, extending the network of motorways, reducing inner-city road traffic, wider use of mini-bus services and introducing schemes for improving the flow of road traffic in urban areas.

Tribal homeland   An area of land in South Africa which has been given by the South African government to black African people as an 'independent' homeland. Such an area is in fact little more than a vast pool of workers for nearby industries.

Urban Development Corporation   An organization set up by the government to speed up the improvement of Britain's worst inner city areas. All Urban Development Corporations have sweeping powers to redevelop land and to build new housing and industrial sites.

Urban land use model   A model which explains the general land use pattern in an urban area and the growth of that area.

Urban sprawl   The unplanned, irregular and often unsightly spread of a city, as people and industries settle where they like. Urban sprawl occurs when there are no laws to control what and where people can build.

INDEX